QUEEN
of All
MAYHEM

QUEEN
of All
MAYHEM

The Blood-Soaked Life and
Mysterious Death of Belle Starr,
the Most Dangerous Woman
in the West

Dane Huckelbridge

wm
WILLIAM MORROW
An Imprint of HarperCollins*Publishers*

HarperCollins books may be purchased for educational, business, or sales promotional use. For information, please email the Special Markets Department at SPsales@harpercollins.com.

FIRST EDITION

Designed by Bonni Leon-Berman

Images in the photo insert are courtesy of the author unless otherwise noted.

Library of Congress Cataloging-in-Publication Data has been applied for.

ISBN 978-0-06-330701-8

25 26 27 28 29 LBC 5 4 3 2 1

LOOK LIKE TH' INNOCENT FLOWER,
BUT BE THE SERPENT UNDER 'T.

—Lady Macbeth

I AM A FRIEND TO ANY BRAVE OR
GALLANT OUTLAW.

—Myra Maybelle Shirley, aka Belle Starr

CONTENTS

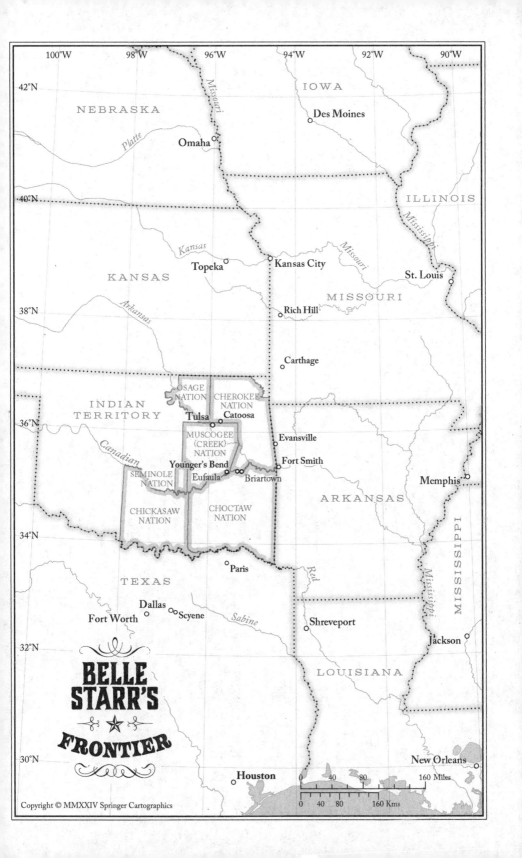

PROLOGUE

A Lethal Twilight

EXACTLY WHAT TRANSPIRED ON that cold and rain-cursed day in Indian Territory, on the silted banks of the South Canadian River, was known to only two people—neither of whom would be in a position to discuss it with anyone by day's end. But between the little that is known and the much that is not, we can imagine.

We know that on the third of February, in the year 1889, just two days shy of her forty-first birthday, Myra Maybelle Shirley mounted her horse following a short visit with friends—a small gathering of Choctaw and Cherokee neighbors, and the white sharecroppers who leased their land. We know that corn pone was served and that local gossip was shared, all of which was fairly standard Sunday fare. We know that she stayed no more than an hour before bidding her hosts farewell and clopping away through the frigid mud and the fading light, back toward her log house at Younger's Bend. And we know that this was the last time any of them would see her alive.

We can imagine this woman sitting straight and proud in her sidesaddle—weary but unbowed after serving time in federal prison, after losing a brother and two husbands to gunfights, and even after having just escorted a fourth husband partway to Fort Smith, to face charges of larceny. Her face is weathered and creased from a lifetime spent running from the law, but the stubborn defiance that burns in her eyes bears testament to a deeper resilience. She has seen everything, done everything, she ever set out to—she has nothing left to prove, to herself or anyone else. We can imagine her in relatively simple attire on this day, forsaking the black velvet and plumed Stetsons she sports in town for the plainer garb she wears among friends. She has even left her favorite pair of pistols behind; she saw no reason to carry them on such a familiar road, so close to home. Especially now that the heydays of her outlaw career are all but behind her and that most of her enemies are either dead or in prison. In the saddle scabbard is her trusty Winchester rifle, with her name and signature brass star emblazoned on the stock, which should suffice. It is a decision that she will soon come to bitterly regret. But ambling confidently beneath the dripping bows of pines, the steam rising from her horse's withers, the path dipping down toward the lulling waters of the South Canadian, her thoughts begin to drift, her mind to wander—

That is, until a shotgun blast jars her from both her stupor and her saddle. A full barrel of buckshot, delivered from twenty feet behind, square into her back. The raw force of its impact throws her from her mount and leaves her gasping in the mud, while her spooked horse whinnies and thunders away, taking her precious rifle—now more so than ever—along with it. Perhaps she summons enough strength, with the raindrops drumming steadily upon the brim of her upturned hat, one cheek buried in wet river-bottom clay, to reach down blindly for a pistol—only to realize that there is no holster at her waist, that there are no ivory handles to grasp or oiled triggers to pull. Perhaps she hears the doomed sucking sound of approaching boots in the mire, perhaps she sees a dark form rising from the crimson corner of a bloodshot eye.

There is a second shotgun blast—this we know—delivered from above, at point-blank range. We can only imagine the sulfurous smell of the black powder, the descending pall of white smoke, the cold pattering of rain, the dying of the light.

The turbulent life of Myra Maybelle Shirley is ending.

But the legend of Belle Starr is about to be born.

INTRODUCTION

The Forgotten Outlaw Queen

WHEN THAT UNKNOWN ASSASSIN squeezed the first trigger back in 1889, blowing Belle Starr from her famous hand-worked leather saddle, they would have had no way of knowing they were inadvertently knocking her right into the pages of history. How could they? At that point, she was only a colorful local character with a checkered past, barely known beyond the frontier settlements of what is today eastern Oklahoma and northern Texas; someone who stirred gossip in neighborhood saloons and provoked headlines in town papers with her ribald antics and frequent brushes with the law. And it very easily could have remained that way, with her name quietly fading into the past, had it not been for one serendipitous event. Two days after her death, the editor of the *Fort Smith Elevator*, a minuscule Arkansas weekly from the ragged edge of Indian Territory, sent off a dispatch about the killing to a few of the large, metropolitan papers. Including, as it were, the *New York Times*.

The timing could not have been better. With the 1880s coming to a close and with the "Wild" quickly leaking out of an increasingly tamed West, eastern urbanites held a voracious appetite for salacious true-crime drama from whatever was left of their nation's vanishing frontier. Yes, heroes sold papers, but villains sold even more, and a *villainess*—particularly an unabashedly stylish one clad entirely in black velvet and flashing an elaborately plumed hat—well, that was simply too good to pass up. Just three days after her death, the rest of America received its first glimpse of Belle Starr, in the form of an obituary on the front page of the

Times, titled "A Desperate Woman Killed."[1] The piece was short and contained as many exaggerations and errors as it did facts. It labeled her "the most desperate woman that ever figured on the borders" (she certainly was not that), stated that she "married Cole Younger directly after the war" (she never married him at all), and also claimed that she "had been arrested for murder and robbery a score of times, but always managed to escape" (also false—she was only ever formally charged three times, for robbery, yes, but never for murder). Yet what the obituary lacked in fact-checking, it made up for in raw titillation. The slim core of truth it conveyed, that a female bandit who ran with famous outlaws had been gunned down in Indian Territory by an unknown assassin, was morsel enough to whet the general public's appetite for more.

Among those intrigued by the murder was Richard K. Fox, owner of the *National Police Gazette*, one of the most popular true-crime tabloids of the day—the word "true" being somewhat loosely applied. But while journalistic integrity may not have been one of the publisher's strong points, knowing how to make a buck was. Recognizing the story's explosive potential, Fox decided a full-length book was in order. A writer was dispatched immediately to Fort Smith, an egregious amount of creative license was taken, and by that summer, a paperback was produced, titled *Bella Starr, the Bandit Queen or the Female Jesse James*. Again, the book was far more invention than fact, and even contained "excerpts" from a fabricated diary. It was a work of bombastic fiction, pedaled as something closer to biography, but the audience for Fox's

---

[1] The word "desperate" did possess an additional connotation in the nineteenth century, particularly in the American West, where it was often used in a similar fashion to the Spanish word *desperado*, to label a person driven to commit reckless and illegal acts out of desperation. Belle Starr may have lived through some difficult economic times, and she certainly committed her fair share of crimes, but at the time of her death, as a generally law-abiding citizen and a custodian of Younger's Bend, she wasn't truly "desperate" in any sense of the word. Quite the contrary, as a matter of fact.

lurid crime dramas didn't much seem to care. The slim volume described her as "more amorous than Anthony's mistress, more relentless than Pharaoh's daughter, and braver than Joan of Arc." It went on to claim that "Mother Nature was indulging in one of her rarest freaks, when she produced such a novel specimen of woman-kind." And it sold by the thousands.

From there, the legend of Belle Starr effectively—to use the parlance of our times—went viral, gaining in grandiosity with each new serialization and with each fresh telling, affixing her place among the mythological pantheon of the Wild West. In the decades to come, there would be novelizations, epic poems, historical biographies, folk songs, and when the technology arrived, even movies. Belle Starr fever may have reached its peak with the 1941 release of an eponymous film, produced by 20th Century Fox, starring the stunning Gene Tierney, who bore no physical or historical resemblance to the raw-boned middle-aged woman who gave up the ghost on the banks of the South Canadian River. Throughout the final decade of the nineteenth century and the entire first half of the twentieth, Belle Starr, the notorious "Bandit Queen," captivated America and captured its collective imagination.

Until, rather suddenly, she didn't. In the postwar years, the name of Belle Starr faded from the national consciousness of the American West. Not entirely—there would always be historians and enthusiasts who knew her story, and her name would continue to ignite sparks of recognition here and there. But her days as a household name, if not a cultural icon, had passed. As to why this occurred, one could posit a number of theories, from the slow death of the Western as a popular American trope, to revisionist historians poking holes in the many biographical embellishments that had gained credence over the years. Perhaps the most convincing reason, however, relates directly to the cultural shifts that were taking place in the United States at that time, as a freshly suburbanized nation stomped the historical mud from its boots and leaned into a new, whitewashed era of cultural puritanism. The cinematic Westerns of the 1950s and '60s—at least the ones made in the United States—held little room for moral ambiguity or complex sociologies. They were ritualized retellings of the creation myth of the American West, one in which brave Anglo-American settlers, pure of both heart and mind, tamed a wild land, cleansing it of materialistic outlaws and hostile Indians through righteous violence. And primary female characters, almost without fail, were paragons of an invented ideal of frontier femininity. Chaste, wholesome, oftentimes schoolteachers or fiancées from back east, they brought decency and lily-white "civilization" to a supposedly lawless and miscegenated land. In effect, they made the West softer, whiter, and safer. More "suburban," one might even say.

With this in mind, it's easy to see how Belle Starr—a whiskey-drinking, horse-thieving, gunslinging double widow, who not only bedded a much younger Cherokee man but also forced *him* to change his surname to match hers upon marriage—might not fit that prevailing paradigm. In the gritty cynicism of a European spaghetti Western, perhaps, and there actually was one such film released in Italy in 1968, retitled in English as *The Belle Starr Story*. But a John Ford movie? As a love interest for Gary Cooper or John Wayne? It's unthinkable. The censors of the era would never have allowed it, and forget about the American public at large. When it came to the pop culture depictions of Western heroines and anti-heroines in the latter half of the twentieth century, she was in effect written out of the script. Annie Oakley would receive her own Irving Berlin Broadway musical, Calamity Jane would be featured in a whole slew of movies, not to mention an HBO series, and Big Nose Kate would have cameos in everything from *Gunfight at the O.K. Corral* to *Tombstone*—she would even be played once by a decidedly petite-nosed Faye Dunaway. For Belle Starr, however, there was nothing but literary tumbleweed and cinematic crickets. She was all but forgotten.

As far as cultural lacunae go, this one was unfortunate. Because unlike her more celebrated frontier sistren, Belle Starr actually *was* an outlaw and a gunslinger and an equal partner to some of the most legendary bandits of the era. Indeed, while Annie Oakley was shooting at glass baubles in staged Wild West shows, while Calamity Jane was stumbling drunk and aimless through Deadwood, and while Big Nose Kate was peeking out from behind the curtains of her bedroom during the Gunfight at the O.K. Corral, Belle Starr was packing pistols and raising hell, from Texas all the way up to Missouri. Her early chroniclers may have taken some creative liberties, but certain facts are incontrovertible. Belle Starr definitely *did* harbor and consort with legendary outlaws like Jesse James and Cole Younger. She *did* marry into a clan of Cherokee warlords, operating, alongside her husband Sam Starr, one of the largest banditry and smuggling rings in the Indian Territory. She *did* ride sidesaddle and sport a pair of intimidating .45s that she lovingly called her "babies." And she *did* face charges of horse theft and armed robbery, even serving prison time for the former, courtesy of the infamous "Hanging Judge" Isaac Parker. Belle Starr may not have received national recognition during her lifetime, but her plumed hat sat squarely in the shaded, overlapping portion of a fascinating historical Venn diagram, containing both storied personas *and* epochal events. Encircling her own blood-drenched biography like barbed wire is the history of Appalachia, of westward expansion, of the forced removal of the Cherokee, and of the Civil War in the Border States. Her life was lived at the crossroads of all of them.

However, even the dowdiest of historians can prove vulnerable to the allures of raw curiosity and human wonder. And when it comes to writing about Belle Starr's life, even more compelling than all that dry and weedy history are the rich mysteries that still attend it. It's true: the story of Belle Starr is rife with unknowns. Not even newspaper articles or census records of the era can be fully trusted. Dates were erased, names were changed, details were invented—sometimes out of carelessness, but often with an agenda in mind. Were one to asterisk every sentence that contained a suspect source or an iffy reference, a book about Belle would become a veritable Milky Way of stars. Practically by necessity, any researched attempt at revealing the details of her life becomes less like writing an academic treatise and more like painting an artistic portrait, shaded as truthfully as possible, while also acknowledging a bit of interpretive brushwork. The West has simply become so mythologized, so aggrandized, that teasing ironclad truths from that tangled skein of frontier yarns is often all but impossible; a little bit of legend will cling to almost any fact. And when it comes to Belle Starr, said legends are usually woven from unanswered questions. Did she really serve as a teenage spy for Confederate guerrillas? Did she fence horses and provide a hideout for Jesse James? Which of the many armed robberies attributed to her did she actually participate in, if any? And did she ever kill anyone in the process?

All of which leads to the biggest mystery of all: Why? Why did a woman who had considerable advantages in life—a good family, a decent education, solid marriage prospects, a clear path to financial security—choose to pursue a life of crime? Belle Starr very easily could have slipped into the character and mien of a Southern belle, marrying a wealthy landowner or merchant, living comfortably in the boomtown of Dallas. Instead, she chose to consort with bandits, flee from the law, live rough among the Cherokee, and stroll through the streets of one-horse towns, laden with guns.

One could blame the societal damage caused by the Civil War, her family's move from Missouri to the Texas frontier, or even the death of her older brother Bud—a trauma, most seem to agree, that scarred her for life. And one would not necessarily be wrong. There is probably some truth in each of these suppositions.

The fullest answer, however, as to why Belle Starr chose the outlaw's way may quite simply be found in her adamant refusal to be cowed by a society that held definitive ideas about how a woman should behave and what she could accomplish. Belle simply had no use for sewing circles or calico dresses; she would not be cosseted inside any farmhouse kitchen or be seen as less than equal to any man. In her own words: "So long had I been estranged from the society of women (whom I thoroughly detest) that I thought I would find it irksome to live in their midst." The very rights and privileges that nineteenth-century America denied her because of her sex, Belle Starr decided to acquire by the gun. She chose a path different from that which was expected of her—a route that shook with thunder, that was drenched in blood. An exceedingly dangerous road, albeit one upon which she took orders from no man.

And *here* one must also be careful. Because the temptation is certainly there, given the currents and trends of our times, to portray Belle Starr as some kind of proto-feminist Robin Hood or some form of Wild West justice warrior. It would make for some catchy storytelling, that's true. Belle Starr, however, was neither of these things. And while she may have been bucking the same sorts of societal pressures, it's hard to imagine that the saloon-loving, Confederacy-sympathizing Belle would have had much in common with the teetotaling Yankee matrons who served as the vanguard of the early women's rights movement. It's far more likely she would have threatened to smash their teapots over their heads. The truth, be it comfortable or not, is that Belle Starr was never out for social justice, nor was she an advocate of any cause—she was in it solely for herself. And in that regard, she bore far less resemblance to any Susan B. Anthony than she did to the Irish, Italian, and Jewish gangsters who would emerge half a century later in the ethnic ghettos of Eastern cities. Individuals who, just like her, knew that because of their identity in America, the life they aspired to could never be achieved through honest means. So just like them—but fifty years earlier—Belle Starr chose to achieve it through dishonest ones. She put down her sewing kit and picked up a gun. And the way of the gun did indeed bring her the very freedom she craved: to love whomever she wanted, to live however she pleased, and to take whatever she felt was rightfully hers. But in the end, as was the case with so many outlaws and gangsters, it also led to her ruin, leaving her to gasp out her last breaths face down in that Oklahoma riverbed, riddled with buckshot—and perhaps even regret. And it is that meteoric rise and vertiginous fall, in pursuit of a kind of liberty and equality that her own country refused to grant her, that makes her story so quintessentially American and as relevant today as it was a century and a half ago.

But there's one more mystery still. A smaller, more personal one, which I hoped, possibly naively, I might solve as well. Growing up, I was often told that Belle Starr was a distant relation on my mother's side—Scots-Irish farmers who arrived in eastern Texas in covered wagons at roughly the same time Belle did, and who, if the stories are true, also had blood ties to the Cherokee Nation. As to the veracity of both claims, going into this project, I honestly could not say. As I suspect is the case with more than a few American families with deep rural roots, the alleged link to Belle Starr is just one square of trivia in an admittedly checkered past. There is no shortage of outlaws and troublemakers dangling—several by the neck—from our family tree. And while some, like my second cousin Lester, the last man to be hung in Macoupin County, Illinois, I know for a fact to be kin, others—well, it's harder to say.

I began this book with the hope that the research involved might shed some light on the matter—and that if I was very lucky, *somewhere* amid all the gunsmoke and betrayal, the war cries and blood spatter, the rumbling of horses and jangling of stolen gold, I might even find an answer.

PART I

THE
FRONTIER

CHAPTER 1

Born into the Whirlwind

ONSENSUS IN AMERICA HAS never come easy. This has been true
throughout our history, and many would argue, it's even truer
today. Indeed, it sometimes seems the only thing we as Americans
have been able to agree upon during the awkward adolescence of
this twenty-first century is our fundamental inability to agree on
anything. The pervading sentiment, splashed across headlines in
digital ink, espoused over the internet by virtual partisans, is that
the United States is a fraught and fractured land—a country riven
by cultural disparity, plagued by vast inequality, and simmering
with the potential for senseless violence.

But as much as we may wring our hands or clutch our pearls
while lamenting the discord of modern American life, the truth
of the matter is this: the climate-controlled, cable-news-watching
country of today is a pale and placid shadow of the brutal dystopia
that stretched and burned between these two oceans in the middle years of the nineteenth century. More of a multicultural battle
royale than a modern nation, less of a functioning democracy than
a class-driven grudge match, the United States in the mid-1800s
was not united in any sense of the word. And few years—at least
up until the advent of the Civil War—would prove more violently
contentious than 1848.

This was the year that a pair of European calamities, a crippling famine and a failed revolution, sent a tidal wave of human
suffering crashing against the seawalls of the Northeast's foundational cities—a refugee crisis unlike any the world had ever

known. The quaint and narrow streets of the old Anglo-Dutch capitals were suddenly inundated with homeless migrants—Gaelic speakers from the wreckage of rural Ireland and German speakers from the shambles of the Holy Roman Empire. Over a million of each would cross the water to escape the death sentence of the Old World, only to find poverty and hard labor in the New. A lucky few would evade the subhuman conditions of the overflowing slums—hellholes like New York's Five Points and Boston's Fort Hill—but many more would not, turning tenements to tinderboxes, entire neighborhoods to powder kegs. Resentments flowed, hatreds abounded. Blood and pestilence both ran rife through the gutters. Typhus, cholera, tuberculosis, dysentery—in the slums of Manhattan, one in four Irish newborns would not survive infancy; in Boston, the overall death rate for Irish immigrants was more than double that of the native-born. The situation was untenable, and the ruling class of old Dutch and East Anglian Protestants who presided over New York and New England would have surely given in to the nativists, the soon-to-be "Know Nothings," and shut off the tap of immigration completely—if only they hadn't needed all those desperate souls to serve as living grist for the mills that were beginning to transform the nation into an industrial colossus.

Farther south—below that imaginary line inscribed in the air by messieurs Mason and Dixon almost a century before—a very different and even crueler system of peonage prevailed. Amid scorching mudflats and malarial plains, three million slaves descended from captured West Africans—Yoruba, Bantu, Wolof, Igbo, Ashanti, and a hundred more—toiled beneath the lash on sprawling plantations owned by the descendants of West Country aristocrats. While the latter struggled to embody a rough simulacrum of the landed English gentry, the former struggled simply to survive. Some estimates put the life expectancy of a cotton hand at that time as low as twenty-two years; more optimistic surveys set it around thirty. Chattel slavery, which produced cotton, tobacco, and sugar, would make the American South the fourth richest "country" in the world, a region wealthier than any other nation in Europe except England. The raw materials it yielded would fund the incipient industrial revolution beginning to reshape the North, and almost single-handedly fuel the textile industry of Great Britain. However, for the plantation slave, upon whose splitting back all this lucre was built, there were only sweltering fields and festering rags, half-rancid pork and moldy hardtack, with a short respite on Sundays to sing out prayers for salvation.

Farther west, on the prairies and in the forests that lay just beyond the cusp of the Appalachians, whole new territories, both purchased from the French and wrested from Native Americans, invited all those willing to bust sod and lay claim. Anglican Yankees from Connecticut, Palatinate Germans from Pennsylvania, Ulster Scots from the hills of Virginia and Kentucky—they came to America's middle in descending order, leaving behind stifling Eastern hegemonies to become yeoman farmers and plow their own acres. In their isolation and detachment from the religious institutions of the coast, a novel cast of creeds took hold, to be dragged westward in the wake of the Second Great Awakening. All along this inland fringe, clapboard churches shivered with a holy fire as the Quakers quaked and the Shakers shook and the Dunkers dunked; canvas tents billowed and tugged at their guylines as early Adventists slipped into tongues and Baptists summoned brimstone and Mormons piled in, trailing their legions of wives. In the ecstatic nature of their worship and in their sense of impending judgment, some of these new adherents saw a plain call to arms. One such impassioned evangelical in Ohio's Western Reserve even went so far as to call himself an "instrument of God," in a holy war that he believed would rid the nation of slavery. His name was

John Brown, and his quest to cleanse the country of its "original sin" would begin that very year with his contribution to the *Appeal to the Coloured Citizens of the World*, a seminal abolitionist text. However, his moral crusade would take a turn to the violent in "Bleeding Kansas," where he and his sons would hack five men to death with broadswords, and end at Harpers Ferry, where the failed slave rebellion he orchestrated—a harbinger of the far greater bloodshed to come—would earn him the hatred of at least half the country, not to mention a gibbet and a noose.

And even farther west still, beyond the bottomlands of the Mississippi, with its relic population of French-speaking Acadians and Creoles, beyond the Indian Territory of Oklahoma, where the "Civilized Tribes" of the Southeast had been forcibly relocated in the most uncivilized of fashions—beyond everything, beyond the pale—lay a land of such staggering vastness and human variety as to boggle the mind of even the most imaginative pilgrim. Some of it was acquired back in the boondoggle of the Louisiana Purchase; the rest had been snatched away from Mexico in a lopsided war won that very year. All of it defied easy settlement or description. This new swath of land, reaching all the way to the Pacific, held more potential and more danger than the steady stream of newcomers could begin to comprehend. Across its middle stretched the Great Plains, a rolling Sahara of grass a *million* miles square, trodden by bison herds 50 million strong and patrolled by borderless horse nations that protected both their quarry and their people with fearsome determination—tribes like the Cheyenne, the Arapaho, the Crow, and the Sioux. In the flatlands of Texas, where fractious settlements of Americanos, Tejanos, peninsulares, and Indios jockeyed for power and occasionally massacred one another, the only seeming common denominator was a shared terror of the Comanche—who in addition to being quite possibly the greatest mounted warriors in history, were also tremendous egalitarians in that they tortured and slaughtered with equal zeal anyone who encroached upon their hunting grounds. Apaches, Tonkawas, Anglos, mestizos—all were fair game. Even freshly arrived German immigrants, having escaped the uprisings of Europe and the tenements of the East, to farm in the rolling hills around Austin, were quickly made aware of the true severity of their trespass. In the time it took a shaky-handed homesteader to reload and fire a smoothbore musket, a Comanche warrior could loose twenty lethal arrows in their direction, all delivered from a horse traveling over thirty miles an hour. The Comanche were perhaps the only tribe that not only avoided losing territory to the colonial ambitions of Spaniards and Americans—they actually managed to win land back, expanding an invisible empire known as the Comancheria that would stretch from northern Mexico all the way to southern Kansas. European diseases and the near extirpation of the buffalo would eventually conspire to end their reign, but in 1848, the Comanche were still the "Lords of the Plains."

And then there was the end of it all: California, where both a continent and manifest destiny ran headlong and did a golden cartwheel into the sea. What had been an unprobed wilderness punctuated by a scattering of Indian camps and crumbling Spanish missions was undergoing an existential transformation, thanks to a secret that had slipped someone's lips in the first month of that year: *there was gold in them thar hills*. With an overland crossing through the aforementioned plains being all but suicidal at that point, most of the early "Argonauts," as the first fortune hunters were whimsically known, arrived from Eastern cities via a five-month-long ordeal on the high seas, going all the way south around Cape Horn. Gold fever spread, and they were soon joined by prospectors from foreign lands as well, including China, where high taxes following the Opium Wars and a string of droughts sent rural laborers with dreams of the Gam Saan—gold mountain—in search of riches across the sea. In no time at all, California mining camps were a veritable Babel of tongues, with French, Quechua, Cantonese, Genoese, Welsh, and even Basque spicing up the prevailing banter of English and Spanish. In the headiness of the rush, the old mission towns of San Francisco, San Jose, and Los Angeles exploded into bustling metropoles. Collectively, they existed in a legal no-man's-land—as an American "possession," California was no longer part of Mexico, but it was not a state or even a recognized territory. In 1848, the place was almost literally lawless. Fortunes were won and lost over single games of faro, claim disputes were prone to being resolved with a gun, and back alleys brimmed with Kentucky whiskey, Peruvian pisco, Mexican tequila, and Chinese opium. But while the discovery of gold may have stoked exponential growth for California's new migrant population, it had the opposite effect on its Indigenous peoples. Uprooted from their traditional lands, deprived of wild foodstuffs, and exposed to new diseases, the tribes of California were all but eradicated in what more than a few historians have deemed a flat-out genocide. From numbers that hovered around 150,000 in that first year of the gold rush, the Native population would plummet to just 16,000 by the century's end. An environmental and humanitarian catastrophe set into motion by an all but useless metal, far too soft to be of much service, whose sole saving grace was its refusal to tarnish.

Such was the state of America in 1848. A chaotic jumble of peoples, clans, religions, and tribes, whirling and colliding in a New World crucible that seemed to scorch as many as it saved. If there was one essentially universal point of consensus, however, one conviction all these haggling combatants seemed to share, it was this: no matter if it was a Bowery beer hall, a Baptist tent revival, an Amish barn-raising, a Comanche tribal council, a Gullah praise house, or a meeting of the Princeton board of trustees, women were not allowed to participate as equals alongside men. If there was one feature that was ubiquitously and undeniably American, it was that the female half of the population was either severely constrained or forbidden entirely from participating in the rituals and affirmations of community and power. And while this very year—1848—has often been cited as the beginning of the women's rights movement, kicked off by a convention of Quaker activists in Seneca Falls, New York, it would still be almost three-quarters of a century before American women would be guaranteed the right to vote, and well over a century until they would be permitted to open bank accounts, attend elite universities, or finance their own homes virtually anywhere in the country.

It was on February fifth of this whirlwind year of 1848 that a baby girl named Myra Maybelle Shirley made her howling entrée. Born into this most beguiling of nations—but even more important, born of it.

As to the family she was born into, it had no shortage of turbulence of its own. The common narrative is that her family—the Shirleys—came from typical Scots-Irish, Appalachian frontier stock, serving, as so many families like theirs did, in the vanguard of Western expansion, their Kentucky rifles and whiskey stills always at the ready. And there is considerable truth in this. The Shirleys did indeed settle in the hills of Appalachia, and they did participate in that Ulster Scots hopscotch that began in Pennsylvania, then cut down into Maryland and Virginia, before funneling through the Cumberland Gap and landing in southern Indiana and the Ozarks. Her mother may have even had some Hatfield blood in her—ties were rumored, but never firmly established. The Shirleys, however, were *not* Scots-Irish in origin. They weren't even really Shirleys. The first of the family's paternal line to arrive in America was Johann Carl Schalle, and he was a Palatine—the

other, lesser-known European ethnic group responsible for settling Appalachia and defining the frontier. Eventually, the name
would be simplified to Shally, and then anglicized to Shirley, but
he and his wife Anna Esther were as German as sauerkraut.

Granted, the Palatines and the Scots-Irish were not totally
dissimilar. Both came from war-torn, highly contested border
regions, and both were drawn to America by the promise of actual land ownership, which was an all-but-impossible feat in old,
monarchical Europe. The two groups even arrived at roughly
the same time, in the early and middle decades of the eighteenth
century. In fact, Johann Carl and Anna Esther Schalle came
to America on a ship in 1739 that cast off from Rotterdam and
stopped briefly in Dublin—it's likely more than a few of their
future Ulster Scot neighbors joined them on that boat. However,
unlike the Scots-Irish, who had considerable experience living
on remote homesteads and fending off armed rebellions, the earliest German-speaking immigrants to land on America's shores
were for the most part Anabaptists and pacifists, fleeing the religious persecution of the old Holy Roman Empire. And as it just
so happened, religious liberty was the major selling point of William Penn's colony. Not surprisingly, a healthy portion of these
refugees from the Rhenish Palatinate would choose to remain
in Pennsylvania, transforming over the next two centuries into
the Amish and modern Mennonites. In fact, shortly after im-
migrating, Johann Carl Schalle—now calling himself Charles—
would receive land grants to farm in Lancaster County, which
today hosts *the* largest Amish community in America. Ironic,
given the propensity for bloodshed and firearms that the Shirley
clan would later display, but true: Belle Starr's earliest American
roots are not to be found in any blood-feuding mountain holler,
but among peace-loving, Pennsylvania Dutch–speaking farmers,
smack-dab in the middle of modern-day Amish Country.

But not all these German-speaking immigrants were content to stay in calm and docile eastern Pennsylvania. Provoked in many cases by the need to acquire cheap farmland—the bulk of the inheritance often went to the eldest son or was split between siblings, demanding a buyout—no small number of Palatines followed their Scots-Irish compatriots into the mountains of Appalachia, with a strong preference for the Shenandoah Valley. And while the Palatines may not have been quite as handy with a musket or a whiskey still, they did have one advantage over the Scots-Irish: they were experienced woodsmen. The Scots-Irish came from a land of stone and thatch—the wilds of Appalachia were foreign to them at the onset. It was the German-speaking Palatines, with their origins in the Black Forest region, who knew how to notch logs for cabins and split rails for fences and build elevated timber corncribs, ample evidence of which can be found dotting the Schwarzwald to this day. So the decision to leave the bucolic comforts of eastern Pennsylvania for the densely forested hills of Appalachia is not quite so puzzling. The Palatines wanted to buy cheap land—especially if they came from a large family, where copious siblings made land inheritance complicated—and they were willing to venture into a wooded frontier to find it.

Johann Carl's son, Johann Peter, was one of seven children. Perhaps for that reason, he left the family farm in Lancaster County and went south and west, to Rockingham, Virginia, right into the heart of the Shenandoah. He would end up settling there with his wife, Anna Elizabeth Kelker—another Palatine from Pennsylvania—and apparently alongside at least one brother, as there is a record of him selling Valentine "Sherley" two horses and one plow near Rockingham on April 29 of the year 1788.

By that time, however, American attitudes toward territorial expansion had changed considerably, as a result of its triumph against Great Britain during the revolution. To avoid angering their French rivals and Native American allies, the colonial British government had always done everything in its power to keep its unruly and decidedly land-hungry American subjects from pushing west across the Appalachian Mountains, into the virgin prairies and forests beyond. However, with the final surrender of British forces to General George Washington at Yorktown on the nineteenth of October 1781, any protests they still had were falling on deaf ears. And with the Louisiana Purchase of 1803, the French no longer had much to say about it, either. The United States of America, still in its infancy as far as nations go, had doubled in size, virtually overnight. Which sent a stream of fresh settlers, a good many of them Appalachians, pouring into what is today the southern Midwest and Upland South, flavoring that part of the country into perpetuity with their fiddles, their corn liquor, and their high nasal twang.

Including, as it were, Johann Peter's son Christian, the first Shirley to push west of Appalachia. He arrived in Floyd County, Indiana, around 1810, after passing through Madison County, Kentucky, where he had spent several years working as a farmer. Of course it's impossible to say—such things are not preserved in land grants or baptismal records—but it's likely that by this point, the essential nature of the Shirley clan was beginning to change. It's probable, given how close-knit Palatine communities were in Pennsylvania, that Johann Peter had spoken German as a first language, despite being born in Lancaster County. It's also reasonable to suppose that Christian Shirley had considerable familiarity with the language as well, as did his wife, Roseanne Canote. But after all that time spent in the western woods of Virginia, and later in Kentucky and southern Indiana, it is equally reasonable to suppose that the Shirleys were beginning to look and sound considerably less like Pennsylvania Dutch farmers and considerably more like backwoods Upland Southerners. Not that they were poor—each generation had managed to buy land and consolidate their holdings before cashing out and moving farther west to improve their lot, the very story of Western expansion itself. But they were certainly picking up Southern sensibilities and sympathies along the way, assimilating, over the course of several generations, into the Anglo-Celtic culture of their frontier neighbors, far as they were from Lancaster County.

Those sensibilities would truly flourish with Christian's eldest son, John "Judge" Shirley: a man who spoke no German, married a Scots-Irish Kentucky woman, and eventually, after moving to a little town on the very edge of the Missouri Ozarks called Carthage, would father the most famous—and fiercest—Shirley of all.

ACCORDING TO THE RECOLLECTIONS of a certain George B. Walker, who lived in the Carthage area during the Civil War years and knew the Shirleys well, "old John Shirley" was "as pleasant a man as you could find." Which may well have been true—as the keeper of a small-town tavern and hotel, John would have needed to have a gregarious public persona. He was, after all, responsible for welcoming guests, keeping them entertained with witty banter, and catering to their whims and needs. But even from the documentary scraps of his existence that survive, it seems that there was more to the man—a burning ambition, an almost aggressive desire to succeed. It is perhaps telling that John wasn't mentioned in his father Christian's will; the bulk of the family farm back in Floyd County, Indiana, went to John's brothers, Denton and Anderson, with small cash allowances for his sister, Elizabeth. How much can be read into this is hard to say. Perhaps there were tensions between father and son, or perhaps Christian believed John had other interests and didn't need the inheritance as much as his brothers. Regardless, it does say something about how John was positioned within the Shirley family: a man apart, he had to make it on his own. He had something to prove. And prove it he most certainly did, upon his arrival in southwestern Missouri.

First, there was his "Judge" moniker, which, given the fact that there is no record of his ever studying or practicing law, might imply a certain self-imposed grandiosity, or at least hint at the public perception of such, something akin to a Kentucky "Colonel." Then there was his penchant for advantageous marriage and divorce. Eliza Pennington, the Kentucky woman of alleged Hatfield blood who would bear him five children—the future Belle Starr among them—was his third wife. He apparently married and divorced two times prior in southern Indiana, which would have been unusual for that time and place. And while it is possible that his first two wives left him of their own free will, to live alone on the edge of the frontier, that seems unlikely. The ambitious "Judge" Shirley was going places, acquiring and discarding spouses as he rose through the social ranks of frontier life. Eliza, his third and final wife, was something of a Southern belle, a respected figure in Louisville society, who brought to Missouri, according to her obituary in the *Dallas Daily Times-Herald*, "all of the Kentucky graces she had learned as a child." She was considered a lady of "social eloquence," who could play the piano beautifully when decorum demanded— although interestingly enough, the same obituary also lays down the claim that the "wild blood of the children was derived from the Pennington side of the house," and that when marital discord occurred, John Shirley always insisted that "the children got their meanness from her." Which, if the feuding Hatfield connection is legitimate, may have held a grain of truth—or may simply have been the rantings of a fractious husband. It's impossible to say.

What we do know is that John and Eliza Shirley arrived in southwestern Missouri at an opportune moment. It was 1839, just two years after the last of the region's Osage had been forcibly exiled west to Indian Territory, as a result of the Sarcoxie War—which in reality wasn't so much a war as an armed bullying campaign against a confused and understandably irritated tribe struggling to make sense of just what, exactly, these strange English-speaking newcomers wanted, so much hungrier for land than the French fur trappers and priests who had preceded them. The answer, unfortunately for the Osage, was for the tribe to simply leave.

With relatively fertile land, abundant timber, and plenty of local creeks for powering mills now available, the environs around Carthage offered ample opportunities for an ambitious pioneer like John Shirley. In 1848, after close to a decade of frontier homesteading, the U.S. government officially granted him a patent on 800 acres southeast of Medoc—a sizable holding for a yeoman farmer. And the prescient John Shirley wasted no time in selling off parcels of his extensive acreage for profit, beginning in 1850 with the sale of 160 acres to David Martin for $700. This would have been a significant amount, given that his entire real estate holdings, as of that year's census, were appraised at a mere $600. With that initial injection of liquid capital, he purchased the following year his first two-acre lots in the nearby town of Carthage, taking the initial step in his transformation from backwoods homesteader to prosperous burgher. In 1856, he sold the rest of his farmland to a Mr. George W. Broome. With the profits from that sale, coupled with the lots he already owned, he founded the establishment that would make his family famous in the region: the Carthage Hotel, known colloquially as "the Shirley House." Within a few years, John Shirley would own not only the hotel but most of the block, including a blacksmith shop and livery stable associated with the business. By the time the 1860 census came around, his real estate holdings had increased from that meager $600 of a decade prior to a respectable $4,000, plus a personal estate of $6,000 more, for a net worth of $10,000—a small fortune by the standards of the day.

Alongside John Shirley's financial prosperity came plentiful offspring. He already had a son and a daughter from his first marriage, Preston and Charlotte, who came with him to Missouri from southern Indiana. By the time the 1850 census was taken, his third wife Eliza had given birth to three additional children, with a fourth and fifth child appearing in the census ten years later, after they had moved to town and opened the hotel. Of Eliza's five children, four were boys: John Allison, Edwin Benton, Mansfield, and the youngest son, Cravens. And right in the center of the brood was the quintessential middle child, Myra Maybelle, who at some point—the verdict still isn't in on when—began to go simply by Belle.

As we well know, Belle was born on February 5, 1848, long before her parents opened the hotel and relocated to town. Her teenage years may have been spent among the manicured lawns and brick storefronts of Carthage, but at heart, she was a farm girl, having spent her childhood on the original frontier homestead outside Medoc. By the time she was born, almost a decade after John and Eliza's arrival, most of the true pioneer labor—cutting down trees, removing stumps, building fences, erecting a cabin—would have already been done. The initial Shirley home had likely been a log house, but by 1848, a more "civilized" clapboard farmhouse had almost certainly replaced it—or been built around it, as was often the custom. As for the farm itself, some sense of it can be gathered from an advertisement that ran for the same tract, several years after John had sold it. The ad, published on March 29, 1861, in the *Southwest News* of Carthage, describes the old Shirley farm as follows:

600 acres of Spring River bottom land, situate in Jasper County about three miles northwest of Sherwood, and on one of the most beautiful streams in the west. There is 100 acres in cultivation, has

on it a small apple orchard, dwelling house, kitchen, stable & c.,
has a good well. The larger portion of it is heavily timbered; stone
coal is abundant in the vicinity, and a more desirable stock farm
could not be found in the Southwest.

Of course, some embellishment may have been added—this is a
real estate advertisement, after all—but assuming reasonable accu-
racy, the Shirley farm comes off as a fairly bucolic place. And some
additional insights can be gleaned from it as well. From the land's
description as a "stock farm," and from the fact that only one-sixth
of the acreage was actually being cultivated for grain farming, it's
safe to assume that under his stewardship, John Shirley had been
engaged primarily in the breeding and raising of horses—a fact
that could also explain Belle's lifelong passion for all things horse-
related, be it riding them, grooming them, or yes, even stealing
them. Her skills in horsemanship—and marksmanship, for that
matter—were likely acquired at a young age, growing up on a stock
and stud farm in the Ozarks, with an older brother to show her the
ropes.

She was, by all accounts, extremely close to John Allison—
known by the family as Bud—and the commonly accepted story,
although there is scant proof to back it up, is that it was he who
taught her to handle both rifle and pistol, taking her riding through
the surrounding countryside at a full wild gallop. True or not, she
clearly had a strong bond with her elder brother, stronger perhaps
than with anyone else in her family. It's easy to envision the two
of them—Belle seven or eight, Bud, just into his teens, the stables
mucked, the day's chores all done—tearing off across the aforementioned apple orchard on their favorite mounts, ducking to
avoid the low-hanging branches, squirrel guns at the ready, laugh-
ing into the purple rush of cold evening air, that tomboyish little girl receiving her first forbidden taste of what the Appalachian

author Thomas Wolfe once described as "darkness, the wind, and incalculable speed." A taste, as it were, that would only whet her appetite. A hunger, it just so happens, that would last her a lifetime.

WHEN JOHN SHIRLEY SOLD his farm in 1856 and relocated his family to the town of Carthage, he did more than improve their fortunes. He fundamentally altered the nature of their existence, from that of country people engaged in agricultural labor to one of commerce-minded burghers, running a business that was inextricably linked to the life of the town. For the young Belle, not quite yet ten, it must have been a startling shift, to go from the crickets and lightning bugs of the woods out by Medoc to the bustle of carriages and clatter of trade that filled the streets of the burgeoning town. And her new role as a hotelier's daughter would have brought her into contact with an entirely new cast of colorful characters, from top-hatted traveling lawyers to high-plumed Southern ladies to broad-brimmed ranchers making their way farther west. Even the Osage occasionally visited Carthage from their exile in the village of Flat Rock Creek over in Kansas, congregating in front of Linn's general store, where they bought tobacco and red calico, bedecked in their traditional tribal finery.

One common misconception is that John's tavern was some sort of crude frontier flophouse, with bearskins and muskets hanging on its log-beamed walls. The fact of the matter is, by 1856, Missouri had been a state for over thirty years, and Carthage had been a county seat for fifteen. Its stately two-story brick courthouse had stood at the center of town since 1849, with a central square hemmed in on all sides by orderly shops and businesses. In addition to Linn's general store, these included the law offices of Johnston and Kerr, Franklin's harness shop, Cannon's grocery, Casey's bakery, Chrisman's saloon, Bulgin's carpentry shop, and Dawson's drugstore, which was soon also to publish, from a printing press in its back, Carthage's first newspaper, *Star of the West*. In fact, its editor was the druggist's own son, Christopher Columbus Dawson, who was known to all as Lum. There was even a specialty shop, run by J. L. Cravens, where one could find everything from whalebone corsets to mule collars. By the time John Shirley opened his tavern-hotel, Carthage was already a bustling "Southern" town, and with its rose gardens, shade trees, and white picket fences, it would have borne far more resemblance to something out of *Tom Sawyer* than out of *Last of the Mohicans*. The Shirleys' establishment was almost certainly quaint and quite possibly even elegant, at least by the standards of the day; it seems to have been regarded as one of the finer hotels in southwestern Missouri. Indeed, at the time, being a county seat meant something—significant trials would have been held at the town's courthouse, festivals and gatherings would have occurred on its greens, and government officials would have passed through its streets on a regular basis. And as the primary hotel and tavern in the town of Carthage, the Shirley House was where important guests would have stayed. The hotel boasted a library of leather-bound books, a polished piano for an evening's entertainment, and meals that almost certainly came with the option of wine. Being a relatively young settlement and close to the frontier, Carthage certainly would have been a *bit* rough around the edges. But as a thriving county seat populated largely by transplanted Southerners, it also would have done its best to affect a sort of genteel antebellum charm—and with their prized hotel as its flagship, the Shirley family would have served as the town's primary ambassadors.

With their new station, however, came the demand for a higher level of education and refinement, for the children in particular. It's unclear how much schooling Belle received growing up on the farm, but aside from some basic letters and numbers courtesy of her mother, the answer is probably not much. And beyond mere book learning, there were the manners and graces expected of any woman of decent upbringing at that time—and with her mother Eliza's "social eloquence" in mind, it's easy to envision a great deal of headshaking and hand-wringing to have occurred through farmhouse windows, every time Belle lit off bareback for the high timber with her older brother Bud, howling into the wind. The move into Carthage coupled with their new position in society presented John and Eliza with the impetus to give their daughter the kind of education they saw fitting for a young Southern lady—namely, a moderate amount of classical study, coupled with ample instruction in comportment and etiquette.

There was only one small problem: no such school in Carthage existed as of yet. Which was why Belle initially received, along with two of her brothers, at least some degree of private tutoring at the town's Masonic Hall—which occupied the second floor of Linn's general store—courtesy of William Cravens, the father, evidently, of the same J. L. Cravens who sold the corsets and mule collars. A former student of Mr. Cravens who studied alongside a ten-year-old Belle would remember her many years later in the *Carthage Press* as "small and dark," insisting that she was actually "a bright, intelligent girl but was of a fierce nature and would fight anyone, boy or girl, that she quarreled with." Beyond her quick temper, however, "she seemed a nice little girl." A pleasant, sharp-witted child with a ferocious temper, who would take on any challenger, no matter their size or sex—even at age ten, Myra Maybelle Shirley was revealing the first traces of what she would one day become.

Then in 1858 community leaders officially opened the Carthage Female Academy, situated on Seminary Street in the southern part of town. The school, which was first chartered in 1855, consisted of a new two-story brick building that cost an impressive $3,000 to build, catering to the daughters of prominent families from all around Jasper County, Missouri. Under the tutelage of Principal Samuel M. Knealand, together with two teachers, a Ms. Walker and a Mr. Hurley, girls were instructed in reading, writing, history, and arithmetic, while also receiving lessons in more erudite subjects like Greek, Latin, Hebrew, and French. Art and music classes were offered as well, which might explain Belle's other lifelong passion besides horses: the piano. And with a polished upright available at the hotel, she would have had ample opportunity to put her musical education into practice.

At first glance, the community's investment in the Carthage Female Academy may seem surprisingly progressive for a small Southern town only a day's ride from the true frontier. After all, the construction costs and staff salaries would have been hardly inconsequential—a sizable investment in the edification of the town's young women. But it deserves at least a mention: the original intent behind such academies was hardly to turn out freethinking, independent career women. These were effectively charm schools for aspiring Southern ladies, designed to give them a touch of refinement so they could wax eloquent at their husband's dinner parties and entertain guests at the piano with some impromptu Beethoven. Or as the headmaster of a similar nineteenth-century institution located in Giles County, Tennessee, put it, the goal of women's education was "to preserve and cultivate the ornamental character of the female sex." And that was precisely what they provided—a final coat of polish and buffing for a class of young women destined to be viewed by society simply as ornaments.

For better or for worse, the Carthage Female Academy would be destroyed less than a decade after its founding in the fire and fury of the national calamity to come, incinerating its records— including any proof of Belle's attendance or how she may have fared as a student. But it seems safe to assume that a young Myra Maybelle Shirley, daughter of one of the town's most prosperous businessmen, would have attended Carthage's only school for females. And it seems equally safe—perhaps even *safer*—to assume that the very first seeds of her rebellious nature were sown around this time; that the same feisty little girl who delighted in fistfighting with boys and racing horses with her older brother began to bristle and fume under the constant stream of admonishment that issued forth from all authority figures present, be it her mother or her principal or her teachers, regarding what "a lady" could and could not do.

Indeed, in parsing the early history of the Shirley family in Missouri, in peering into these formative years, one can almost feel the defining substance of an inchoate Belle Starr beginning to form and rise like yeast. A farm girl, still a bit wild and countrified, fond of horses, familiar with guns, suddenly soaking up the style and sophistication of townsfolk, while at the same time feeling the first pull of the wider world beyond—wondrous glimpses of which are caught in the jangling beads of the visiting Osage, the silverworked revolvers of itinerant gamblers, and the plumed fans of velvet-clad doyennes lounging in the hotel parlor. A girl who has all the Germanic drive and ambition of her father, coupled with her mother's Scots-Irish temper and Southern flair for drama. A girl who is constantly being told in no uncertain terms that *No, a lady can't do that*, despite every fiber of her being telling her *Yes indeed, a lady can.*

All the basic ingredients were there. In the flinty soil of southwestern Missouri, the germinating seed of Belle Starr had been planted. The only thing missing was a tipping point. A rupture. An event that would upend the societal norms and rules that constrained her, to the point where what was righteous and what was legal were no longer clear, let alone interchangeable. And that rupture would not only come on the advent of her teenage years—it would burn the town of Carthage down around her.

CHAPTER 2

Carnage Comes to Carthage

H OW DOES ONE EVEN begin to tell the story of the American Civil War? Where does one begin, when it comes to a conflict that would shred a callow young country to pieces, killing 2 percent of its entire population—620,000 souls—before finally giving freedom to another 4 million? One could start with the climate-based agricultural patterns of the North versus those of the South, or the culture-based immigration patterns of the Dutch and East Anglian merchants who first settled the cities of New England and New York, as opposed to those of the progeny of post-feudal English gentry who landed in Virginia and the Carolinas. And of course, one could also choose to begin with the introduction of African chattel slavery to the American colonies, an "original sin" that wasn't original at all, but borrowed, right alongside John Rolfe's famous tobacco seeds, from the Caribbean plantations of the Spanish—who in turn had borrowed and adapted it during La Reconquista from the Moors. The truth is, there is no simple slit in the curtains of history through which one can slip in and comprehend that cruel and bloody stage; it's simply too sprawling, too vast. However, the aforementioned real estate advertisement for John Shirley's stock farm can serve as a small but compelling peephole through the dark velvet of time, providing rich historical insights, with just those few lines of type, that a textbook never could.

The ad that appeared in the *Southwest News* of Carthage, on March 29, 1861, offers for sale "600 acres of Spring River bottom land." A full accounting is given of that stock farm, from the stable to the "dwelling house" to the kitchen structure; even a "good well" is mentioned, useful for drawing drinkable water. One thing that is not included in the inventory of features and structures, however, is slave cabins. And there's no reason such a detail would have been purposefully overlooked—the *Southwest News* was a notoriously proslavery publication, and the occupation of the town by Union troops was still months away. In fact, the advertisement even included, as an unsettling addendum, that the land itself could be paid for in slaves, "at the highest cash price." But there is no mention of slave quarters as part of the property. The reason behind this omission is almost certainly a simple one: the pioneer, homesteader, and stockman John Shirley, when he worked the farm in the 1850s, did not own slaves. None were mentioned on that original 1850 census, when his real estate holdings were appraised at a meager $600, and given his situation at that time, it's not surprising. He likely could not have afforded to own human property, and his own offspring provided plenty of free labor—there is a reason, after all, rural frontier families tended to be on the large side.

While it's difficult to say precisely how much John had been exposed to slavery over the course of his life while his family bounced across Virginia, Kentucky, and Indiana, the answer is probably not a great deal. Palatine German immigrants were well known for being against the institution of slavery, even when they moved south out of Pennsylvania into the Shenandoah Valley. And regardless of any inherited distaste for the practice, slavery would have been virtually nonexistent on the Appalachian frontier of Kentucky, where he spent his early years, and flat-out illegal in Indiana, where he had spent most of his adult life prior to Missouri. On paper, this John Shirley does not appear a likely candidate to support slavery or the incipient notion of Southern secession. He was neither a slave owner nor deeply Southern, having grown up in border states, descended from yeomen Pennsylvania Dutch farmers.

But as demonstrated by the census of 1860, taken ten years later, John Shirley was changing, both on paper and in his daily life. This John Shirley, who lived comfortably in town, who owned a prosperous hotel and tavern, who could claim a sizable fortune and multiple real estate investments to his name, *did* own slaves. Two are listed on the census, later identified as Jordan Gloss and Leanner Shaw, for whom he paid $611—the total value of his real estate holdings just ten years before—and who resided in a lean-to on the west side of the building. As to why he made the sizable investment to purchase human beings to work in his hotel and tavern, it's hard to imagine it was purely out of "necessity." Running a relatively small inn with a stable attached would almost certainly have demanded less manual labor than his stock farm had out by Medoc. And his family was only growing in size, with more children to assist with chores. But that perhaps is precisely the point: the new John "Judge" Shirley, a town father and self-made Southern gentleman who openly embraced his new social position, would have embraced the practice of slavery as well, as a form of "keeping up appearances" among his well-heeled clientele, if nothing else. He probably didn't want his wife or his children scrubbing pots, sweeping floors, or shoveling horse manure anymore; such things were now considered beneath them. He was invested in the institution of slavery wholeheartedly, as an inseparable component of his newfound identity, even though he was hundreds of miles away from any significant plantation economy, and despite the fact that it didn't necessarily make much economic sense. And forget about morality—that apparently didn't trouble him at all.

This stubborn adherence to the preservation of human bondage, in service to some misconstrued societal ideal, was shared by many in the border state of Missouri. Including, as it were, John

Shirley's two teenage children, Belle and Bud, both of whom had come of age during the Bleeding Kansas years of the 1850s, in a town still within riding distance of the settlement at Pottawatomie Creek, where the abolitionist John Brown and his sons had hacked five men to death with broadswords. Officially, the Civil War wouldn't begin until 1861, but on the border that separated Kansas and Missouri, right where the Shirleys lived, violence between abolitionist and proslavery settlers had been raging for half a decade. Belle and her older brother Bud grew up steeped in that violence, and their community was riven by it. Their own father, who was described years later by Kansas's *Fort Scott Weekly Monitor* as a "very bitter confederate" and who apparently even tried several times to kill a local pro-Union Irish immigrant named John Crow, would have surely inculcated them throughout those years with an intense distaste for abolitionists, Northerners, federal representatives, and anyone else who sought to deprive him of his human property. The children of the Shirley clan may have inherited their patriarch's ambition and drive, but they also were heirs to his allegiances and his hatreds. And in the case of Belle and Bud in particular, this meant that when the winds of war finally came to Carthage, they would both be swept up, both carried away.

THE LEGALITY OF SLAVERY may have been at the heart of the dispute that provoked the Civil War, but Western expansion was the catalyst that turned it deadly. By the 1850s, the tide was turning against America's "peculiar institution." The wave of immigrants from Germany and Ireland arriving in Northern cities, coupled with the rapid growth of industrialization that sparked the demand for their labor, created a country that was geographically top-heavy in terms of both population and resources—the delicate balance of powers that had allowed slavery to persist in the South into the latter half of the nineteenth century was shifting. Add to that the fact that many countries in Europe, a continent that Americans had always taken great pride in denigrating as ideologically backward and socially repressive, had already outlawed slavery along with the slave trade. Great Britain, America's tyrannical bogeyman since the Revolution, had abolished slavery in 1833, and France, the nation that had helped the colonials achieve their "liberty" during said revolution, had done so in 1848. For the United States of America, a country that claimed to be a global bastion of freedom, the fact that 4 million of its residents—more than 12 percent of its entire population—lived in bondage was increasingly becoming a source of national shame, at least in the states where slavery was banned. Abolitionist sentiment was growing, rendering the position of Southern states—whose agro-industrial economies were largely dependent on slave labor—all the more tenuous.

Which meant that as settlement expanded westward and new states with congressional votes were added on, ensuring the continuation of the delicate balance of those powers that had prevented slavery from being outlawed became paramount, a consuming Southern obsession. The famous Missouri Compromise of 1820, which admitted Missouri as a slave state while admitting Maine as a free state, had also laid down an invisible border along the 36°30' parallel, with the intention of ensuring an equal distribution of slave and free states in the decades to come. The violence that erupted in the Bleeding Kansas border wars between 1854 and 1859, right on the Shirleys' doorstep, was effectively the first stitches popping in that fragile compromise.

When Kansas had first come up for statehood—with the potential to determine which faction controlled the U.S. Senate—and the decision was made, courtesy of the Kansas-Nebraska Act of 1854, to let the residents themselves vote for whether slavery would be legal there, chaos ensued, as settlers from both camps poured in and had at it. A Civil War in miniature raged for half a decade, with a tenuous peace being achieved at last thanks to the efforts of the new territorial governor John W. Geary. That peace was shattered, however, on both a local and national scale, with the election of Abraham Lincoln in November of 1860. The idea of a president openly hostile to any territorial expansion of slavery was too much for most slave states to brook. Before his inauguration could even take place, seven Southern states would leave the Union, Kansas would be admitted as a "free" state with little political resistance, and all hell would break loose. By April 12 of the following year, as a result of the Confederate attack on Fort Sumter, America was officially at war with itself, and impassioned young men from both sides of the Mason-Dixon were lining up to fight.

One such young man was nineteen-year-old John Allison Shirley, better known as Bud. He was one of many Confederate sympathizers who called Carthage home, and who had bristled for months at the candidacy and election of Abraham Lincoln. Carthage did have a smattering of pro-Union men, individuals like Norris C. Hood, Archibald McCoy, Dr. J. M. Stemmons, and of course John Crow, the same Irish immigrant who John Shirley would later attempt to kill. But the majority of the town, as one might expect of a frontier settlement composed primarily of Southern transplants, was sympathetic to the nascent Confederacy. A copy of the *Southwest News* from March 29, 1861—the same issue, incidentally, that included the advertisement for John Shirley's old stock farm—offers a few tantalizing hints at just how intense anti-Unionist sentiment ran. In one editorial, Abraham Lincoln is described as "six feet four in physical stature and four feet six in mental stature." Another article containing the minutes from a town hall meeting urges the secession of Missouri, promising to welcome any Northern troops with "bloody hands to hospital graves." There is also an ominous advertisement, courtesy of the metalworks of Parkinson, Long &

Co., printed as a reassurance to local teamsters that the company would continue to smelt and ship lead, "so that waggoners can be supplied with loads at any time at custom prices." Lead, evidently, being the one commodity everyone knew would soon be in high demand and short supply.

However, the most interesting line of print from that March 29, 1861 issue of the *Southwest News,* the one most relevant to the fates of both John Allison and Myra Maybelle Shirley, was a public announcement that ran as follows: "The Border Rangers drill every Saturday from this on. Let everyone be at his post tomorrow as there is important business to transact." These two sentences, terse and seemingly innocuous as they were, contained for the town of Carthage the very first cold tang of the whirlwind to come. Because they were, in effect, a call to arms, summoning all men of fighting age to gather and begin training in defense of the Confederate cause. The Border Rangers unit was the initial pro-Confederate militia of Carthage, Missouri, likely a relic of the Bleeding Kansas days, and this issue of the *Southwest News* calling for its renewed assembly in preparation for battle was almost certainly passed around the parlor of the Shirleys' hotel, to be read and nodded over by family members and guests alike. John Shirley, by this point in his mid-sixties, would have been far too old to drill with the militia and train for the war that lurked just two weeks in the offing. But his son Bud was of prime fighting age, and it's easy to imagine the father—and Belle, too, for that matter—watching from the front porch of the hotel with a piquant mix of pride and longing as Bud, later described by fellow volunteer George B. Walker as a young man "medium sized, dark complexioned and who weighed probably 160 pounds," marched toward the village green to join the other Border Rangers, a pistol at his waist and a rifle-musket over his shoulder. And he must have made an impression, as Walker also described him as "as good a companion and as brave a man as you could find anywhere." But an interesting addendum—Belle left her mark as well. As part of the same account, Walker had this to say about his comrade's teenage sister: "although she was small for her age she was rather a pretty girl and everybody liked her." It's not difficult to imagine the young men of Carthage trading winks and smiles with their friend's beloved younger sibling as they marched past the hotel, standing as straight and tall as they possibly could, doing their best to convey the same sense of regimental nobility that their total lack of uniforms belied.

As for Jordan Gloss and Leanner Shaw—the two young slaves that John Shirley had purchased for $611 to work at his hotel and stable—it's impossible to know what they were thinking as they watched the aspiring Confederate volunteers assemble in Carthage, guns raised high, yelping their shouts of rebellion into the cool spring air. The Border Rangers would have drilled right beside the brick courthouse, which itself had been built using slave labor, and at which public slave auctions occurred each New Year's Day, with the keening call of the auctioneer almost certainly audible from the hotel. Regardless, it seems safe to say that Jordan and Leanner would have had a reaction very different from that of Belle and her father and would have experienced a different kind of longing. Jasper County, of which Carthage served as the county seat, did not, by Southern standards, have many slaves—only 350, out of a population of 6,883. The Confederate cause, for those who supported it, was far more of an ideological concern than an economic one. Southwestern Missouri was a place of forested hills, unused prairies, and small family farms, not of sprawling lowland cotton plantations. But for those 350 individuals who knew what it was to be considered and treated as less than human, the stakes could not have been higher, and their hope for freedom, expressed far less publicly but felt no less intensely than their masters' desire for war, must have burned and trembled within.

There was a common sentiment prior to the war, and that persisted long after, that slavery in the border states—Missouri in particular—was somehow less harsh, more "humane" than the bondage that prevailed farther "down the river," where humans were treated like disposable grist for the massive plantations that turned out the cotton the rest of the country craved. However, to dispel any notions that the inherent violence that pervaded the plantation slavery of the Deep South wasn't equally pervasive in Missouri—Carthage, in particular—the events that transpired during the summer of 1853 offer a shocking rejoinder.

The story broke in newspapers around the state: a certain Dr. Fisk, after allegedly receiving a large sum of money from a business partner, had been murdered outside his home. His house was burned down shortly thereafter, with his wife and two-year-old child still inside. In the aftermath of the heinous crime, the citizens of Carthage were convinced, based solely on an item of bloodstained clothing found at the cabin of a slave named Colley, that he, along with another slave named Bart, had conspired to commit theft, rape, and murder, and then burned down the house to conceal their crimes. As to the validity of the accusations, there never was any trial or court appearance. Nor was the business partner who had provided the money ever seriously investigated or considered a suspect. Instead, after stringing one of the accused slaves up on a rope to elicit a confession—coerced under torture—the citizens themselves decided that the two men under suspicion deserved to die. Consensus could not be reached on the appropriate means of execution, and a vote was held on the town square, with those who favored hanging marching to one corner of the lawn, and those in favor of burning gathering at the other. A decision was finally reached by popular vote, and three days later, the largest crowd ever seen in the county assembled at a natural "amphitheater" formed by a ring of hills outside of town.

Local slave owners forced their slaves to attend the public execution so that they, too, could see what happened to any person of African descent accused of revolting against the social order—in fact, they even reserved for them the seats closest to the stakes. At precisely three o'clock, the two condemned men were marched in and chained together between two posts, while cordwood and kindling was piled around them. As the fire was being lit—by two other slaves, commanded to do so by their masters—Colley began singing hymns, while Bart screamed and pleaded for his life. According to witnesses, they struggled for a few minutes before being smothered by the flames. An hour later, after the fire had burned down, there was little that remained, and what little that did was washed away shortly thereafter by a summer cloudburst that soaked the spectators on their way home and drenched the entire county in rain.

It's impossible to say if John Shirley or his family witnessed the two men being burned alive on the outskirts of Carthage on that stormy August afternoon in 1853. The Shirleys were still living on the stock farm out by Medoc at that time, although it was recorded that people traveled from as far away as fifty miles to attend. It's not known if Jordan Gloss or Leanner Shaw, who would later become the legal property of John Shirley, sat in the front row on the orders of their previous master. They probably would have still been children at the time, although that may not have been a deterring factor. What can be stated with some certainty, however, is that virtually everyone in the community—white and Black, free and slave, secessionist and unionist—would have been familiar with that story, even eight years later. And while many in Jasper County would waver or seek compromise in the tumultuous days leading up to the war, everyone knew that the fight to come was ultimately about the preservation or eradication of the institution of slavery, with all the violence, suppression, and coercion that went with it.

At least in that one regard, everyone was on the same ideological page; everyone knew exactly what was at stake.

WHEN WAR FINALLY DID come to the border states, it did not come cleanly. Unlike states whose geography and allegiances were less ambiguous—Mississippi, say, or Vermont—the states that existed both spatially and politically between the North and the South fractured along far messier lines. And in few places was this truer than in Missouri, a state with a mixed Southern and Northern population and tremendous cultural gaps between its cosmopolitan, immigrant-filled cities, and its demographically Southern and Appalachian hinterlands. A merchant from Chicago would have felt right at home walking through the bustling ethnic markets of downtown St. Louis, a cotton farmer from Georgia equally at ease in the state's flat Bootheel region, and a moonshiner from the Blue Ridge just as content in an Ozark mountain hollow.

Little wonder, then, that when the moment came to choose sides, clear consensus did not come with it. As Mark Twain, perhaps the most famous Missourian of all time, would recall: "Out west there was a good deal of confusion in men's minds during the first months of the great trouble—a good deal of unsettledness, of leaning this way, then that, then the other way. It was hard for us to get our bearings." Missouri's governor, Claiborne Fox Jackson, epitomized this stance, publicly vacillating throughout the spring between supporting secession while also maintaining some measure of neutrality; he initially wanted to keep Missouri out of the war, but he clearly harbored Confederate sympathies. Jackson would force the federal government's hand, however, just two months later, when he began gathering state militia troops on the outskirts of St. Louis, uncomfortably close to the city's fortified arsenal. General Nathaniel Lyon, recently promoted by Lincoln to take charge of all U.S. military affairs in the state, beat him to the punch and surrounded "Camp Jackson" with his own pro-Union army of recent recruits—most of whom, interestingly enough, were German immigrants who had fled the same revolutions that had wracked the remnants of the Holy Roman Empire the year Belle was born. In the end, Governor Jackson's state militia yielded to General Lyon, and the arsenal was secured, ensuring that the city of St. Louis, along with its crucial control over Mississippi River traffic, would remain in Union hands.

Southwestern Missouri, however, where the Shirleys called home, was another matter entirely. The federal intervention at Camp Jackson had galvanized public sentiment there. The region was a hotbed of Southern sympathizers, and just across the state line from the unambiguously Confederate armies of Arkansas, a state that had seceded the same day that Missouri state militia forces had convened outside St. Louis. An infuriated Governor Jackson, still smarting from the humiliation of the Camp Jackson debacle, officially declared the creation of a State Guard—a full-on Confederate militia—and prepared for war. When the same "Yankee Dutch" troops who had surrounded his militia forces outside St. Louis went on to occupy the state capital of Jefferson City and oust him from his role as governor, his course was set. Jackson fled from the federals with his ragtag recruits, making a hasty course for Missouri's southwestern frontier, where he hoped to organize and train his secessionist State Guard while officially joining up with the Confederate forces from Arkansas. In hot pursuit of him, however, was a feisty Union colonel named Franz Sigel, himself a recent immigrant from the German town of Baden. His mission was to cut off Jackson's State Guard before they could establish themselves in the region and link up with Confederate troops from across the southern border. A clash was all but inevitable, and the town where it would take place was Carthage, Missouri.

On July 5, 1861, a date remembered for the presence of the Great Comet that hovered ominously and unusually bright in the summer sky—an augury, some believed, of the calamity to come—that confrontation finally took place, in a stretch of prairie and timber ten miles to the north of town. The Battle of Carthage, as it has come to be known, rarely receives much ink in histories of the Civil War, overshadowed as it has become by the much larger and more official Battle of Bull Run that would occur just two weeks later. The Battle of Carthage itself resembled a prolonged skirmish between two hastily gathered and poorly armed state militias far more than it did an organized, uniformed conflict between gray-clad Confederates and blue-blazoned Yankees. The Missouri State Guard volunteers were mostly poor farmers with squirrel rifles and old shotguns, and the Union troops were primarily German immigrants from the slummier quarters of St. Louis, carrying unfamiliar weapons yanked at the last minute from the city's arsenal. "We resembled a rabble more than soldiers," a Private John T. Buegel would write in his journal regarding the battle. "Each wore whatever clothes they chose to wear. They had become torn on the march. In place of trousers, they had slipped on flour sacks. Others had no shoes and were walking on uppers or going barefoot. Still others had no hats and used flour sacks for head coverings." And these were Union soldiers—the Missouri State Guard volunteers would have been even worse off than that.

The Battle of Carthage was anything but a well-orchestrated series of brilliant maneuvers. A Chancellorsville or a Vicksburg, it was not. It was, however, the first true taste of violence for the Shirleys, and for Belle in particular. Specifics about the family's involvement in the battle are scant; the printing presses of the *Southwest News* would be commandeered to serve the Confederate war effort shortly after the engagement, and recruits to the Southern cause had been so haphazardly added, few records remain of exactly who from Carthage joined in the battle. It seems probable, if not certain, that Bud Shirley and his fellow Carthage Border Rangers fought in some form on the side of the pro-Confederate Missouri State Guard. And it is a historical fact that when the tide began to turn against the vastly outnumbered Union forces of Colonel Sigel, he retreated with his men southward back toward the town of Carthage itself, with both sides eventually facing off in the town square—*literally* on the doorstep of John Shirley's hotel. The thirteen-year-old Belle would have surely heard the encroaching thunder of artillery shells and crackle of gunfire as the battle lines approached. Before being dragged into the root cellar, where many residents were hiding, she may have even watched through a crack in the shutters as the smoke billowed across the village green and as ricochets spat fragments of brick and bloodied men screamed for help in a tortured mix of English and German. It was recorded that in the artillery barrage that followed, one errant shell even struck the bell of the Carthage Female Academy, filling the town with a single haunting knell. One would think that such an experience might turn a young girl away from a life of guns and violence—but in the case of Belle, it seemed to have the opposite effect.

COLONEL SIGEL's 1,100 UNION troops were better armed, better organized, and more disciplined than Governor Jackson's Missouri State Guard. They were also outnumbered, though, by roughly five to one. Volunteers from the surrounding Missouri countryside, not to mention proper Confederate reinforcements from Arkansas, had all poured in just prior to the engagement, swelling the secessionists' ranks. When it became clear to Sigel that he could not hold Carthage against Jackson's superior numbers, he had no choice but to beat a hasty retreat, fleeing with his troops for the nearby village of Sarcoxie, the Missouri State Guard hot on his heels.

The citizenry of Carthage was largely jubilant. Women were already welcoming panting state guardsmen in the streets with food and water before the last of the Union troops had even fully retreated—the Rebels, for by now they were surely that, paused only long enough for a quick gulp from a gourd before resuming the chase. By the time the smoke cleared, the American flag installed over the brick courthouse by Sigel's forces the night before had been ceremoniously replaced by the Confederate Stars and Bars, and wounded men from both sides were being treated together in a makeshift hospital established within. When the courthouse became full, the additional wounded were taken over to the Shirleys' hotel, although five injured Union soldiers were first kept on a lawn and later crammed into a corner of a separate room—probably at the behest of John Shirley himself, whose antipathy for the North and for the federal government had certainly not been lessened by having German-speaking troops from St. Louis occupy and bombard his "Southern" town. This sentiment was likely shared by his teenage daughter Belle, who in addition to having just absorbed from the secessionist victory a newfound appreciation for the redemptive, perhaps even ecstatic, power of violence, also possessed a newfound hatred for Yankees. But her beloved older brother Bud had survived the battle, and she was surely grateful for that fact—and committed to helping him, in whatever way she could, win the war.

But for that, she would have to wait. Neither the spirit of revelry nor the new Confederate occupation of Carthage lasted very long. Claiborne Fox Jackson, the self-proclaimed leader of a Confederate state government in exile, briefly tried to run his operations from southwestern Missouri, but realized within the first few months that it was not practical. The region was much too close to superior Union forces for comfort; Arkansas was a far safer solution. However, when the Confederate government abandoned Carthage in the fall of 1861, and Jackson left for Arkansas with much of his State Guard in tow, there was no longer any compelling reason for Union forces to attempt to occupy the town, either. With fierce battles raging farther east, largely on the other side of the Mississippi, precious resources and men could not be spared at that time to occupy a hostile frontier town with relatively little strategic or material value. Jasper County did have some lead mines, which had been fully exploited by Jackson's Confederate government during its brief tenure there, but the North was anything but short on ammunition—they had lead and powder to burn.

So during the last months of 1861, the county seat of Carthage was essentially abandoned by both sides. No armies occupied it, and no civil body governed it. A town fraught with sectarian divides and bitter resentments became, almost overnight, a completely lawless place. There was suddenly a vacuum of power in Carthage, and in the anarchy that ensued, friends and neighbors, people who formerly would have held summer ox roasts together, mingled at church picnics, and attended one another's birthday parties, all at once had license to do unspeakable things to each other.

Ironically, one of the first examples of this new frontier anarchy came courtesy of George W. Broome, the very man who had purchased John Shirley's stock farm back in 1856. A Georgia native, Broome was a notorious secessionist and dealer in slaves—he had even offered to exchange farmland for them on multiple occasions. He owned ample acreage, ran a popular general store, and was considered prosperous in the community, a fact that may have sealed his doom. In August of 1861, a band of marauders murdered George W. Broome in his home, stole forty head of horses, and burned his house to the ground. This act may have been a politically motivated attack on behalf of Northern jayhawkers,[1] it may have been rural banditry aimed at profit, or it may have been both—it's impossible to say. Regardless, a posse was formed in response, and suspicions immediately landed on a local clan of pro-Union Irish immigrants, three brothers in particular, named John, Austin, and Isaac Ireland. John was kidnapped and lynched by the mob on the spot following a mockery of a trial, while his two brothers were subsequently tracked down and killed near the Kansas border. A crude frontier crime and the extraction of crude frontier justice, in a place where such incidents would have been unthinkable only a few years before—at least as far as free white residents were concerned.

With the arrival of 1862, the situation deteriorated further. The exiled Confederate state government was now functioning out of Arkansas, and with the term of the 11th Cavalry of the Missouri State Guard expiring in February, the volunteers from Carthage and its environs who still wished to fight had a choice: enlist with the official Confederate Army in Arkansas and fight the Union forces farther east, or return to Missouri and join one of the guerrilla bands that were cropping up and terrorizing any manifestation of the federal government they could find. At first this had meant only Union troops and resources, but it quickly became understood among most Confederate-aligned bushwhackers that this included Union sympathizers as well. Northern families left Jasper County by the dozens, fearing for their lives, including the Hoods, a prominent family whose daughters had been schoolgirl friends with Belle, as it soon became clear that the line between the guerrilla insurgency and bald criminality had blurred. Horses were stolen, houses were burned, and eventually, entire farms were

---

[1]   Per a newspaper reporter traveling through Kansas in 1863, a jayhawker was a Unionist who professed "to rob, burn out and murder only rebels against the government." They were the mortal enemies of the Confederate-aligned bushwhacker guerrillas who fought across much of southern and western Missouri.

commandeered. The wife of one targeted Unionist, a Mrs. Lazarus Spence, would recall of this period:

> *After the [confederate] soldiers left we were visited from time to time by bushwhackers who acted polite enough at first and paid in confederate money, like the soldiers, for what they took. As the weeks passed, however, they changed their attitude and took whatever they wanted without paying for it. I felt my husband's life was no longer safe. . . . One day we heard that some bushwhackers from Granby were coming to kill my husband and so we hid out in the brush. . . . The situation seemed to be getting worse instead of better and on December 23, we decided that we would not stay another minute but leave while Mr. Spence was still alive.*

Stories like this were commonplace in southwestern Missouri toward the end of 1861 and the beginning of 1862, with former friends and neighbors going at one another's throats because of their political allegiances and views on slavery. It is likely during this period that John Shirley attempted to kill his neighbor, the Unionist and Irish immigrant John Crow—an attack that apparently caused the man to flee Carthage and move across the state line, into the more Union-friendly Kansas, where he would spend the rest of his days.

From those two options—enlist with the regular Confederate Army or return to Jasper County and join up with a guerrilla band—Bud Shirley chose the latter. One likely factor was that with his aging father well into his sixties and with his older half brother Preston off in Texas, Bud, whether he liked it or not, was the man of the house at a time when sectarian violence was raging in Carthage. And the situation was becoming only more volatile as the various Native American groups who had long since been driven out of white-held lands made the very understandable decision to take advantage of the chaos and align themselves with the cause that best suited their needs. Many Osage, living in exile in Kansas since being forced off their ancestral lands in Missouri during the Sarcoxie War of 1837, joined up with federal regiments like "Ritchie's Indians" and took to raiding the homesteads of their usurpers, dressed in full war paint and traditional regalia. Many Cherokee and Choctaw parties from Indian Territory in present-day Oklahoma, on the other hand, raided for the Confederate cause—a decision that may seem counterintuitive, given the racial component of Southern secession, until one takes into account that many Cherokee and Choctaw themselves possessed slaves, not to mention an abiding hatred for the federal government, whose Indian Removal Act more than thirty years prior had driven them west. All these aggrieved parties would descend on southwestern Missouri with payback, both literal and figurative, on their minds. And whether such fears were warranted or not, the notion of vindictive Indigenous people on the warpath was the ultimate atavistic horror for families with deep frontier roots like the Shirleys. And so, with Confederate bushwhackers and Unionist jayhawkers raging a bloody guerrilla war, with farmhouses being burned and entire families being butchered, and with tribes that hadn't been seen in the area in more than a generation taking up arms against their former oppressors, it's no wonder that Bud Shirley decided to come back to Carthage.

There was another, more specific reason—or perhaps even target—that may have also drawn Bud Shirley back home. By the spring of 1862, federal forces under the command of Lieutenant Colonel Powell Clayton had begun making forays into Jasper and neighboring counties from their home base in Kansas, ostensibly with the goal of gathering foodstuffs and breaking up precisely the kind of guerrilla bands that Bud Shirley sought to join. For the first time since Colonel Sigel had turned tail back in July, real uniformed Northern forces were showing their faces again right in the Carthage square, confiscating wheat from the town's mills and imprisoning locals suspected of harboring Confederate sympathies in the town's brick courthouse. And adding insult to injury, Colonel Clayton had been tasked by Missouri's resident pro-Union government—not Claiborne Fox Jackson's Confederate government in exile—with aiding in the formation of a formal pro-Union militia, emboldening the region's Union families to take up arms and make public displays of fealty, not to mention seek retribution. To young men like Bud Shirley, who had witnessed the defeat of Sigel's Northern troops and seen Confederates take control of the town, this surely felt like backsliding, like losing what had been fought for and hard-won. In his eyes, the same foreign invaders he had already chased off once were again occupying his home—and he wanted them gone.

There was one rather obvious impediment, however, to Bud Shirley's homecoming to Carthage. As Colonel Clayton's frequent visits to Jasper County during the spring of 1862 began to resemble less a series of foraging missions than an actual military occupation, the Union commander began to adopt one of the anti-guerrilla tactics that occupiers so often do: arrest, question, and harass virtually any young male of fighting age, regardless of whether they were part of the insurgency or not. The account of the aforementioned George B. Walker, who was not yet involved in any bushwhacking during his first encounter with Union troops, serves as a good example of what any fighting-age man would have experienced on a regular basis during the spring of 1862 in Carthage:

> There was a full regiment of union cavalry in the town, and they gave the impression of being well drilled, efficient troops. I was eighteen years old at the time and had taken no part in the war

but was living quietly on my father's farm. One day I had occasion to go to Carthage for something and while I was there the federal cavalrymen arrested me and put me in the court house, this being where they kept their prisoners. I was confined here all night and in the morning was taken downstairs and before Colonel Clayton. . . . The colonel then asked me my name, age, where I lived, and some similar questions. Finally he ordered me released. "Go on home and be a good boy," he told me, "and come in here every other day and report to me . . . just so that I will know that you are behaving yourself."

This was precisely what Bud Shirley would have faced as a twenty-year-old man living in Carthage, and it was exactly what made any sort of armed resistance against Union forces so challenging. With Colonel Clayton keeping tabs and imprisoning any suspect male who crossed his path, gathering intelligence on the numbers and positioning of federal forces was rendered all but impossible. Any young man would have been regarded with suspicion and detained and questioned accordingly.

And in fact Bud Shirley did run into precisely that problem, narrowly escaping a fate even worse than George B. Walker's while in Jasper County in 1862. According to Mrs. C. C. Warner, another local resident, Bud and two other Confederate sympathizers named Berry Bedford and James Moorhouse were spotted and approached by a group of "federal men" in the woods near her farm. Bud and James were able to get away "by running through a field," although the apparently less fleet-footed Berry was not so lucky—he was captured by the federal men and taken into custody. The terrified Mrs. Warner, witness to the entire incident, was told that the captive was in no danger and that she should return to her home. And Mrs. Warner complied, although as she would later recall, her skittishness was well warranted:

Soon after we got back, however, we heard a volley of shots and some of the men came by the house and told us we could have our man now. As expected, we found him shot to death. We took the door from the tenant house close by and got the dead man onto that. Some of the men who had remained behind helped us do that, for it was a pretty heavy job for girls to do. We then sent word to the Bedford home and his little boy brought a wagon on which we placed the improvised stretcher and took the dead man home.

This anecdote illustrates, in vivid tones, the wartime social dynamic in Jasper County: All men were presumed to be natural combatants, while women were generally viewed as innocuous bystanders. And it was at precisely this moment when a young and decidedly *female* Myra Maybelle Shirley found her niche. Her gender may have prevented her from taking up arms against the Northern "invaders"—surely a source of constant frustration for the headstrong and hot-tempered teenager—but it also gave her, probably for the first time in her life, a kind of liberty and access that was unavailable to her same cohort of young men. Essentially, the very thing that had kept her from engaging in the fight that she craved suddenly worked to her distinct advantage. As a teenage girl, Belle could travel without arousing suspicion, without being imprisoned or questioned, without risking a quick bullet in the brain. And this in turn made her, almost instantly, an incredibly valuable intelligence asset for the inchoate Confederate insurgency in Jasper County, Missouri.

Which in turn leads to the first of the many mysteries that attend the legend of Belle Starr: Was she actually a Confederate spy? The answer, based on the historical evidence at hand, is that yes, she did indeed engage in espionage on behalf of the Confederate insurgency, going on reconnaissance missions and passing along the intel to Bud and his guerrilla band. Although contrary to legend, it is very unlikely that she or her brother ever rode or fought with Quantrill's Raiders. Western Missouri was, from a community perspective, a small world, and while the Shirley family definitely knew and befriended some of the famous miscreants and roughriders who raided alongside the legendary—and rightfully vilified—Confederate guerrilla chieftain William Quantrill, and probably even hosted them at various times in their hotel, it is doubtful that Bud or Belle ever joined with his outfit. The evidence is not definitive per se—it is hard, after all, to prove a negative—but convincing enough, circumstantial as it may be.

First, no documentary record, no primary source, no eyewitness account places Belle or Bud at Quantrill's side during his ravaging and raiding of the Missouri and Kansas countryside. In his recounted memoir *Three Years with Quantrill*—one of the few surviving firsthand accounts from a Raider—former Missouri guerrilla fighter John McCorkle goes into considerable detail about the Confederate irregulars who joined up with Quantrill's band, including minor and famous figures alike. And he makes no mention of Myra Maybelle or John Allison Shirley—which would be a considerable oversight on his part, given that he devotes entire chapters to other soon-to-be Western outlaws who fought alongside him, men like Jesse James and Cole Younger. Which is to say nothing of Cole Younger's own autobiography—and he will play a part in the Belle Starr saga soon enough—because he knew the Shirleys quite well and discusses the family at length in his recollections of Missouri during wartime, making no mention of either Belle's or Bud's ever fighting with him as part of Quantrill's band. It would be a shocking coincidence indeed if both of these former Raiders somehow forgot that they had fought alongside one of the most infamous female outlaws of the Wild West era or her relatively well-known older brother.

Second, there is the question of logistics. Though William Quantrill would reave and pillage all along the Missouri–Kansas border, eventually even dipping down south into Texas and east into Kentucky, his guerrilla band was very much a product of the Little Dixie region of central western Missouri and the corresponding parts of Kansas where its Southern sympathies spilled across the state line. Most of the band's core members hailed from this pro-Confederate pocket in the northern half of the state, centered roughly around the area of present-day Kansas City. And many of its worst atrocities occurred there, including the Lawrence Massacre, where some 150 unarmed pro-Union men and boys were slaughtered, and in some cases mutilated, by Quantrill and his followers. In general, the guerrilla bands that formed in Missouri were very much homegrown organizations empowered by the Confederate Congress's Partisan Ranger Act of 1862, as well as the act's subsequent local offshoots. A military proclamation for Missouri, issued by the Confederate government in Arkansas in November of that same year, would state:

> For the more effectual annoyance of the enemy upon our rivers and in our mountains and woods all citizens of this district who are not subject to conscription are called upon to organize themselves into independent companies of mounted men or infantry, as they prefer, arming and equipping themselves, and to serve in that part of the district to which they belong.

The key wording here being "in that part of the district to which they belong." These bands, whose formation was initially encouraged by the exiled Confederate government, were specifically designed to be comprised of local guerrillas, because locals knew the "mountains and woods" described above like no other and were in the best position to ambush and sabotage the occupying Northern troops. They were, by design, *local* organizations. So in 1862, with Confederate-sanctioned militias and guerrilla units forming left and right, it would have made little sense for either Belle or Bud to randomly decide to leave behind the familiar mountains and woods of Jasper County, and instead ride 150 miles to the north and join Quantrill's local Jackson County guerrillas—especially not when they had their very own homegrown guerrilla bands forming right in Carthage at that very same time.

Instead—and unlike the Quantrill stories, there are eyewitness accounts and documentation to back this up—Bud and Belle Shirley did the logical thing. They stayed in Jasper County and participated in the popular insurrection against the quickly mounting federal occupation, which, toward the end of 1862 and beginning of 1863, was coalescing into an organized armed resistance. That same proclamation of 1862 which encouraged Confederate partisans to engage in the "effectual annoyance of the enemy" also came with specific instructions on how to begin:

> *When as many as ten men come together for this purpose they may organize by electing a captain, one sergeant and a corporal, and will at once commence operations against the enemy, without waiting for special instructions. Their duty will be to cut off Federal pickets, scouts, foraging parties and trains, and to kill pilots and others on gunboats and transports, attacking them day and night, and using the greatest vigor in their movements.*

Fortunately, a great deal of the oral history of the federal occupation of Carthage was later recorded by the local writer and historian Ward L. Schrantz. And it is thanks to his carefully transcribed accounts that we have some idea of what Bud, and to a lesser extent Belle, were up to during this period. Essentially, Bud Shirley and his pro-Confederate comrades followed the orders of the Confederate proclamation. The same George B. Walker who began the war as an innocent bystander being imprisoned and questioned by federal troops had, by 1863, become a full-fledged combatant, right alongside his good friend Bud Shirley. By the spring of 1863, both he and Bud had been "formally sworn into the service of the Confederate states as soldiers," joining a company of thirty men formed right in the town square of Carthage, of which another local, Jim Petty, had been elected captain. Of course, while they may have considered themselves proper soldiers fighting on behalf of the Confederate state government in exile, to the Union troops garrisoned in southwest Missouri, they were simply bushwhackers, un-uniformed terrorists operating outside the rules of war and worthy of neither mercy nor quarter. The original intent of Captain Petty's newly formed Carthage company had been to join up with the brigade of Colonel Joseph O. Shelby, a Missouri Confederate operating out of the relative safety of Arkansas. It was a move that would have given them the proper uniforms and official Confederate status they desired. But with southern Missouri now rife with Union forces sent to protect the border against Confederate incursions—including the freshly arrived Major Edwin B. Eno, commander of the 8th Missouri Union Cavalry and future bane of Bud's and Belle's existence—braving the gauntlet to join Colonel Shelby in Arkansas was all but impossible for the moment. So Bud Shirley and his band stayed local, camping in the woods and laying low at safe houses between their ambushes and sabotage raids. Belle, meanwhile, did what younger sisters of resistance fighters so often do during military occupations, be it in Belfast, Berlin, or Baghdad—she used her unique position as a female noncombatant to pass messages, gather intelligence, and warn her older brother when enemies were near.

Determining the exact nature of Belle's clandestine wartime activities, by dint of their secret nature and thanks to a lack of wartime documentation in general, is challenging. Unlike Bud, for whom there is at least a smattering of attributable firsthand accounts and documentary sources, there is little beyond oral tradition when it comes to his younger sister's activities, much of which was haphazardly recorded in her early biographies, marked by both wild exaggeration and pure fabrication. But while such oral histories, passed down by neighbors and distant relatives, garbled and embellished over the years, should certainly not be taken as anything resembling historical fact, they shouldn't be completely discounted, either. Oftentimes, strands of likely truth can be extracted from them—most often when multiple independent reports corroborate some specific story or fact.

One such instance of this may be Belle's encounter with Major Edwin B. Eno of the 8th Missouri Union Cavalry. The incident allegedly occurred while he and some of his officers were staying with the Ritcheys, a wealthy family in the nearby town of Newtonia known for their Union sympathies. Two early versions of the story exist, one first appearing in S. W. Harman's *Hell on the Border*, which was published in 1898, less than a decade after Belle's death, and another in Homer Croy's *Cole Younger: Last of the Great Outlaws*, originally published in 1956. The former gives no direct source for the story, although the latter was recounted to Croy during a visit to the original Ritchey Mansion. The two stories contain conflicting dates and details, but the essential substance of the anecdotes is the same. According to the Harman account, which places the event in February of 1862, Major Eno effectively imprisoned Belle briefly at the Ritchey house after capturing her during a scouting mission, to prevent her from warning her brother of his troops' movements and his intention to attack his guerrilla band. According to the Croy version, which claims the incident took place exactly one year later, Belle showed up unexpectedly at the house on horseback and pretended to be lost, in order to spend the night with the Ritcheys and gain intelligence on the major and his outfit. The circumstances vary, but the core of the story is the same: a teenage Belle stayed at the house while Union troops were quartered there, gathering useful information on their numbers and positions while also, on a somewhat lighter note, making use of the Ritcheys' expensive piano. As the oral history from the Ritchey family went:

After supper the people went into the parlor where there was a square rosewood grand piano. Belle obligingly sat down and played. Everybody thought this was delightful. After the music she again talked pleasantly, now and then asking a question. The sum and substance of these questions had to do with the Union troops and how many were there. She learned also that the Richey [sic] house was being used as headquarters for Major Eno and his officers, that enlisted men were using the stone barn and the stone mill as barracks; in addition, some of the men were encamped in the town of Newtonia. Belle smiled brightly; it was interesting to know such things, she said.

In addition to her piano playing, both versions of the story have her slipping out of the Ritchey home shortly thereafter, cutting cherry switches with which to crop her horse once outside and then galloping off toward home. In the Harman version, she rides so swiftly, she is able to warn her brother of Major Eno's impending attack, while in the Croy version, her cutting the switches is a signal for her brother's waiting guerrilla band to attack, upon which they bombard the house and blast it to pieces.

In both instances, the stories contain errors, as one might expect from any oral tradition told and retold countless times over the years. The date couldn't possibly be correct for the Harman version—Major Eno wasn't in Newtonia in February of 1862—

and the details of the Confederate bombardment of the Ritchey mansion in the Croy version are suspect as well, given that virtually no small, mobile guerrilla band of "irregulars" operating in Jasper County in 1863 would have had access to that kind of heavy artillery. The house had likely sustained most of its wartime damage the previous year, during the First Battle of Newtonia, when the 31st Texas Cavalry, fighting alongside the 1st Cherokee Battalion, took up defensive positions in the Ritchey mansion and were shelled by Union howitzers accordingly. However, despite the discrepancies and the obvious inaccuracies, a sense can be gained of the kind of activities Belle was likely involved in while Union troops were occupying Carthage and nearby towns. Using her status as a female noncombatant to gain proximity to Union troops, engaging in reconnaissance, and then employing the equestrian skills she acquired growing up on a stock farm to race back to the guerrilla positions and share the intelligence with Bud—this seems a likely summary of how she participated in the war, and far more realistic than the tall tales of her sporting a pint-size Confederate uniform and spyglass, whispering military secrets directly into the ear of William Quantrill.

And when it came to using her status as a female noncombatant to gain proximity to Union troops, there's at least some evidence that she may have taken it even one step further and capitalized on her unique position as a young, attractive girl in a place crawling with uniformed teenage boys generally deprived of feminine company. Having been raised on a stock and stud farm, Belle was undoubtedly aware of the birds and the bees, and in wartime, surrounded by rebel guerrillas and occupying Union forces alike, she would have been keenly aware of both the power and the danger her own burgeoning sexuality as a sixteen-year-old girl posed. Such was likely the case in an incident described in the February 5, 1903 edition of the *Carthage Evening Press*, as recounted by an "old soldier" who served in the 3rd Wisconsin Cavalry Regiment, when it was passing through Jasper County as part of a Union counterinsurgency expedition. The story is worth printing in its entirety, both because of the insight it provides and for sheer entertainment value:

The 3rd Wisconsin regiment was stationed about Carthage during the war and did a good deal of scouting over the country, often running into Carthage. Whenever the opportunity presented for any information in regard to the movements of the federal soldiers to be of any benefit to the bushwhackers who were often encamped in out-of-the-way corners, the notorious Belle Starr, or Myra Shirley as she was then known, would mount her horse and go like the wind till the message was delivered. Then she would come back through the lines ready to seek more information.

Being a woman it was hard to follow her movements. Two of the members of Company I of the regiment being Jasper county boys, from the vicinity of Sarcoxie, they knew whom they were dealing with.

On one occasion when the regiment ran into Carthage on a scout, as was often the case with the boys, they arranged to have a dance at night. One of the boys above spoken of and another soldier by the name of Coulson decided that they would go after Miss Shirley and her chum Miss Eliza Loving and escort them to the dance which was to come off somewhere on the public square.

The two ladies were found at the residence of Judge Chenault, who lived somewhere on the public square . . . somewhere near what is now the junction of Grant Street and Howard Avenue.

Mrs. Chenault strenuously objected to the girls going, and not wishing to go contrary to her wishes the girls entered into an agreement with the boys that they were to leave and were to return with an officer with orders for their arrest, which they did, being accompanied by Lieut. Calvert, then in command of the company, now a resident of Independence, Kansas. The girls were promptly placed under arrest and escorted to the dance, after which they were returned home and released.

The story rings true because of one intriguing detail: the fact that Belle and her friend Eliza agreed to go to the dance only if the boys returned with an officer and contrived "orders for their arrest." It would have been critical to Belle, deeply embedded as she was with militant Confederate sympathizers, that her actions not be interpreted the wrong way and that she appear to go unwillingly with the Union boys. However, given her family's hatred for the Union and the occupying troops, it seems equally certain that she was not attending a dance with Union soldiers, whom she despised with a passion and did her best to help her brother kill, for her own amusement. The chance at that kind of proximity to federals, to flirt with them and try to uncover their numbers, locations, and plans, must have been too good to pass up. As to what intelligence she gleaned from the dance, we'll never know, but she would have surely shared it with Bud and his band.

It's difficult to prove but also quite possible—if not probable—that Belle's intelligence gathering led directly to one of the most hair-raising encounters of Bud's guerrilla-fighting career. According to George B. Walker, shortly after their company had formed, he was approached at their camp in the woods outside Carthage by both Captain James Petty and Bud Shirley, the latter having just returned from a secret visit to see his sister and the rest of his family in town. During this visit, most likely after talking to Belle, Bud had learned the location of a pro-Union safe house southwest of the town square, where Northern militiamen were hiding out. Bud in turn passed the intelligence on to Captain Petty, and based on this tip, his commanding officer decided to gather a party of eleven guerrillas, George and Bud included, and storm the house.

The intelligence was sound—there was indeed a band of pro-Union militiamen staying at the domicile in question. However, the low-quality pistol caps the guerrilla band relied upon were not. They were vulnerable to moisture, and, in George's own words, "sometimes became worthless and failed us when we needed them most." And this evidently was precisely one such unlucky occasion. No sooner had they arrived in front of the Union militia's hideout than the bold Captain Petty took a rifle bullet to the head and "slid from his horse, instantly killed." With the element of surprise now gone, George and Bud snapped their pistols frantically at the Union gunman standing in the doorway, but neither got off an actual shot—their caps failed to explode, their guns completely useless.

From there, it only got worse. The half dozen militiamen they initially suspected to be in hiding actually turned out to be "at least thirty-five that had been crowded in that house eating dinner," and who, roused by the noise, "were now coming out of every door and window." Outnumbered and with faulty pistol caps, Bud and George had no choice but to whirl their horses around and gallop away in retreat, while the Union militiamen, enraged and pouring onto the street, blazed away with their rifles and pistols. Bud managed to escape unharmed, but George received a ball through the shoulder, a wound that, though excruciatingly painful, he did survive.

In the wake of the botched raid, the guerrilla band was left both directionless and leaderless, with the Union militias primed for revenge. Their salvation would come, however, courtesy of Shelby's Raid, a sabotage-minded surge of cavalry that swept up into Missouri from Arkansas, under the command of the very Colonel Joseph O. Shelby with whom the guerrillas had failed to join the previous spring. According to George B. Walker, "One of the lieutenants took command of our company and when Shelby came through on his raid in October we joined him." This does seem to dispel the oft-repeated tale that Bud was a captain and took the lead of his band. If that had indeed ever been the case, his friend George would have surely recalled such a fact. It does, however, raise an interesting possibility. For years, the common consensus has been that Bud and Belle both stayed in Jasper County for the remainder of the war—and it was definitely in Jasper County where Bud's military career would come to an end. But is it possible that John Allison Shirley, aka Bud, actually joined Shelby's uniformed Confederate forces, as George B. Walker's testimony seems to indicate? It's known that the advent of the year 1864 was relatively quiet in Missouri, in large part because most of the guerrillas had left for the season. Some, like William Quantrill and his followers, went to lick their wounds in Indian Territory, alongside sympathetic Cherokee and Choctaw fighters; others departed for Arkansas with Shelby's forces, to wait out the winter in less hostile lands. Essentially, the entire southwest of Missouri was temporarily emptied of insurgents, as the cold weather and leafless trees presented too many dangers for small bands of clandestine fighters accustomed to hiding out in the woods and foraging for food. Belle almost certainly stayed behind with her family in Carthage, as there simply would have been no place for a teenage girl in the Confederate Army. But is it possible that Bud actually fought alongside Colonel Shelby in Arkansas during those months?

There is one intriguing piece of evidence that suggests *perhaps* he did, and it's not a yellowed newspaper article or tattered Confederate regiment roster. It's a photograph, or more specifically an ambrotype, that's long been overlooked by biographers and historians—in part because it was in a private collection for most of its existence, but also because a penciled inscription on the backing, identifying the figure in the portrait as "Edwin B. Shirley," Belle's *younger* brother, is patently incorrect. Edwin would have been fourteen at the time the portrait was taken, and the young man it depicts, sporting a dapper havelock-style cavalry cap, with a surprisingly sophisticated M1855 Colt revolver carbine clutched in his hands, is clearly older than that. According to the University of Virginia Small Special Collections Library, which currently holds the artifact in its archives, the young man it depicts is in fact "John 'Bud' Shirley, Missouri Irregular and 8th Missouri Cavalry, CSA." The interesting point there being not his status as an Irregular, or guerrilla—that has already been well established—but the claim that he fought with the 8th Missouri Cavalry, an official Confederate regiment based out of Arkansas and composed primarily of former Missouri State Guard members.

As to the authenticity of the photograph, it's difficult to verify in any substantial form. The young man depicted does display a passing, perhaps even familial resemblance to an existing photograph of Belle Starr when she was young—same long, narrow nose, same pained, piercing eyes, same thin, grim mouth—although that doesn't prove a great deal from a historical perspective. And the National Park Service Soldiers and Sailors Database does indeed include a John A. Shirley who fought for the Confederacy with the 8th Regiment, Missouri Cavalry, although it does not say which years—so perhaps the claim is correct, although there were likely other John A. Shirleys in Missouri at that time. It's impossible to say with any certainty, although the existence of the ambrotype does raise a compelling possibility, if nothing else.

What is certain is that by late spring of 1864, Bud was in Jasper County—perhaps having returned from Arkansas or Indian Territory, perhaps having never actually left Missouri. He was once again engaged in guerrilla activities as part of a rebel band camped out in the woods north of Carthage, ambushing Union patrols and harassing Union sympathizers. By this point, Bud Shirley was personally known and sought after by Northern militias and troops, he and his friends being "noted bushwhackers" who were increasingly in danger any time they showed their faces. "Shoot on sight" was the order of the day; after three years of massacres and atrocities committed by both sides of the conflict, quarter was neither given nor taken. And those three brutal, bloody years had indeed taken their toll, on the bushwhackers in particular. An aura of desperation and doom was beginning to surround the Rebel efforts, both on a smaller local scale and on a larger national one, as the cause of the Confederacy was increasingly resembling a lost one. Vicksburg had been surrendered back in July of the previous year, and the Battle of Gettysburg, General Robert E. Lee's last-ditch effort to bring the fight to the North, had ended in defeat for the Confederates soon after. Ultimately, despite having put up a ferocious fight, the agrarian feudal South, like some relic of the Middle Ages, simply couldn't compete with the modernized industrial colossus of the North, with its seemingly endless supply of immigrant soldiers and labor. The Confederacy was starved for both men and resources, its armies barely able to limp into battle. And in Jasper County, while the guerrillas were being captured or killed off in scores, more Union reinforcements and arms kept pouring in. Prospects for the Rebels were looking increasingly dim, and crouched in the woods outside of Carthage, sharing the last scraps from the hotel kitchen with her starving and bedraggled older brother, Belle almost certainly would have realized this, too.

When the end finally came for John Allison Shirley, on the twentieth of June, 1864, it was not heralded by war banners and bugles, or accompanied by any glorious cannonades or cavalry charges. Rather, it came ingloriously and over supper, as he and another guerrilla, Milt Norris, were being fed at the home of the Stewart family, known Confederate sympathizers living in nearby

Sarcoxie. A company of Union militia camped out in Cave Springs had been tipped off that the two notorious bushwhackers often came to the Stewarts' house for meals, and they had subsequently staked out the residence, in effect laying a trap. And the next time Bud and Milt were spotted sneaking in from the woods for a clandestine meal, the house was quickly surrounded by militia troops and the command was given to open fire. The two Rebels bolted, both with mouths probably still full of smoked ham or cornbread, sprinting from the house and scrambling to reach the nearby brush. Milt Norris, by some miracle, made it, receiving only a scratch on his side from a rifle ball while leaping over the back fence, clutching at the wound as he vanished into the trees. Bud, however, was not so lucky. He was in midair, halfway over the fence and just a few strides from safety, when the fatal rifle cracked and the lead tore through his body, freckling the split rails in blood. He was dead before he even hit the ground, the war ending for him right then and there.

It would be difficult, if not impossible, to pinpoint any one moment or event that signaled Belle Starr's transformation from an educated, well-bred young lady from a respectable family into a gunslinging, horse-thieving, bandit-carousing outlaw. It was a gradual process marked by fits and starts, punctuated at wide intervals by the various traumas and pressures that shaped her identity. However, if one *were* to try and find a moment when something changed, when something snapped, rendering that happy little girl from the stock farm in Medoc forever irretrievable and a far darker, far more violent character all but inevitable, it was probably at the death of her beloved older brother. The same brother who had taught her to ride and to shoot and to do so many of the other things that nearly everyone else in her life had told her were off-limits to someone like her, that were unbecoming of a lady. The same brother that she had spent the better part of the war supporting and informing, passing on messages and materials following each midnight run, each heart-racing ride across enemy lines. They shared something even stronger than kinship or blood ties—they were comrades-in-arms, having risked their lives together for the same lost cause. She never said as much herself, but Bud was probably the person closest to her in her life. And when the news broke that he had been gunned down by Union militiamen at a farmhouse outside Sarcoxie, the sixteen-year-old Belle took it very, very badly.

Exactly how badly can be gleaned from the recollection of a Mrs. Sarah Musgrave, a resident of Sarcoxie whose version of events was recorded by Ward L. Schrantz in *Jasper County, Missouri, in the Civil War*. She described the following scene in the aftermath of Bud's killing:

> *[Milt] Norris came to Carthage post haste and told the Shirley family of Bud's death. Next day [Bud] Shirley's mother and Myra Shirley, the 16-year-old sister of [Bud] Shirley, appeared at Sarcoxie, the latter with a belt around her waist, from which swung two big revolvers, one on each side. She was not timid in making it known among those she saw that she meant to get revenge for her brother's death. As is well known in Carthage, Myra Shirley is the girl who afterwards acquired bandit fame as Belle Starr, and became famous in literature under that name. So even in her early youth she was showing the character which afterwards made her notorious.*

The brashness of Belle, the sheer bravado, to do such a thing is remarkable. And the scene is so cinematic as to beggar belief— Hollywood couldn't concoct a better origin story for a burgeoning outlaw. And yet that is what happened in Sarcoxie, Missouri, on the twenty-first of June, in the year 1864. A teenage girl rode into a Union-held town to collect her brother's corpse, at a farm surrounded by federal troops and militiamen, openly brandishing a gun belt with two revolvers and seeking vengeance for her brother's murder. There are a number of imaginatively told versions, taken from folklore or invented by her early biographers, as to why that vengeance was never extracted. One version even has her yanking the triggers at the Yankee soldiers to no avail, the caps long since removed from the pistols to prevent her from actually using them. But the likeliest explanation is simply that the Union men in the area granted her wide berth, with no man present in any sort of rush to get into a gunfight with a teenage girl—a gunfight, given Belle's reputation, they were not at all certain to win. So instead of a pistol duel, there was simply the prelude to a funeral, as the corpse of John Allison Shirley was loaded unceremoniously into a wagon, while Eliza Shirley wept and while Myra Shirley glared. As to why John "Judge" Shirley, the father, wasn't there, Sarah Musgrave doesn't say in her account. Perhaps in an era of banditry and lawlessness, he couldn't leave the hotel unattended. Or perhaps the death of his favorite son, in the service of a cause that he himself had foisted upon him, was more than he could bear.

Given what happened next, it may have been the latter. With his hotel business in shambles after three years of war, with his son dead and buried in a pine box six feet under, with his own dreams—all but realized only a few years earlier—of becoming a prosperous Southern gentleman ground into the dust, John Shirley reached his breaking point. He could take no more. And as such, he made the previously unimaginable decision to leave it all behind. Together with his family, he abandoned his war-ravaged hotel and the lots he had once rented to the town's assorted businesses; he loaded up a pair of canvas-covered wagons and quit

Carthage forever. His eldest son Preston, from his first marriage, was homesteading in north central Texas, a place of refuge for many displaced Missourians, and John Shirley chose to give up and join him.

As for Belle, one can only guess how she reacted to the jarring move, gazing out from an ox-drawn Conestoga wagon as everything she had ever known rocked and then faded into the haze of distance. She likely felt considerable sadness, but given her sensibilities and predilections, it's hard to imagine there wasn't some excitement, some fulminating sense of the unknown yonder, to go along with it. Texas, after all, was the *true* frontier—a place where cattle drives brought cowboys yelping into faro halls and bison herds without end swallowed the horizon, while Comanches ran roughshod over entire towns and fought horse to horse against mounted Rangers. The notion must have stirred something in Myra Maybelle Shirley's blood, if nothing else. Even if she was leaving her hometown behind.

THE DECISION TO LEAVE Carthage and abandon their hotel business was almost certainly a difficult one for the Shirleys. But in the end, in one of the sad ironies of the town's troubled history, it didn't matter. On September 19, just a few weeks after the Shirleys' departure, General Sterling Price, leading 12,000 Confederate troops out of Arkansas, made a last-ditch attempt to retake the state from Union forces. He failed miserably. What he did manage to achieve, however, was a massive reconcentration of federal troops in southwestern Missouri, sending the region's guerrillas running for their lives, desperate to join any uniformed Confederate outfit they could find. And in the chaos of their hasty departure, it was decided that if the Confederates could not occupy Carthage, then nobody would. On September 22, following that ill-conceived order, a band of fleeing bushwhackers burned the entire town to the ground. Including what remained of the Shirleys' hotel, including, even, the Carthage Female Academy. Over the course of one day, the municipality was all but erased from existence. In fact, the war had practically erased the entire county. In 1860, the census had put the population of Jasper at 6,883 people. By the close of the war in 1865, there were only 30 men to be found within county lines. Meanwhile, in Carthage, the blackened brick chimneys—the only parts of the houses that had survived the conflagration—stood alone as strange, haunted columns in which owls now nested, filling the vacant nights with their mournsome calls, and the village green—where Belle had once played and where Bud had once drilled—became totally overgrown with tangled foliage, reverting back to a den for wolves and a bower for deer.

Beyond reducing his entire existence to ashes, the war that John Shirley had so vehemently supported—the necessity of which he had so incessantly drilled into his two eldest resident children—had by its bitter end killed one and forever changed the other. But it also did something else. In her dealings with Confederate guerrillas, and thanks to her relationship with her bushwhacker brother, Belle had come into close contact with two kinds of people previously unknown to her. The first was an entirely new species of frontier outlaw: horse-riding, gun-wielding criminals with a unique guerrilla skill set acquired while fighting the Union. Robbing trains, running down stagecoaches, holding up banks—novel forms of banditry that were soon to find a whole new expression once these bitter and violent young men, without gainful employment or a cause to fight for, fled the ruins of Missouri and went west. And second: Belle had become acquainted with the Cherokees and Choctaws who came up to Missouri from Indian Territory and fought for the Confederacy. She probably would have met young Cherokee and Choctaw braves serving in Indian brigades alongside the other uniformed Confederates, and she certainly would have heard stories from other guerrillas of what they had encountered when they fled to Indian Territory to escape Union forces—a convenient hideout following a successful raid.

With the entire world she knew now burned to the ground, with all convention and expectation now reduced to rubble, with the same Carthage Female Academy that had inculcated her with a woman's societal limitations now dust and cinders, there was nothing left to compass Belle's course except the north star of her own burning ambitions. The war had traumatized her, and it had damaged her, but it had also, in its own destructive, cathartic way, liberated her. Sitting at the helm of her family's covered wagon, reins firmly in hand, bumping and rolling over the rutted sod on her way to Texas, she surely knew that she was about to set foot in a wild place where the rules were not yet written, where she could chart her own dark and glittering course. And while she may not have realized it just yet, those two encounters—with guerrilla-trained outlaws and Cherokee war parties—were soon to reshape her destiny in a host of incredible new ways, taking her to the outer limits of both wonder and violence.

CHAPTER 3

The Bloodiest of Meridians

G IVEN THEIR RESPECTIVE HISTORIES, it seems strange—counterintuitive, even—that Texas should have remained a sparsely settled and relatively lawless frontier, while Missouri had long since been transformed into a facsimile of the more populous states back east. After all, Texas was first claimed by the notoriously evangelistic and economically intrusive Spanish way back in 1519, with serious efforts at establishing missions beginning as early as 1690. The French, on the other hand—better known for their somewhat lax approach to Upper Louisiana—wouldn't begin sending scattershot Jesuits and fur trappers to Missouri in earnest until a full century later. It would stand to reason that the Spaniards, with their conquistadors and their encomiendas and their hundred-year head start, would have long since accomplished in Texas what they were able to do in Central and South America in just a few decades. That is, to establish a closely controlled, intensely bureaucratic colony with haciendas and urban markets funneling riches back to the Iberian metropole. The Spanish had mastered this technique across an entire continent and a half, and yet in Texas, it never took hold. While towns like Carthage were putting up brick storefronts and white picket fences, while a city like St. Louis was teeming with commerce and brimming with fresh immigrants, huge swaths of Texas—which by 1865 had already been a state for *twenty* years—were still largely uninhabited and totally ungoverned.

Many theories for this lag have been posited, from a paucity of precious metals to an inadequate climate for lucrative Spanish plantation crops like tobacco or sugar. However, there is one far more clamant and visceral reason that so much of Texas had been and still remained, even by the 1860s, beyond the pale of European or American settlement. *Fear.* Early settlers, be they Spanish, Mexican, or Anglo, all regarded the idea of establishing a remote homestead on the vast plains of central Texas with universal horror. And the source of this fear, what made this existential dread possible, was ironically something that Europeans themselves had brought: the horse.

Prior to colonization, the Native peoples of Missouri—at least those residing in the forested hills that covered much of the state—did not, as a rule, ride horses. Even the Osage, renowned for their equestrian skills while living as nomads on the prairies of Kansas, tended to ditch their mounts and adopt the lifestyle of Eastern Woodland cultures upon their migrations into southern Missouri. Horses simply weren't practical for mobility in a forest, and most of the game that woodland tribes hunted—such as wild turkeys and white-tailed deer—needed to be stalked on foot. On the Great Plains, however, just a bit farther west, where the grasslands stretched into a vertiginous infinity and bison herds thundered along without end, Native people *did* ride horses. And one tribe rode them better than virtually anyone on earth.

It's hard to say exactly when the first escaped Spanish mustangs found their way into Comanche hands—it was likely some time in the first decades of the 1700s—but the consequences of mastering that new technology were immediately clear. Before the horse, the Comanche were impressive in neither numbers nor stature. They were migrants, a wandering offshoot of the Shoshone, bullied by other tribes as they wandered south in search of a homeland. However, when they realized the full potential of a mounted offensive wielding their bows and lances, everything changed. Astride their swift Spanish ponies, they swept into the Southern Plains and crushed anyone who stood in their path. In effect, thanks to their new combination of mobility and firepower, they established an empire, themselves becoming colonists, presenting the other Native tribes they encountered with a choice: serve as their vassals, supplying tribute and supporting them in times of war, or face apocalyptic consequences. And the Comanche were nothing if not true to their word. According to the account of Domingo Cabello y Robles, an eighteenth-century colonial Spanish governor of Texas, the Lipan Apache, a military powerhouse that had thrived on the Southern Plains since long before the arrival of the Comanche, were nearly decimated and exiled from the plains for good following an epic nine-day battle that occurred in 1724. What the Comanche did to the Lipan Apache, they would also do to the Tonkawas, to Spaniards, to Mexicans, and when Anglo-Americans finally began to arrive in the 1820s, to them as well.

Like most colonial empires, Comancheria, as their sprawling territory came to be known, was built on a previously untapped natural resource: the buffalo, a seemingly unlimited source of food, fuel, and materials to which the Comanches' unparalleled horsemanship had given them sudden access. Buffalo, after all, were almost impossible to hunt on foot. With horses to both hunt and defend their wild stock, however, the Comanche were able to establish a monopoly on this resource in the Southern Plains, eliminating any party that endangered their access to it, regardless of whether it was a band of Pawnees encroaching on their herds or Anglo-American homesteaders turning their grassland into farmland.

A prime example of the Comanches' aggressive "shock and awe" tactics is the Great Raid of 1840. The campaign, designed by the brilliant war chief Buffalo Hump as retaliation for the slaughter of a number of tribal leaders at a bungled treaty negotiation, was almost certainly the largest Indigenous raid in the nation's history. With a war party that may have consisted of as many as a thousand mounted Comanches, Buffalo Hump in effect subjected the towns and cities of central Texas to his own Native American version of blitzkrieg, killing, burning, and looting his way across the land to send the foreign invaders a calculated message. His campaign culminated in the sacking of the port city of Linnville on the Gulf of Mexico, hundreds of miles from where it had begun, in an attack so sudden and so brutal, the townspeople had to flee from the incoming horse charge into the ocean, swimming for their lives and clambering onto boats. In the end, Buffalo Hump and his war party would literally wipe Linnville off the map, while also riding away with some 3,000 stolen horses—a massive windfall in a society that measured wealth almost exclusively in horseflesh. Ironically, some of those horses, and their descendants, probably ended up in Missouri. St. Louis was one of the biggest markets for Comanche horses, with the very same Osage who had been pushed out of the state often acting as their middlemen.

For white settlers—for any intruders, really—the message was unmistakable: stay out of Comancheria or risk total annihilation. Any homesteader, vaquero, or wayward Apache brash enough to cross that invisible border and encroach upon Comanche resources uninvited was openly inviting a fate far worse than death. The Comanche, like many tribes of the Great Plains, imbued with divine significance the torture and mutilation of their enemies. It was a ritualized and necessary component of war, crucial for diminishing the risks of spiritual reprisals, and useful for the reclamation of personal honor. While a child did have a decent chance of being adopted and even loved by the tribe, and a young woman might be kept on as a slave or ransomed for horses, most adults captured by a Comanche war party could look forward to some combination of being scalped, flayed, gang-raped, castrated, and burned alive—shortly before being riddled like a porcupine with arrows.

The frontier town of Scyene—today part of Dallas—where the Shirleys settled upon leaving Missouri was outside the territory traditionally designated as Comancheria. But not by much. The famous raid on Fort Parker in 1836, in which Cynthia Ann Parker was taken captive by a combined band of Comanche and Kiowa, occurred just ninety miles to the south, a distance that would have been nothing to a highly mobile mounted war party, whose striking range was some *four hundred miles*. And the Civil War had left many of the forts that dotted the Texas frontier all but abandoned, as soldiers were called back to fill the Union ranks—which in turn had allowed many tribes, Comanche and others, to expand their territory unopposed. Granted, by the mid-1860s, the true apex of Comanche power was already past; European diseases had done considerable damage to their martial hegemony, and several bands had surrendered to life on reservations. Yet across much of the Southern Plains, their prowess as mounted warriors remained legendary, their moonlit raids still a mortal threat. And this legacy was precisely what had left so much of Texas pristine, wild, full of bison, and devoid of settlers. What had made it, in effect, the perfect blank slate for an aspiring outlaw with an extant taste for danger to reinvent himself. Or *her*self, as the case may be.

This period—what is colloquially known as "the Wild West"—did not last long: twenty years, give or take a few, covering the two decades just after the Civil War. This was a period when the abolition of slavery meant new Western statehoods were no longer stymied by congressional disputes, and when recent advancements in steam engines and repeating weapons enabled the formerly inaccessible plains of the "Great American Desert" to be cleared of both bison and Indigenous peoples in the cruelest of fashions. It was during these two powder-burnt decades that the legend of

Belle Starr would take root, nourished by that almost mystic Western triad of what would prove to be the woman's three greatest passions: horses, outlaws, and the Indian Territories.

And as far as the outlaws were concerned, the Shirleys would not have to wait long—the bandits would come to them.

THERE WAS A SIMPLE reason beyond mere wartime allegiance that the transplants from Missouri clung so closely to one another on the Texas frontier: many of the established Texans did not want them there. This proved especially true in the case of Belle and her immediate kin. The Anglo-Texans among whom they landed may have shared a common Southern identity and Appalachian pedigree, but the Shirleys, like many Missourians, were seen as outsiders upon their arrival. Despite their similar origins—Stephen F. Austin, known as the "Father of Texas," was himself a Missouri man—many of the Shirleys' neighbors had already been in Texas for two generations by the end of the Civil War, having come to the region in the 1820s with the first wave of English-speaking settlers. In fact, their initial Anglo-American settlement had been established at the invitation of colonial Spanish authorities, who had thought, much like William Penn, that these stubborn Scots-Irish frontiersmen would provide a natural buffer against "Indian raids" and foreign invaders. Little did they know that those same stubborn Scots-Irish frontiersmen would outlast them all and take the place over. By 1865, these were people who had beaten back the Mexican government and the Plains horse tribes alike, who had briefly seen their beloved state become a republic, and who remembered the Alamo. As Texans, they were proud and expansive, and they understood, after four decades of surviving on solitary farms and ranches, scattered across horrifically vast plains, the value of unity. In short, they were winners; their destiny had already manifested itself.

While the majority of these Texans were indeed Confederates, the Civil War had barely grazed their state compared to what it had done to Missouri. Even the cotton industry in Texas had thrived throughout the conflict, with the state's proximity to Mexico allowing it to evade the blockades that prevented most of the South from reaching foreign markets. Meanwhile, the refugees who arrived from places like Jasper County had seen their family members slain, their houses burned, and their livelihoods destroyed. This trauma would turn John Shirley, once remembered fondly by Carthage residents as being "as pleasant a man as you could find," into the "very bitter Confederate" described years later by the *Fort Scott Weekly Monitor*. Approaching seventy, he was essentially starting a farm from scratch on a wild frontier—just as when he arrived in Missouri from Indiana as a much younger man.

Upon their arrival in Scyene, following an exhausting wagon journey south through ravaged and war-torn lands, the entire Shirley clan almost certainly resided temporarily with Preston, John's son from his earlier marriage, who had already established a farm in the area. His dwelling may have been a sod house, a crude clapboard structure, or possibly even a dugout—essentially a hole in the dirt covered with logs, a relatively common low-cost housing solution among settlers at that time. A far cry, in any case, from the polished piano and leather-bound books of the Shirleys' hotel back in Carthage. Eventually, the family was able to procure their own piece of land a mile outside of town near the South Mesquite Creek, where, after likely suffering in another dugout seething with dust and flies, they cobbled together enough funds to build a respectable clapboard house of their own and begin working the land, raising corn, hogs, and John Shirley's old mainstay, horses. John toyed with the idea of opening another hotel and reliving his glory days, but like so many of his dreams, this never panned out. Their family business and fortune both gone, the Shirleys were back to eking out a living as subsistence farmers.

And not surprisingly, given their volatile history and embittered nature, they got off to a bad start within the community. Apparently, they were regarded as somewhat selfish and inconsiderate by their Texan neighbors—gregarious plains folk unaccustomed to the clannishness and surliness of these new arrivals from the Ozarks. It's easy to imagine that the southern Missouri war refugees pouring into the area were regarded by the established Texans in a manner not entirely dissimilar from how Dust Bowl migrants in California would be perceived by the locals just two generations later: impoverished, uncouth, haunted by what they had lost, and prone to desperate acts of survival. The farms in the area all relied on a single communal well, and according to the account of one neighbor, the Shirleys had a habit of unapologetically dragging up massive barrels on sledges and draining the well dry, leaving no water for the other families—a dangerous act on the dry Texas plains. Beyond their simple lack of consideration, there seemed to be a consensus that there was something peculiar about the Shirleys, this swarthy, standoffish, vaguely shell-shocked family who had little interest in socializing with neighbors or integrating within the community. They generally kept to themselves, except when other Missourians visited, and otherwise did what little they could to repair the innumerable damages that the war had visited upon them.

One of the first tasks John and Eliza set themselves to once the farm near South Mesquite Creek was up and running was to get Belle—now nearly seventeen—back in school, to make up for the lost years during the war when she had been racing her horses behind Union lines and passing on intel to Confederate guerrillas. She briefly attended classes at a one-room prairie schoolhouse presided over by one of their neighbors, a Mrs. Poole, but her attendance was irregular, and she was regarded by her classmates as being dark and pretty but "rather wild." Her parents may have tried to force her to attend, but by this point, it's likely that any attempt to control or compel Belle to do anything would have been in vain. Wars have a habit of making children grow up too fast, and not only had Belle grown up—she'd grown beyond anyone's control. During the war years, she'd had her first taste of danger, and of a forbidden freedom previously unknown. She'd come to learn the dark and addictive thrill of a midnight run. The thunder of hooves, the smell of spent powder, the gleam of gunmetal—there was no going back from that.

And then there was Dallas. Located less than ten miles from the new Shirley farm in Scyene, the largest outpost in the area was a true frontier town in the classic Western sense. With a population approaching two thousand by the war's end, it was far larger than any urban center Belle had ever spent time in, and its broad packed-earth main street was lined on both sides by a motley assortment of saloons, gambling halls, restaurants, and clothiers. The arrival of the railroad in 1872 would truly turn Dallas into a boomtown, but by the end of the Civil War, it was already experiencing significant growth. This was spurred in part by migrants like the Shirleys who were fleeing the ravages of the conflict—both white settlers and a large number of recently freed slaves. But the other main catalyst in the frontier town's rapid expansion was the sudden importance of the state's burgeoning cattle industry. The Civil War had taken a disastrous toll on many types of agriculture practiced in the Lone Star State, but in addition to boosting the local cotton industry, it had also proven a boon for cattle ranchers, many of whom returned from the war to discover that their temporarily feral herds of longhorns had grown substantially in their absence—with an increased demand for beef in Eastern cities to boot. The Chisholm Trail and the Shawnee Trail both funneled herds of longhorns from across South Texas up north to Kansas stockyards, and both passed close to Dallas, keeping the town regularly supplied with cowboys fresh from a drive, looking to spend their money in all the irresponsible ways youths so often do.

To Belle, a girl on the cusp of turning seventeen who was fond of music, dances, and dangerous young men, the allure of the town—just an hour away from Scyene if taken at a trot—must have been indescribable. Carthage had been close to what was considered "the frontier," and it was indeed a stopping-off point for many heading west. But it had never been Western in the way that Dallas was. Carthage, with its quaint brick storefronts and white picket fences, resembled most Southern or Midwestern towns, with its residents sporting Southern and Midwestern fashions. But amid the dusty streets and swinging saloon doors of Dallas, Belle would have seen sombrero-wearing vaqueros, brilliantly bandanaed cowhands, buffalo hunters dressed head to toe in buckskins, and saloon girls of every stripe clad in lavish dresses and feathered caps. She would have heard jangling dance-hall pianos, the stomping of bootheels across pine, volleys of jubilant pistol fire, and vivid retellings of the latest Kiowa or Comanche raid. The year 1865 may have been a catastrophic one for much of the South, but it was a banner year for what might be described as Western culture. To wit, it was the same year that John B. Stetson released his first Boss of the Plains cowboy hat, that "Wild Bill" Hickok participated in the first-ever quick-draw gunfight, that Oliver Winchester began work on his famous repeating rifle, and that Jesse Chisholm created the legendary trail that would take cattle drives from San Antonio all the way to Abilene. Belle was there for the start of it, and she was there at the heart of it. She almost literally watched the Wild West being born, and she soaked up its flamboyant style and ribald spirit with unrepentant relish. Her father, the aspiring Southern gentleman in exile, may have withered in defeat or grimaced in disgust before these rustic new surroundings, but Belle was drawn to them like a moth to the flame.

There is a photograph that still exists—a portrait—of Belle full in the flower of both her young adulthood and her new Western identity. Her face is youthful and callow, some might even say beautiful, with eyes that, though seemingly bearing traces of pain, also manage to radiate a steadfast hope. This Belle is a far cry from the haggard, plains-hardened woman who would appear in later daguerreotypes, after the whiskey and raw winds had taken their toll. Around her neck, she is loosely kerchiefed by a silken foulard; atop her head sits a broad-brimmed stockman's hat perched back at a confident rakish angle. Her dark hair hangs unbraided and un-adorned in a manner befitting Wild Bill himself. It's worth noting that her entire mien is not just Western—it is *masculine* Western, with nary a bonnet or a corset or a jabot collar in sight. Such a getup was not befitting a lady, and wearing it in a frontier town would have surely provoked stares, if not hoots and hollers. But Belle evidently did not care. She was no poseur, no dilettante. She would come to inhabit the costume wholeheartedly and embody the lifestyle, warts and all.

However, to cross over completely—to fully become a bandit of the Western stamp—she would require an escort. Someone to usher her across the invisible line that separated the decent folk who trundled behind mules and lived in sod houses and suffered through Sundays on raw pews made of pine, and the indecent folk, who wore a full brace of pistols and used their bandanas to hide their faces and who tugged the corks out of celebratory whiskey bottles with their teeth. And in the case of Belle, she would have not one but two such ushers, forming a love triangle whose violent geometry would change the course of Belle's life, and fundamen-tally alter the shape of frontier banditry in the West.

Back in 1863, when the tide was truly beginning to turn against the Confederacy and the Union was starting to win back substantial swaths of Rebel territory, President Abraham Lincoln found himself faced with a conundrum: how to *re*unite the United States of America once the fighting was finished. And in the end, he reached the difficult conclusion that the only way to rebuild a house divided against itself was to forgive those who had sought to rent it asunder. The result was the Proclamation of Amnesty and Reconstruction, a sweeping and many felt excessively generous plan to pardon those who had participated in the rebellion and designate funds to rebuild their war-ravaged lands. In effect, the common everyday soldiers who had served in the Confederate Army would not be charged with any sort of treason or suffer penalties for damages incurred during their service to its cause.

This decision may have laid the groundwork for reconciliation and even established a path back to normality as a country. However, it did contain one troubling oversight: it left unclear how ununiformed guerrillas in Union-held states like Missouri were to be dealt with after the war. The scruffy irregulars who ambushed Union positions and assassinated Union sympathizers may have been true Confederate soldiers in their own minds, but to Missouri authorities, they were nothing but criminals and brigands. Which in turn meant that when the war ended, almost an entire generation of young men, trained in the art of guerrilla warfare and exceedingly comfortable with lethal force, faced the very real prospect of criminal prosecution if they stayed in Missouri. This was a possibility for nearly any guerrilla who had fought for the Confederate cause, but it was an especially pressing threat for those who had served in notorious bands like Quantrill's Raiders—the guerrilla outfit made infamous by the aforementioned Lawrence Massacre, in which 150 unarmed Union men and boys were executed. Granted, there were plenty of atrocities committed by Union paramilitary groups as well, such as the sacking of Osceola by James H. Lane and his ruthless Kansas Brigade. But it was the Confederate-aligned guerrillas who faced the most legal peril, particularly in light of the new Drake Constitution adopted by the Missouri state legislature on April 8, 1865, which granted sweeping amnesty to federal militias, but not their Confederate counterparts.

With this prosecutorial sword of Damocles hanging over their heads and with their own local economy still in total ruins, many of these former bushwhackers fled the state and sought a living using the one viable tool still at their disposal: their guns. They already had ample experience sticking up Union arms depots and holding up Union treasury convoys. They even had a familiarity with Indian Territory and North Texas, places William Quantrill and many other guerrilla leaders had used as hideouts following a big raid. It was simply a matter of taking those skills and that knowledge, formerly reserved for exploiting the weaknesses of federal troops, and applying them instead to the public at large. And as it just so happened, thanks to the massive postwar migration of Missourians into the area around Dallas, they had not only kinship ties binding them to the region but also a string of potential safe houses where they could lay low for a while after a big score.

Bud Shirley may have never served under William Quantrill, but the Shirleys themselves knew men who did. As innkeepers, they had formed close relationships with many of western Missouri's established families, garnering a reputation for their hospitality—at least as far as their own kind was concerned, with "their own kind" meaning Confederate sympathizers with a violent distaste for the federal government. And thanks to Bud's involvement with the guerrilla insurgency, they had also become well acquainted with his general cohort of young fighting men. In fact, the Shirleys may have even offered them direct assistance in their activities. There is a record of a Jasper County civilian court petition from July 31 of 1865, in which William G. Bulgin, former owner of a carpentry shop in Carthage, accuses John Shirley, John F. Festal, and John L. Fuller of banding together "with other persons for the purpose of over throwing the laws of the County & for the purpose of robbing peaceable citizens of their property." Specifically, he claims that this trio of Johns ransacked his home and later burned his property, to the tune of $415 in damages. Granted, the Shirleys had already fled to Texas by that point, and the lawsuit almost certainly went nowhere. But this, taken together with the claim that John Shirley had attempted to murder the pro-Union Irish immigrant John Crow, seems to strongly indicate that the entire Shirley family offered material support, if not violent involvement, when it came to local Confederate guerrillas in need. They would have been known among Missourians as people a desperate bushwhacker could count on—during the war and after as well.

All of which helps to explain how Cole Younger, the notorious gunslinger, cattle rustler, bank robber, and future partner of Frank and Jesse James, ended up riding into Belle's romantic orbit. As to when their paths first crossed, by Younger's own account, recorded in his autobiography, *The Story of Cole Younger, by Himself*, the first time he met her was just before the end of the war. He writes: "In the spring of 1864, while I was in Texas, I visited her father, who had a farm near Syene [*sic*], in Dallas county. Belle Shirley was then 14, and there were two or three brothers smaller." Cole Younger's relationship with John Shirley likely went back to that first Battle of Carthage in July of 1861, a conflict in which he had served as a private in the Missouri State Guard, quite possibly right alongside John's son, Bud Shirley. Being stationed in Carthage in the days before and after the battle, he would likely have come to know one of the town's most prominent citizens and Confederate sympathizers. He may have even had a drink or a meal at the Shirleys' tavern, in the heady, jubilant days following their victory over Colonel Franz Sigel and his "Yankee Dutch." Which was why, evidently, while passing through Scyene, Texas, in 1864, he remembered the Shirleys' legendary Missouri hospitality and decided to pay the elder John Shirley a visit.

There is, however, one small but glaring problem with his timeline. Unless the Civil War records of Jasper County are severely mistaken—which isn't beyond the realm of possibility—the Shirleys were not in Texas in the spring of 1864. Bud Shirley would not be gunned down by a federal militia in Sarcoxie until late June of that year, and John Shirley wouldn't sell his belongings, pack up his wagons, and flee the ruins of Jasper County until weeks later, likely arriving in Texas in late summer or early fall. Furthermore, by the spring of 1864, Belle would have been a striking and savvy dark-haired sixteen-year-old—definitely not the rascally fourteen-year-old Cole Younger casually describes, tussling around the farm with her younger brothers, Edwin, Mansfield, and Cravens. Both of these distinctions—the chronology of the visit prior to the war's end and the age of Belle at the time—seem of the sort that a twenty-year-old Confederate guerrilla would have been likely to remember. And even the timeline presented elsewhere in his autobiography contradicts his recounting of events. He does mention doing some scouting for General Henry E. McCulloch in North Texas in the fall of 1863, but by November, he was already long-gone. His self-described wartime itinerary for the first half of 1864 has him chasing down cotton thieves for General E. Kirby Smith in Louisiana, engaged in a grand reconnaissance mission for General John S. Marmaduke in central Arkansas, crossing all of Kansas to cut telegraph lines with a Colonel Jackson in Colorado, fighting Comanches and Apaches while passing through what is today New Mexico, and finally dipping down into the Mexican state of Sonora, to catch a boat and embark on a secret Confederate sabotage mission in the Pacific Northwest. In short: Cole Younger, in the spring of 1864, was by his own account an exceedingly busy young man. It's hard to identify any reason, let alone a free moment, that would have compelled him to embark on a weeks-long journey into northeastern Texas. And even if there were, it doesn't seem possible, barring some critical error in the historical record, that the Shirleys would have even been there to begin with.

Which begs the question: Why would Cole Younger purposefully misrepresent such seemingly inconsequential facts? That he visited the Shirley farm at some early point in his rollicking, gun-slinging career seems genuine; he even correctly identifies the fact that Belle had three younger brothers at the time, which would not have been common knowledge. But why would an outlaw with a scandalous reputation subtly fudge the date he first met Belle and her age at the time? One possible answer, to the first part of the question at least, may have to do with the context within which Cole Younger wrote his autobiography. Penned when he was almost sixty, after having served fifteen years of what was supposed to be a life sentence for armed robbery and murder, Cole Younger's book was a last-ditch—and fairly feeble, by virtually any standard—attempt at rehabilitating his image. He freely admits his time spent during the war with William Quantrill and William "Bloody Bill" Anderson and confesses to palling around later with his old war buddies, Frank and Jesse James. But beyond that, he claims that he only killed honorably and heroically on the field of battle; he accepts no accountability whatsoever, preferring to depict himself simply as a man who "fought as a soldier who rights for a cause, a creed, an idea, or for glory." Which, to anyone even mildly familiar with Quantrill's Raiders or the James-Younger gang, is patently absurd. Cole Younger was a prominent member of the most ruthless guerrilla band in the Civil War, and following that, a leader in one of the most violent—and prolific—criminal gangs in the history of the West. He fought alongside war criminals known for scalping and disemboweling their enemies; he rode at the front of an out-law band famous for leaving the corpses of bystanders in its wake. Today his name is most often associated with photographs taken later in his life, portraits of a bald, doughy, weak-chinned man in an almost comical bow tie. The true Cole Younger, however—and the same Cole Younger that Belle would have first met, still dusty from the trail when he darkened her door—can best been seen by earlier photographs, like the one taken shortly after his wounding and capture by Minnesota police in 1876. This younger, leaner it-eration of the man sports a drooping outlaw-style goatee, mutton-chop sideburns, and a thousand-yard-stare that makes it clear why bank tellers were so quick to turn over their money. He didn't just posture as a dangerous man—he truly was one.

This was exactly the perception that Cole Younger was trying to whitewash, if not completely erase, when writing his autobiog-raphy decades after his felonious heyday. Crimes were omitted and details were changed to absolve himself of liability—which very well could be the case with his first visit to the Shirley farm. An alternate scenario, and a possibility that is at least worth consider-ing, is that the initial meeting between Cole and Belle in Scyene described above actually took place two years later, when the bud-ding young outlaw finally had an exceedingly *good* reason to flee Missouri and take temporary shelter among Confederate sympa-thizers in Texas. According to Cole Younger's written account, he had fled Missouri in great haste in the summer of 1866, when a vindictive sheriff who blamed him for killing his son during the war—of course Cole Younger pleads his own innocence—obtained a warrant for his arrest and assembled a posse to string him up. And there may indeed be some truth to this version, as portrayed in his autobiography.

But there could also be another explanation for this sudden

burst of heat from local law enforcement, more than a year after the war had ended. Coincidentally, it was also during the spring and summer of 1866 that a string of bank robberies and holdups was committed across Missouri by what was widely known to be a band of former Confederate bushwhackers. This included the now-infamous Clay County Savings Association robbery of February 13, which is generally regarded as the first daylight, peacetime bank robbery in U.S. history, as well as the June 13 jailbreak of two former members of Quantrill's Raiders in Independence— both of which resulted in fatalities. While no concrete evidence ever emerged proving who *exactly* participated in the crime spree, it's long been suspected—and there were rumors of this even at the time—that Cole Younger, as well as his war buddies, Frank and Jesse James, took part in at least some of these early heists. In fact, there was even an oral tradition, later repeated by Western chroniclers like Burton Rascoe, that Cole Younger, along with three of his brothers and Jesse James, stopped in Scyene on their way back from San Antonio, where they had exchanged some of their stolen Missouri gold for currency from a Mexican broker. This version of the story has them riding into Scyene in July of 1866 and staying for a few days with their old friends, the Shirleys. In his memoir, Cole Younger insists that upon fleeing Missouri in the summer of 1866, he spent much of the next year bouncing around the Deep South and hiding out among sympathetic friends in Louisiana. But for a man who was known to change details and dates to protect himself and his accomplices from criminal liability, perhaps Louisiana was a convenient placeholder for Texas.

Hiding his tracks as a criminal may explain the discrepancy in dates. As for Belle's age, there could be an ulterior motive at work there as well. By the summer of 1866, or at least shortly thereafter, Belle would have had another man in her life: Jim Reed. He, too, was a former member of Quantrill's Raiders from

Missouri, someone that Cole Younger had fought beside during the war and knew quite well. It's likely that Belle met Jim Reed long before Cole Younger—long before moving to Texas, even. Years later, in an interview Belle Starr gave to the *Dallas Morning News*—just after her arrest for committing armed robbery disguised as a man, no less—the claim was made that "When less than 15 years of age she fell in love with one of the dashing guerrillas, whose name she said it was not necessary to give." From details presented later in the interview, it's clear that the "dashing guerrilla" in question was Jim Reed, not Cole Younger, as some of her early biographers presumed. If this point is accurate—and it should be stated that the article in question does include a few errors and exaggerations, as one might expect from a Wild West newspaper looking to sell copies—then she would have first met Jim Reed back in Missouri during the war, prior to her family's Texas migration. His own family, evidently prosperous by the standards of the day, had a farm outside Rich Hill, to the north of Carthage. It's not known exactly how or when Jim first met Belle; it's possible he, too, was a wartime acquaintance of Bud. What is certain, however, is that after the war, he and some of his family members packed up the wagons for Texas, and that by 1866, he was living on a farm in Collin County, half a day's ride from the Shirley homestead in Scyene. Which means that if Cole Younger did happen to pass through Scyene in the summer of 1866 while fleeing an arrest warrant in Missouri, it's not at all unlikely that the now eighteen-year-old Belle would have been in the midst of a courtship with, if not formally engaged to, his old wartime comrade Jim Reed. And that, given the salacious rumors that were to percolate in the years to come, may explain his desire later in life to disavow any romantic association whatsoever, and portray her as a carefree young teen upon their first meeting.

As to what Belle saw in Jim Reed, it's difficult to say. True, he was a former Confederate guerrilla, like her late, beloved brother, and he came from a respectable Southern family. But based on the path of his life to come and on the slightly less tangible perception gleaned from his old daguerreotype portraits, he simply comes off as bearing the taint of a ne'er-do-well. Unlike Cole Younger, the dangerous, steely-eyed young war hero and stickup artist, destined for a long and legendary career as an outlaw, the gangly, mustachioed Jim Reed evinces something more weasely and feckless—perhaps even doomed. The type of man who didn't know how to lie low or resist a provocation, who could readily get pinched after a big score for some minor irrelevant crime. There are stories, oft repeated in much of the early Belle Starr literature, claiming that John Shirley forbade the marriage. They even go so far as to claim that the couple had no choice but to elope, and were married on horseback, in a secret outlaw ceremony officiated by the notorious gunslinger John "King" Fisher. Variations of this tale appear often enough and in disparate enough sources that it may contain *some* grain of truth.

What is known, because there's a marriage license to prove it, is that eighteen-year-old Belle and twenty-year-old Jim were formally and officially married on November 1, 1866, by the Reverend S. M. Wilkins of the Corinth Presbyterian and Community Church, located in Collin County, where the Reeds resided. The Corinth congregation wouldn't build its first proper church structure until well after the war—services were usually held at the local schoolhouse or a private home—so it is possible that the ceremony occurred in front of one of said structures, contributing to the story of an outdoor wedding. If the November weather was foul enough to muddy up the black prairie soil and ruin new shoes, it may have even been held on horseback. And the gunslinger John Fisher was a native of Collin County and a known criminal accomplice of Jim Reed's, so it's not beyond the realm of possibility that he may have been passing through when the wedding occurred, even volunteering to hold Belle's horse steady during the exchanging of vows, as the *Dallas Morning News* would later claim. It's simply one of those moments in the Belle Starr story where myth and fact are so tightly intertwined as to be impossible to fully disentangle.

Whatever affections Belle still felt for Cole Younger following that first visit to her family's farm, and whatever violent urges still itched at Jim's trigger fingers following the Civil War, were both temporarily put on hold as the newlyweds sought domestic bliss in Scyene—an ambition that, unsurprisingly, was not to pan out. Legend, not to mention more than a few of Belle's early biographies, have her being stolen away by her disapproving father following the elopement, to be placed at either a relative's farm or a boarding school, only to be stolen back by Jim Reed and whisked away to Missouri. There's no evidence to back up this soap opera version, and it's difficult to imagine a headstrong, pistol-packing Belle being kept against her will by anyone, let alone her own father—a man who had been unable to control or contain her during the Civil War years, when she was still in her mid-teens. If John Shirley did hold that much animosity toward Jim Reed, he did a relatively poor job of chasing him away or sabotaging the marriage. It appears Jim actually made a feeble attempt to help out at the Shirley farm and may have even supplemented his income with a stint as a saddle salesman in Dallas—neither of which met with any lasting success. Shortly thereafter, the newlyweds packed up their things and left Scyene behind.

Rather than any sort of wild elopement, a far more likely explanation for the couple's departure from Texas is that Belle and Jim faced the same challenges there that young couples have grappled with since time immemorial. Jim Reed was a twenty-year-old man with no *legal* trade or métier to fall back on, and without enough money in the bank to purchase land of his own—a crucial factor for financial independence on the frontier. If the ambitious and social-climbing John Shirley harbored any misgivings about his new son-in-law, Jim Reed's financial insolvency, more than anything else, was the likely source. And there is some evidence that John Shirley was struggling to pay the bills himself, and not in the best position to support the young couple or have them under his roof. In the September 21, 1867 issue of the *Dallas Weekly Herald*, he placed an ad, looking to sell "Six yoke of first class oxen and a No. 1 wagon" on what he believed were "reasonable terms." Oxen were valuable draft animals, critical for farming and transport, and the decision to unload such a significant resource would not have been arrived at lightly. Additionally, Edwin Benton, Belle's younger teenage brother, was beginning to gain a reputation around Dallas for stealing horses—an unusual choice of crime for a young man whose family was known as stock farmers and should have had horses to spare. So it's certainly possible that the entire Shirley clan was facing difficult financial straits and wasn't in an ideal position to assist or house the young married couple.

Which in the end took Belle and Jim right back to Missouri. Rich Hill, to be precise, where the Reeds had lived prior to the war, and where they still had considerable kin and owned their own land. By 1867, the prosecutorial fervor against former Confederate guerrillas had abated somewhat, and formal Reconstruction efforts had begun. The state, though hardly a paragon of prosperous tranquility, was no longer the scorched, apocalyptic wasteland it had been just three years earlier, when bushwhackers, jayhawkers, and partisan bands of Native Americans had lit up the night in an unchecked orgy of violence. Jim took to farming alongside his brothers, but his efforts at domestic stability in Missouri were to be even more halting and ineffectual than those of Texas. In no time at all, he was consorting with his same wartime crew, many of whom had already made the leap from former Confederate guerrilla to full-fledged outlaws. When not planning heists or hiding out from the law, this lost generation of Missouri war veterans spent their days racing horses, gambling, drinking, and carousing. The hedonism of Fort Smith, Arkansas, and the lawlessness of Indian Territory, both just a few days' ride to the south, held considerable appeal to these violent young men so fond of wagers and whiskey, and Jim Reed was more than happy to join them. Once again among his old Civil War friends, once again raising hell across his old Civil War stomping grounds, Jim began vanishing for weeks at a time, leaving his young wife alone for long and uncertain stretches.

If Belle felt the desire to join her new husband on his sprees—and knowing her, she almost certainly did—such longings were soon to be stymied by a far more practical concern. For in the early months of 1868, on the eve of her twentieth birthday, Belle learned that she was pregnant.

OF ALL THE GLITTERING mysteries and flashing unknowns that seem to gold-tassel the black velvet of Belle Starr's legend, none, with the possible exception of the identity of her eventual killer, have generated as much speculation or debate as the identity of her daughter's father. Rose Lee Reed, better known as Pearl, a sobriquet applied by her doting mother, was born sometime in early September at the Reeds' farm in Rich Hill, Missouri. There's some evidence that motherhood, at least at its onset, calmed Belle's more adventurous urges and brought out a strong maternal instinct. Years later, residents of the area would recall her riding into town in her signature sidesaddle fashion, her infant daughter held close, to attend services at the Bethel Baptist Church. Apparently her tender devotion to young Pearl made an impression on them, as she caressed and cooed at the infant all throughout the preacher's sermon, unable to take her eyes off the child. Noticeably absent from such recollections was Jim Reed, who appears to have seldom been at home during this period, if his ensuing criminal exploits are anything to go by.

It's difficult to say exactly when the rumors first began circulating. But at some point, possibly during their marriage, but definitely following Jim Reed's death, there were whisperings—perhaps even instigated by Belle Starr herself—that Cole Younger, not Jim Reed, was Pearl's real father. That the same dashing guerrilla and feared outlaw who had climbed off his horse, slapped the dust from his hat, and ambled up to the Shirley farm shortly after their arrival in Scyene rekindled some kind of romance with her when their paths crossed again several years later, on the western prairies of their native Missouri.

As for Cole, he flatly rejected such claims, or indeed any romantic association whatsoever with Belle. In his autobiography, penned decades later, he would insist that following the death of her husband, she once again "came to Missouri and traveled under the name of Younger, boasted of an intimate acquaintance with me . . . and at this time declared that she was my wife, and that the girl Pearl was our child"—an assertion he dismisses as "a fabrication." In fact, Cole describes only three meaningful interactions with Belle that he can recall: the first while visiting the farm in Scyene back in 1864, a second while calling upon both Jim and Belle in 1868, when she was already heavily pregnant and living in Missouri, and a third again in Texas in 1871, when the couple was on the run from the law. He unequivocally denies that anything untoward or improper ever occurred between them, although he does acknowledge that Belle, even when married to Jim, did have something of a schoolgirl crush on him. Shortly after helping the young couple by giving them some of his Texas cattle in 1871—quite possibly freshly rustled—Belle approached him and confided in him of her "troubles." As to whether these troubles were marital or economic, Cole does not specify, but their conversation did prompt a family servant named Aunt Suse to warn him off, declaring that "Belle's sure in love with you, Cap'n Cole. . . . You better be careful." Evidently this revelation convinced Cole that caution was indeed in order, and according to him, he "thereafter evaded the wife of my former comrade in arms." By his own account, Cole Younger, ever the dashing Southern gentleman, did the right thing and steered clear of the starstruck young wife of his old war buddy, Jim Reed.

For the most part, contemporary historians and biographers have accepted this version, insisting that the claims of Cole Younger's paternity were more likely than not just another sordid tale invented to help sell tawdry newssheets and dime novels to a scandal-crazed public. They accepted his denial at face value and struggled to find any specific point in that outlaw polka that occurred between North Texas and western Missouri in which the steps of Belle Starr and Cole Younger would have coincided.

And this very well may be the case. Perhaps the most obvious possibility is also the most accurate: Jim Reed, the husband of Belle, the man who cohabited with her, was the father of their first child together, Rose Lee Reed, better known as Pearl. Given the amount of exaggeration and invention that has surrounded the creation of the Belle Starr legend, it's easy to dismiss the seemingly incredible rumors of another famous outlaw fathering her child as precisely that: incredible rumors. It would by no means be the first wildly improbable myth tacked on by creative storytellers. All of this may well be true, *except*—there are photographs of all the parties involved. And while yes, visual resemblance is certainly subjective, and no, it's not at all a solid foundation for historical conclusions, few would deny that Pearl, especially in her youngest portrait, bears a *striking* resemblance to Cole Younger. They don't just share certain features—they look like direct kin. This is in stark contrast to the son Belle would give birth to three years later, James Edwin Reed, who at least in photographs does look a great deal like his legal father, Jim Reed. Even Belle remarked on the resemblance, writing in a letter to her in-laws—Jim's parents—that Eddie, as their son was called, "is said to resemble Jimmie very much." Pearl, meanwhile, would even go so far as to start using the surname Younger later in life, and while historians have put forth several explanations for that, none seem quite as straightforward as the possibility that the rumors were simply true.

Beyond the physical resemblance and change of surname, there is a fair amount of what might be considered as circumstantial evidence to support the claims of Cole Younger's paternity as well. For example, there are the reports that at her funeral, Belle was laid in the coffin and subsequently buried with one of her most prized possessions cradled in her hands: a pearl-handled .45 revolver that Cole Younger had once given her. And then there are the recurring instances of people not horribly distant from Belle Starr's orbit believing that there was something linking these two individuals beyond mere acquaintance. The original obituary in the *New York Times*, for example, was based on a dispatch sent from an editor of the *Fort Smith Elevator*—someone who very well may have known Belle personally—which claimed she had been married to Cole Younger. Younger's name seems to crop up again and again, and while that's hardly the basis for a biographical conclusion, it is at least worth considering the old adage: where there's smoke, there's fire. And one would be hard-pressed to deny that at the very least, there is something smoldering when it comes to the overlap between Belle Starr's and Cole Younger's stories as outlaws.

Which begs the question: Did their paths actually overlap geographically and chronologically, in a way that could account for an unplanned pregnancy? Specifically, where were Belle and Cole nine months prior to Pearl's birth in September of 1868? Belle, it has been established, was already living on land the Reeds owned in Rich Hill, Missouri, having left Scyene with her husband to try their hand at farming. Is it possible that Cole Younger, who had fled Missouri in 1866 to escape arrest and possibly a lynching, was once again in the area in late fall of 1867? During the month of December—nine months prior to Pearl's birth—to be more precise?

As it turns out, by Cole Younger's own admission, it is. And ironically enough, it is in trying to clear himself of a famous bank robbery that he also potentially implicates himself in Pearl's paternity, although when one reads through his autobiography, it's easy to miss. In presenting an alibi for why he couldn't possibly have been involved in the notorious Russellville, Kentucky, bank robbery of March 20, 1868, he states that he was with his uncle, Jeff Younger, in St. Clair County, Missouri. Why was he back north again, after claiming to have been hiding out in Louisiana the year before? According to Cole, he had been staying at a farm in Carroll Parish "until 1867, when chills and fever drove me north to Missouri." So by his own account, in 1867, he was living in St. Clair County, Missouri—right next door to Bates County, where Belle was living on a farm outside the town of Rich Hill. If the autobiography is accurate, in December of 1867, when Pearl was conceived, Belle and Cole were living only miles apart. And if the stories about Jim Reed's wayward behavior are also true, it's likely Reed was frequently galivanting around Indian Territory with his outlaw friends, away from home for weeks at a time. Which means the opportunity for Belle and Cole to have rendezvoused certainly presented itself, if not the desire to do so.

As to whether such a rendezvous actually occurred, however,

one can only imagine. Short of exhuming graves, or at the very least subjecting living relatives to genetic testing, there's no way to prove Pearl's paternity either way. However, it is not difficult to imagine a displaced, neglected Belle, left alone on a barren farm in western Missouri while her husband was off on a jag somewhere, being nothing short of delighted when Cole Younger, a celebrated Confederate war hero and newspaper-worthy outlaw, came riding up to her door, paying a Yuletide visit to the attractive daughter of an old family friend. His appeal would have been obvious: He was handsomer than Jim Reed, more gallant than Jim Reed, and more famous than Jim Reed, and after what was likely a string of successful bank and stagecoach robberies, he was almost certainly wealthier than Jim Reed. Essentially, he was everything that Jim Reed aspired—but failed—to be. For a Missouri girl born into a family of Southern sympathizers and irresistibly drawn toward Wild West bravado, it's hard to imagine a male candidate more appealing than Cole Younger.

If such a tryst did take place, though, and if Cole Younger was the father of Belle's first child, it does raise the question of why initially Belle, and later Cole, refused to acknowledge it. From Belle's perspective, even beyond the obvious and potentially violent implications of marital infidelity, it's worth considering exactly who these people were. Broadly speaking, all the parties involved hailed from Missouri and were essentially transplanted Appalachians with roots in the Upland South. Revenge and clan-based blood feuds were inextricably linked to their code of honor—a fact that had already resulted in and would continue to produce a tremendous amount of bloodshed in their families. And these weren't just any frontier families. The Reeds, notorious outlaws in their own right, were closely aligned with the Fishers. This included their wedding guest, John "King" Fisher—a stone-cold killer whose gun was alleged to have "thirty-seven [notches], not counting Mexicans," and who was even rumored to own a pair of tiger-skin chaps made from an escaped circus Bengal that he had personally killed. The Youngers, meanwhile, themselves among the fiercest fighters in the West, were all but kin to the Jameses, including Frank and Jesse, who need no introduction at all. They were quite literally the most dangerous outlaws operating in America at that time. And then there were the Shirleys—definitely not ones to shy away from gun violence, either—who had ties to them all.

Reed, Younger, Fisher, James, Shirley: These weren't just prominent frontier surnames. These were five of the most infamous and dangerous outlaw clans of the Wild West era. Even if Belle knew with certainty that Cole Younger was the father of her first child, she could have been equally confident in the blowback such a revelation would have caused. In effect, her husband and his brothers would have been duty bound to go after Cole Younger and his brothers. Which easily could have sucked John Fisher and his relations, Jesse James and his brother, and all the surviving Shirley men into a spiraling vortex of violence that would have spilled blood from Missouri all the way down to Texas, making the Hatfield-McCoy feud look downright quaint in comparison. And Belle, being the shrewd and perceptive woman that she was, would have also known the likely outcome of such a bloodbath. Namely, lots of Reeds, Fishers, and Shirleys gasping out death rattles in the dust, while the members of the James-Younger gang stood over their bodies with smoking pistols. Simply put, the James and the Younger brothers were a lethal force, guerrilla warriors and bandits nonpareil. They were an organized gang of highly trained killers who would take on anyone from Union generals to Pinkertons without batting an eye. There simply would have been no defeating them. Which easily explains why, as a young mother still married to Jim Reed, Belle may have chosen to remain silent and stay with her husband, rather than become a widow and watch her entire family get annihilated. Of course, she would eventually become a widow anyway, thanks to an entirely different blood feud involving Reeds and Fishers. But perhaps that only goes to prove the point. These were men with incredibly delicate senses of honor and incredibly twitchy trigger fingers, something that Belle knew all too well, because she was one and the same—she was no different. A point she had proven four years earlier in Sarcoxie, when she'd worn a brace of pistols into town and challenged her brother's killers to a duel.

As for Cole Younger, his reasons for denying the affair in his memoir would have been closely aligned with his reasons for denying his involvement in the Lawrence Massacre and denying he'd ever robbed a bank in Missouri. As a paroled convict reaching the end of his life, his main priority was to rehabilitate his image and secure his legacy. With the advent of the twentieth century and with the events he had witnessed turning from living memory into recorded history, he essentially tried to change the narrative. He positioned himself as a born-again Christian, he depicted himself as a gallant war hero, and he flatly denied responsibility for any misdeed that might besmirch his name—like fathering a child out of wedlock.

As to what *really* happened between Belle and Cole, while rich ground for speculation, it shall have to remain part legend, part mystery. For better or for worse, the only two people who ever knew the whole story of that rumored affair ended up silenced by buckshot or demented by prison. If love did exist between them, out there alone on the frozen prairie, it was of the sort that burned so intensely as to have no future. And perhaps Belle carried both the joy and the pain of that moment with her right up until the very end, destined to face eternity with her bruised fingers forever laced around its pearl-handled reminder.

UNFORTUNATELY FOR BELLE, WITH the arrival of new life came the loss of life as well. Whatever peace and sense of purpose motherhood may have granted the twenty-year-old were not to last, as two crises impinged on those first halcyon days following the birth of her daughter Pearl. The first was the death of yet another brother, once again in a hail of gunfire. Edwin Benton, two years Belle's younger, had already gained something of a reputation in the environs of Scyene as a troublemaker, after falling in with a rambunctious crowd. Texas towns were crawling with such young men, displaced by the Civil War, scarred by violence, in thrall to the frontier delights of whiskey, faro, and saloon girls. All of which cost money, something juvenile delinquents like Edwin Benton acquired much more easily through dishonest means than honest ones. At some point in 1868, after having already had several teen-age brushes with the law, Edwin was caught red-handed during an escapade and, according to the *Dallas News*, "was shot off his horse near Dallas." A horse, evidently, he had recently stolen. Another crack of a rifle, another torso ripped through with lead, another Shirley, hardly into manhood, spilling down into the dirt, gasping out his last. Some biographers have surmised that Belle traveled back to Texas for the funeral, but that seems unlikely. Bodies were buried quickly on the frontier, and even if time had permitted her to return to Scyene to see her brother laid to rest, the difficulty and cost of the voyage for a nursing mother with limited financial means almost certainly would not have. Belle likely learned of her younger brother's killing from a letter received weeks after it occurred, and probably had little recourse but to stare solemnly out a brittle-paned farmhouse window, holding her infant daughter close to her breast as her throat tightened and the tears welled.

Her husband Jim was unlikely to have been a source of much comfort, as the second crisis came courtesy of his own frontier galivanting. The *exact* details of what transpired on the border of

Indian Territory across the winter of 1868 and spring of 1869 are unclear. Different stories explain the bloodshed that would occur, involving everything from gambling disputes to saloon brawls to insults aimed at honorable ladies. But the crux of the matter seems to be that two opposing criminal gangs, one led by the infamous Fishers of Collin County, and another by a clan of ruffians called the Shannons, were both vying for control of the lucrative smuggling and bootlegging business to be had in the lawless outskirts of Fort Smith, Arkansas. It was the modern-day equivalent of two enemy cartels going to war over a valuable drug corridor, each seeking to destroy the other and corner the market. Apparently, long-simmering tensions had finally erupted when Finnis Shannon, son of the family patriarch Granville Shannon, took it upon himself to walk into a saloon, pull his pistol on "Major" Fisher—alleged to have been John "King" Fisher's own brother—and blow his brains out all over the bar.

When the Kingfisher, who had been out of town on a gambling spree, returned, a full-on gang war ensued in Indian Territory and neighboring Arkansas, during which William Scott Reed, the brother of Jim Reed and a close friend of the Fishers, was killed by Shannon men. This in turn triggered exactly the kind of blood feud that *could* have occurred had any marital infidelity been discovered involving Cole Younger. Because Jim Reed, duty bound by the same code his people had brought over from the shadow-haunted moors of northern Britain and then dragged stubbornly across the raw hills of Appalachia, was morally obliged to settle the blood debt that had been incurred and slay his brother's killers. Which, with little thought to the well-being of his young wife and infant daughter, he did. Bound by blood to avenge his kin, Jim Reed rode south into Indian Territory, joined up with his old friends in the Fisher gang, and on the second of June, across the Arkansas line in the town of Evansville, aided in the assassination

of two members of the Shannon gang by the names of Noah Fitzwater and Newton Stout—and rather thoroughly at that. Fitzwater
was shot twenty-one times, and Stout a half dozen. It's impossible
to say how many of those twenty-seven rounds were fired from
Jim Reed's smoking pistols, but the likely answer is a substantial
portion.

In the killing of the two Shannon men, Jim may have restored
some balance to the Reed clan's canted sense of honor, but he
threw his own familial situation back in Missouri into total dis-
array. He was now a man wanted by federal lawmen and frontier
gangsters alike. Besides the very real risk of being charged with a
double homicide by the U.S. marshals in Fort Smith, the Shannon
family had also put a $1,000 bounty on his head. And that was
just the beginning of Jim's troubles. The gang's ringleader, John
"King" Fisher,[1] the very friend and gunslinger who was alleged to
have presided over his marriage to Belle, was already facing federal
charges for smuggling whiskey into Indian Territory. It was not
at all unlikely, given Jim Reed's previous involvement with John
Fisher and his dealings with the Cherokee, that he risked being
implicated as well. Which in turn could have unveiled a whole slew
of criminal charges stemming from his days spent rollicking in the
Indian nations, while Belle was home alone with their new baby in
Rich Hill.

---

[1]   There has been some debate as to whether the John Fisher involved in the
Shannon-Fisher feud was actually the legendary outlaw John "King" Fisher from
Collin County, Texas. In a Letter to the Editor that appeared in the *Fort Smith
Weekly Herald* on June 26, 1869, written by Finnis M. Shannon himself, he specifically refers to the outlaw in question as John K. Fisher, and describes in detail
how the gunslinger had recently killed his own father-in-law, a Dr. McKinney,
and later fired "30 or 40 shots" into his house, while he was seeking cover—all
revenge for Finnis having killed J. M. Fisher earlier that year in a saloon encounter. Granted, it's not impossible, but it seems *extremely* unlikely that there would
be another gunslinger named John K. Fisher who happened to be good friends
with the Reed brothers from Collin County, Texas, and who happened to ride
with them around Fort Smith, Arkansas.

So Jim Reed did the one thing, beyond accumulating arrest warrants, he was adept at: He turned tail and fled. After ambushing Fitzwater and Stout and rendering their bodies to almost literal mincemeat—according to Finnis Shannon's published account, the assassins had concealed themselves overnight in an old corncrib before leaping out and pumping their targets with an obscene amount of lead—he and John Fisher left Evansville for good. Upon gathering their horses, the fugitive duo made a mad dash for Indian Territory, "whooping and swearing" upon leaving behind the Arkansas line "that they were at home." Which in a sense, they were. Indian Territory wasn't just beyond the jurisdiction of local authorities; it was beyond the pale, a place where rival clans ruled by seasoned warlords issued their own edicts and extracted their own tribal justice. Clans, as it were, that were also known to shelter outlaws when it was in their own interest and proper tribute was paid. Jim Reed, like Cole Younger and Jesse James, had relationships with powerful Cherokee and Choctaw figures that went back to his time with Quantrill's Raiders, when they'd fought together for the same Confederate cause and wintered together on the same tribal lands. No town sheriff or mob of angry citizens would dare follow the Fisher gang—which beyond John and Jim, also included characters as unsavory as Calvin H. Carter, Charles Bush, and Charlie Roberts—into that hornet's nest. A U.S. marshal, perhaps, once an official writ was in hand and a substantial posse was behind him. But with federal charges looming and the Shannons on the warpath, Jim Reed knew that both of those were likely on the way.

Once he'd caught his breath and no doubt celebrated the extraction of his revenge with considerable whiskey, it likely dawned on Jim Reed that he wasn't the only one in danger; Belle and Pearl were also at risk. The Fisher-Shannon feud had escalated to the point where no family members were safe—even the Fisher women were fleeing the town of Evansville—and Jim would have certainly realized that if he had been willing to ride all the way from Missouri to Arkansas to settle a blood debt, there were members of the Shannon gang willing to pay that debt back in kind. And federal involvement was also only a matter of time. John Fisher was already on the U.S. marshals' radar for smuggling, and once the smoke cleared, Jim was all but certain to be included as an accomplice. The wake-up call, however, to the very real danger he and his family were in came courtesy of a certain Captain Anderson of Crawford County, Arkansas. Under direct orders from Powell Clayton, the state governor himself, Captain Anderson tracked down two other members of the Fisher gang hiding out in Indian Territory and killed them in a gunfight. Even if Jim wasn't personally involved in the shootout—and he may have been—he certainly heard about it and probably realized quite quickly that he was in fact an extremely *wanted* man, with federal marshals, state militias, and frontier gangsters all gunning for him. With this in mind, Jim Reed left Indian Territory and hurried back to Missouri to warn his extended family and to make sure Belle and young Pearl were both safe before he went into hiding.

Given Jim's propensity for gallivanting solo, it seems unlikely that bringing them along whilst fleeing from the law was his original intention. It's more likely that Belle insisted, in part because she didn't want to be left alone with his in-laws while he was on the lam, but also because his final destination surely appealed to her innate sense of adventure.

It's possible Jim's choice of Los Angeles was purely practical. With the exception of Mexico, California was about as far from the law as a fugitive could realistically get. But there may have been another factor as well. The year prior, with their own significant

share of federal heat bearing down on them thanks to their suspected involvement in the notorious Russellville bank robbery,
Frank and Jesse James had made their own way to California, hiding out at their uncle's ranch in Paso Robles—and possibly robbing a few stagecoaches to boot. It's not unlikely that Jim Reed
knew about his war comrades' whereabouts and used their flight
from the law as inspiration for his own. Perhaps he even hoped to
link up with them in California, not knowing that by the time he
got there, they would already be on their way back to Missouri,
rested and ready to rob more banks.

Virtually nothing is known about Jim and Belle's journey to Los
Angeles. Years later, a woman claiming to be the granddaughter
of Belle Starr, under the pen name Flossie Doe,[2] would make the
claim in the *Dallas Morning News* that Jim crossed the country
on horseback, while Belle and young Pearl made the trip via stagecoach. This is possible, although unlikely. Reaching the West Coast
without *some* rail travel would have been extremely burdensome, not
to mention impractical. The first transcontinental railroad, linking
Omaha and Sacramento, had opened just that year. The rail journey
took just four days and cost $65 for a third-class seat, while the same
voyage by stagecoach took twenty-five days and cost around $200.
And if they did travel separately, Belle and Pearl would have arrived
in Los Angeles weeks ahead of Jim, which would have been considerably dangerous. By the fall of 1869, the town was still relatively raw

---

[2] Flossie Doe is believed to be Flossie Epple, the granddaughter of Belle Starr
that was put up for adoption shortly after her birth. Initially named Mamie by
Pearl, the infant was given to a Wichita orphanage and adopted by the Epple
family of Newton, Kansas. There is no reason to assume that the article that
appeared in the *Dallas Morning News* was written by an impostor, but many
have questioned how accurate some of the information it contains actually is,
given that Flossie did not have any connection to the Belle Starr name until discovering her true identity as an adult. Any stories included in her article would
have come to her secondhand, from friends and relatives of Belle's, although that
doesn't necessarily mean they should be discounted completely.

and dusty, with a population of just over 5,000 people. Full rail connection for Los Angeles wouldn't arrive until the completion of the Southern Pacific line from New Orleans seven years later, meaning that when Belle stepped off that final stagecoach from Sacramento, her toddler in tow, it was still a rugged frontier settlement.

The *Los Angeles Herald* would describe the place in these days as "undoubtedly the toughest town of the entire nation," thanks to its inordinate number of "fights, murders, lynchings and robberies." A place for a mother and an infant daughter traveling unaccompanied, it most definitely was not. But then again, this was the woman who would become Belle Starr—a bandit queen who ruled over her own roost of outlaws, offering shelter and provision to some of the most dangerous men in the West. Maybe she felt right at home strolling through the gritty frontier streets of the old Spanish mission town, with its volatile mix of Anglo, Mexican, Chinese, and Native peoples. A place where strike-it-rich gold miners gouged each other's eyes out over single games of poker; where Californios drew blades to settle scores in the midst of reeling fandangos; where rival Tong societies engaged in open warfare in the Chinatown alleys; where Gabrieleño men, the sole survivors of an obliterated tribe, gathered on Saturday nights between Arcadia and the Plaza, to drown their immense sorrows in cheap brandy and brawl and sing until the first light of dawn. The jagged crests of the San Bernadinos would have been unlike anything Belle could have imagined growing up in the gentle foothills of the Ozarks; the sunlight glinting off the blue blaze of the Pacific must have stolen her breath. It's possible Los Angeles itself made Dallas seem quaint, even provincial in comparison. Perhaps the place suited her just fine.

As to how Jim Reed supported his family during his brief tenure in Los Angeles, that's not certain, either. Legends have him working in a gambling parlor or tending bar or even robbing stage-coaches in the scrubby hills of Los Nietos. Whatever he did, he appears not to have done it especially well, because by the early spring of 1871, he was facing accusations of passing counterfeit bills around town. Which was extremely poor timing, as it coin-cided with the arrival of the couple's second child, a boy. On Feb-ruary 22 of that year, Belle gave birth to James Edwin, named for his father—this time, apparently, there was no doubt about the infant's paternity—as well as Belle's dead brother, the horse thief blasted off his saddle in Scyene. However, Belle had precious little time to enjoy her second go at motherhood. By the end of March, a slew of federal counterfeiting charges against her husband were looming, with the potential to include his Arkansas revenge kill-ings as well. Having no wish to stick around and find out how deep the law would dig—those charges were bad enough, and they were probably just the tip of the iceberg for an inveterate hoodlum like Jim Reed—he once again urged a no-doubt-irked Belle, who now had a three-year-old *and* a newborn to care for, to pack up her things and get ready to run.

There is a story, repeated in some of the early biographies, of Belle disguising Pearl as a boy as they raced across the country on a stagecoach, to dodge authorities on the lookout for a young mother with a daughter. There is also a claim, made by the same Flossie mentioned previously, that while Jim made his escape in the dead of night via horseback, Belle and her children caught a Pacific steamer and took the long route home, around the tip of Cape Horn. Both are certainly possible, but likely invented. Belle and Jim probably left California the same way they came in: to-gether on a crowded, jostling third-class rail car bench, traveling under assumed names, exhausted and red-eyed from a total lack of sleep, only this time with Belle balancing two screaming children on her knee instead of just one.

WITH CALIFORNIA NO LONGER safe, and with Missouri and Arkansas both off-limits, Belle and Jim returned to the one place where they both had kin and friends to help shelter them—Texas. This time around, though, the young couple was in far worse straits. Belle's family, surely aware of their son-in-law's exploits and flights from the law, was in no great rush to enable him further with housing or money. If John Shirley had had no initial reservations about his daughter's being married to the Reed boy, he certainly did now. Belle approached him for assistance upon their return, asking for livestock and land to set up a farm of their own, but she was rebuked in no uncertain terms. Shirley the elder, with both the wisdom and cynicism the hard years since the war had given him, saw Jim Reed for the troublemaker he was. Not that John Shirley was a saint by any means, but he'd always managed to stand on his own two feet and provide for his family. And apparently, by the summer of 1871, he'd had enough of his son-in-law's failings.

Assistance for the couple would eventually come, albeit from a very unlikely source. Since the fall of 1868, Cole Younger had been living in Scyene, Texas, along with his brothers Jim and Bob. In his autobiography, he attributes the Texas relocation to the need for a milder climate to suit his mother's poor health—which, of course, he blames on the Yankee militias that had burned down her house and subjected her to "exposure." He goes on to claim that upon settling in Scyene, he and his brothers went about "gathering and driving cattle." A more honest accounting might involve him fleeing to Texas after robbing a string of Midwestern banks and establishing a home base in Scyene to take advantage of the ample opportunities for cattle rustling that existed so close to the major drives.

Cole does admit to helping out his old friend Belle and his war comrade Jim when they approached him for assistance. In fact, it was during this time that Belle took Cole aside and told him of her "troubles," specifically as they pertained to her father's not wanting to help her husband out. Belle, knowing Cole's "influence with the father," asked the Confederate guerrilla and war hero—a man whom her father respected and admired—to intercede on their behalf. Which he did. It seems Cole spoke to the cantankerous John Shirley, likely swapped a few war stories from their Carthage days over warming sips of whiskey, and convinced him to give the young couple some land to start their own farm. Not only that, Cole even "cut out a lot of the calves" from one of his two herds so that Belle and Jim could have some livestock to help get them on their feet. There's a very good chance the unbranded and untraceable calves were birthed from cows that he and his brothers had stolen, but Cole doesn't mention that. He doesn't mention specifically what he and Belle talked about, either, but he does make the claim that it was after this encounter that he realized Belle was in love with him and made the decision to stay away from her in the future. If the rumors were true, however, and if he was in fact the father of Pearl, then Cole Younger may have had very different motivations for helping out his former lover. It could have been out of guilt, or perhaps even to buy her silence. Or maybe it was sheer tenderness—that's possible, too.

If it was difficult for Cole Younger to stay away from Belle, he would not have to bear this burden for long. An incident from earlier that year, described in his autobiography, had already made a long-term future in Texas for the Youngers seem unlikely. It was back in February, in a scene right out of a Hollywood Western, that Cole's brother John had gotten drunk in a Dallas saloon and "shot the pipe out of the mouth of a fellow named Russel." John then proceeded to go outside and fire wildly in the air, to the laughter and cheering of the other rowdy customers. For outlaws like the Youngers, this kind of behavior may have constituted harmless drunken shenanigans and nothing more. However, the now-pipeless and badly shaken Russel did not see it that way at all. He promptly reported the shooting to the sheriff, Charles H. Nichols, who rode out to Scyene the next morning, to arrest John Younger.

As to what happened next, as is so often true in these kinds of stories, there are multiple versions. In Cole Younger's version, his brother and the sheriff were both attacked by a vigilante brother of Russel, killing the sheriff and wounding John. Again, it's impossible to know with any certainty, but a more fulsome version is probably the one that appeared shortly after the killing in the *Dallas Daily Commercial.* It describes how John Younger asked Sheriff Nichols if he could have a quick breakfast before being arrested. Sheriff Nichols, in an act of extreme naiveté, consented, upon which John "stepped to the door and fired at Nichols with a shotgun, the load taking effect in the colonel's neck." After unloading his shotgun into the sheriff's throat at point-blank range—and the sheriff, miraculously enough, was able to get off one final shot through all the gurgling and spouting blood before losing consciousness, wounding his attacker in the arm—a winged John Younger leaped onto the lawman's waiting horse and galloped off for Indian Territory, "where the trail was lost." Sheriff Nichols, just twenty-eight years old, died shortly thereafter and was buried the next day. John Younger, meanwhile, himself not yet twenty, had acquired a $500 bounty on his head for this act of cold-blooded murder, a price set by the governor of Texas himself. And it may be worth noting that this was not the first man John Younger had killed. Shortly after the war, at just fourteen, he had shot a former Union militia member right between the eyes after the Northerner insulted him and slapped his face—with a frozen mackerel fish, of all things. It would almost be comical if it weren't so horrific.

But this is who the Youngers were. Despite the sanitized anodyne version of his family that Cole Younger tried so desperately to depict in his autobiography, the actual historical record leaves scant room for doubt. Perhaps they were loyal to their friends, generous to their kin, and gallant to ladies, as gangsters so often are. But at the end of the day, they were true outlaws, the archetype that all future Western gunslingers and cinema bandits would follow. They drank when they wanted and they caroused where they wanted and they stole what they wanted. And they would kill without a scintilla of hesitation or regret anyone who didn't back down, who stood in their way, at least until the day their luck ran out. If nothing else, they were pure and unwavering in that regard, in their devotion to that overarching principle of the outlaw creed. To quote Cole Younger, when he was finally arrested almost half a decade later, following the last failed bank robbery of a storied career: "We tried a desperate game and lost. But we are rough men used to rough ways, and we will abide by the consequences."

Cole Younger was not an honest man, but he was, in his own peculiar way, a principled one. And with his brother having fled town as a wanted man, and with local law enforcement suddenly viewing his family as the equivalent of modern-day cop killers, he and his two remaining brothers made the decision in the spring of the following year to take their herds of what were very likely stolen cattle and skip town as well. Confederate war hero or not, Cole understood that he was no longer wanted in the community, and he saw a more promising future in driving the cattle north to Kansas, then cashing out and reconnecting with the James brothers back in Missouri—essentially, to get back to doing what the Youngers did best. Together, they would form the James-Younger gang and become perhaps the most legendary—and successful—criminal enterprise of the Wild West era, robbing banks, trains, and stagecoaches almost beyond counting, while amassing a fortune and a full scrapbook's worth of newspaper clippings in the process.

Belle, however, would never see Cole again. For the heartbroken mother of two, that chapter of her life was over, with the man that she had pined for since girlhood vanishing north in a cloud of dust and a din of cattle, his mounted silhouette diminishing slowly against the dying light of a setting prairie sun. But while the future that called to Cole above the bellowing of bulls and lowing of calves may have been great, Belle had a destiny of her own that was just starting to curl a beckoning finger. Her days as a long-suffering housewife were coming to a close; her nights as a true outlaw were about to begin.

CHAPTER 4

Baptism by Fire

ONE OF THE LARGEST cash heists in the history of Indian Territory occurred on the night of November 19, 1873, on the border between the Creek and the Choctaw nations. Some $32,000 would change hands before the evening was through, a windfall almost beyond imagining for most outlaws of the era, a once-in-a-lifetime score. And the only thing more shocking than the sheer magnitude of the haul was the brutality by which the thieves acquired it.

Watt Grayson, a prosperous local rancher and former slave owner, had spent much of that day entertaining the questions of a curious white visitor interested in purchasing some horses. This in and of itself was not an unusual scenario for the nearly sixty-five-year-old stock farmer, who was well-known for the quality of his horseflesh. However, in addition to being a prominent rancher, Watt Grayson also had a long record of public service in Creek tribal government. He was regarded among the Muscogee Creek as one of their nation's more affluent citizens, and rumors had long circulated—perhaps courtesy of political rivals—that he had skimmed considerable sums from tribal coffers over the years. Regardless of their veracity, these stories were intriguing enough to pique the interest of a number of the road men who frequented that corner of the territory. Two of these men, accomplices of the first visitor, arrived toward evening, "well mounted and heavily armed." And upon joining their friend and confronting the old rancher, the entire tenor of their conversation changed in an instant.

Snarling now and spitting curses, the three bandits held Watt Grayson and his family at gunpoint and demanded all the treasure he had on the premises. A number of servants, both African American and Métis, looked on in horror, but were powerless to intervene. A trunk was finally produced by the Graysons and pried opened, revealing two thousand dollars in gold and silver currency. But the gunmen were unsatisfied—they must have been tipped off—and demanded to know where the rest was hidden. When Watt Grayson claimed that the trunk was all he had, they dragged him to the stables, tied his hands behind his back, and hung him from a tree limb. He thrashed and kicked in the darkness until he lost consciousness, at which point the rope was released and he collapsed onto the dirt. When the old man came to, the outlaws once again demanded the location of the remaining gold—and Watt Grayson again refused to answer. This rope-torture was repeated six times, each time with the same result. It was only when his assailants threatened to hang his wife in front of him that he finally relented. When the old man was able to stand again, swaying unsteadily in trousers that were almost certainly soiled, they unbound his hands and let him lead the way. Clutching at his ravaged throat, he took the gunmen back to the house and showed them where two kettles were buried beneath the floor, each one packed to the brim with gold.

Accounts would vary as to how much the three bandits actually stole. Initial reports stated it was less than $4,000, while later, more official claims would put the total at $32,000. If the rumors of financial malfeasance were true, it's possible Watt Grayson initially misled authorities to hide his misappropriation of tribal funds. After all, $32,000 was an extraordinary amount for even a tribal leader and successful rancher to squirrel away, although the fortune certainly could have been achieved through honest means as well. Regardless, the very next day, a profoundly shaken Watt

Grayson, with the rope burns still fresh on his neck, would write a desperate letter to his friend W. H. Rogers, in which he begged for help from U.S. marshals and put up a $2,500 bounty on the heads of the three outlaws. His descriptions of two of the men were vague, recollecting one by the "Bay mare with white spots" he was riding, and another by his "light hair and little whiskers." One of the outlaws, however, he got a good look at: a man with "Brown eyes, Brown hair and whiskers, with a roman nose, wearing gray clothes rather worn. Age about 30 or 33." While it's impossible to know for sure, and he wouldn't have *quite* been thirty—it's almost certain that the dark-haired man with the roman nose and worn clothing was none other than Jim Reed.

As for Belle, she wasn't far away, either. By her own account, re-corded in a sworn statement made two years later in Dallas before U.S. commissioner Benjamin Long, she was waiting in the woods outside Watt Grayson's ranch during the heist. She was most likely standing lookout while also holding fresh horses to assist in the gang's escape, although she doesn't confess to this, for obvious reasons. She does admit to knowing the identities of the men in question, including her husband and two of his outlaw friends, "W. D. Wilder and Marion Dickens." She also admits to discuss-ing the plan with them in advance and to meeting them in the woods just after the crime, when they told her that "they had ac-complished their object and had the money to show for it," shortly before "they sat down upon the ground and began counting it." A sum, according to her, that was just under $32,000, with some in currency but most in gold. It's possible she may have even been di-rectly involved in the robbery itself—some of the early biographies have her disguised as a man and waving pistols at the Graysons—though Watt Grayson's descriptions of his three attackers seem to preclude a dark-haired, whiskerless woman's participation in the actual holdup.

But let there be no mistake about it. On that chill night in late November, Belle—waiting silently in the shadows for the bagmen to return, gloved fingers drumming nervously against her leather holster, the ghost of her own breath silver in the moonlight—was indeed part of the crew. She was there when they planned the heist, she stood guard outside the ranch while they executed the robbery, she sat with them while they counted the money, and when it came time to flee, she would do that as well. A posse of enraged Creeks rode after the outlaws in hot pursuit and chased them across the Canadian River, but the trail was lost on the road to Fort Gibson, at which point they got away. In making her escape, however, in fording the chill waters of the Canadian on horseback, saddlebags jingling with purloined gold, Belle had crossed more than just a river. She had finally crossed over to the other side. She was an outlaw now. And she must have enjoyed the sensation, because this was just the beginning.

THE GRAYSON HEIST *SHOULD* have been the score of a lifetime. If Belle's account is accurate and the loot was split three ways, Jim Reed made off with just over $10,000 in what was mostly untraceable gold—several hundred thousand dollars in today's currency, on a frontier where farms were mostly self-sufficient and land was cheap. A seasoned professional criminal could have been set for life, investing in land, buying up lots in town, creating a front. Jim Reed, however, was neither seasoned nor professional, and in the end, squandered most of the money in exactly the ways one might expect. According to Belle's sworn statement made in Dallas two years later, she knew of "no part that could be recovered" of Grayson's stolen gold, her husband "having spent or disposed of all that he had," leaving her "in a destitute condition." A local deputy marshal by the name of W. H. Anderson substantiated her testimony, stating that Reed and his friends were "notorious for horse racing" and often "lost large sums of money in that way." He believed "it had all been gambled off and otherwise spent," with one of the men known to have lost $3,000 in gold on a single race.

Given Jim Reed's habits and environs, this kind of profligacy should have come as no surprise. Dallas was booming by the end of 1873, having just experienced a surge of growth thanks to the recent arrival of both the Houston and Texas Central and the Texas and Pacific railways. These new rail connections turned what had been a raw frontier outpost into a rollicking cattle and cotton town teeming with saloons, theaters, gambling parlors, and brothels. It was in Dallas, after all, where Doc Holliday would transition from country dentist to full-time gambler, becoming one of a *hundred* professional gamblers believed to have operated in the town at that time. It was also in Dallas that efforts on behalf of Mayor Benjamin Long to clean up "Boggy Bayou," the town's infamous red-light district, would result in a three-day-long gunfight, as furious johns barricaded themselves in a gaming house to protect their beloved dens of iniquity. This was the type of place Dallas was going into the year of 1874, and Jim Reed was precisely the kind of man it attracted. None of which was good for a marriage that was already strained. While the rumors of Belle's affair with Cole Younger would remain just rumors, Jim Reed would take it upon himself to find a mistress in a very open and public way.

Jim and Belle had been on the rocks since returning from the Grayson heist in Indian Territory. His unwillingness to share the gold, coupled with its subsequent squandering in gambling parlors and bordellos, was the most likely cause. An exasperated Belle, having finally reached her breaking point, ended up returning to her family's farm in Scyene, where John and Eliza had been looking after young Eddie and Pearl. While his wife resumed her maternal duties, Jim Reed was content to bounce around Dallas for a few months, living high on the hog with the last of their gold.

That is, until Dallas finally became too dangerous as well. As it turns out, carousing around town and spending money left and right was not the best way to avoid attention from authorities. People began talking, and soon Jim Reed had federal heat bearing down on him from both the Grayson theft in Indian Territory and the Shannon killings in Arkansas—to say nothing of the various private bounties hovering over him as well. By February of 1874, Reed, having been identified by multiple witnesses, had formal writs against him seeking his arrest for both crimes, as well as a powerful Creek tribal leader and a clan of frontier gangsters all willing to pay handsomely for his head on a stake. Time was running out for the former guerrilla, and with his loot all spent, he decided to skip town yet again. Only this time, Jim Reed would join his familiar cadre of Missouri outlaws in San Antonio, almost three hundred miles to the south, and he would take a local girl named Rosa McCommas, his new mistress, along for the ride. The McCommases were old neighbors of the Shirleys, and it's likely that Belle knew Rosa, a local beauty eight years her junior, quite well—which probably added insult to the injury of being replaced by a "younger woman" at the age of just twenty-six.

However painful and disappointing the entire episode was, it served as a reminder for Belle of two valuable lessons. First, the importance of establishing her own financial security independent of a man: to have her own income, to invest in her own land, to have a home that she could call her own and that no one could prize from her grip. And second, never to be cut out of a major score again. From then on out, she would be an equal partner in all her criminal endeavors, and eventually, once she had gathered her own crew, even the boss. Never again would she get chiseled out of what she felt was rightfully hers, be it a disputed horse, a sack of stolen gold, or a title claim on Younger's Bend. And while her husband's betrayal and philandering surely smarted, in the end, severing ties with the recalcitrant Jim Reed would prove to her benefit. Indeed, this fugitive husband of hers, feckless to the last and forever on the run, would soon run out of road.

HAD JIM REED SAVED some of the ten thousand in gold he'd stolen off Watt Grayson, had he and Rosa McCommas taken up with decent folk, had they used the ill-gotten funds to buy a house and some land, had he settled down to pursue his passion for breeding fine horses the way his father-in-law had, Jim very easily could have built a decent life for himself in San Antonio, living to reach a ripe old age. But of course he did none of these things, because decency was simply not in his nature. Jim Reed was an Anglo-Celtic wild man of the frontier stamp, a whiskey drinker, a gunfighter, and a cardplayer. Perhaps it was the adrenaline rush of a fresh score that he could not resist. Or maybe it was the lure of the gambling dens and brothels, which burned through money. Or maybe he was also in some ways jealous of the James-Younger gang, men who had served with Quantrill just like he had, left Missouri for the Texas frontier just as he had, and yet somehow seemed so much more successful in their ventures, pulling off bigger scores, earning bigger headlines. Perhaps he was seeking something more impressive, to prove his own mettle and show that he was their equal—a heist that would truly make his mark on the West. If this was the case, though, then Jim Reed should have been considerably more careful regarding what he wished for. Because he was about to get it.

On the evening of April 7, 1874, with dusk just setting in, he along with his outlaw friend Calvin Carter, as well as a nephew of Carter's with too many aliases to count, robbed the Austin–

San Antonio stagecoach line. The stage in question was carrying eleven total passengers and a fresh load of mail—seemingly a standard haul. And with their faces hidden behind bandanas, a six-shooter clutched in each hand, the three outlaws demanded the money and jewelry of all on board. When the last of the riches had been handed over, they cut loose the horses and turned their attention to the mail sacks, hoping they might contain some paper currency. Finding little of value there and realizing they were in a race against the incoming night, they cut their losses and broke for the hills. The bandits galloped away amidst a pale swirl of letters into the indigo twilight, making off with close to $3,000 and four gold watches.

As far as scores go, it was not a major one. The Grayson haul had been an order of magnitude larger—$3,000 was the amount that Jim Reed and his associates would bet on a single horse race. But what made the robbery notable wasn't the amount that was stolen, but who it was stolen from, something that Jim Reed, in his haste to pull off a noteworthy caper, probably did not stop to consider. In this case, they weren't just stealing from a small-time rancher in the Creek Nation; they had actually robbed a major stagecoach line, not to mention the president of the National Bank of San Antonio, who happened to be a passenger. Unlike the Grayson robbery, which was only mentioned in passing in a number of local papers in the vicinity of Indian Territory, the stagecoach robbery made the *New York Times*. On April 9, 1874, two days after the stickup occurred, it reprinted the following from the *Galveston Daily News*:

> *A special dispatch from Austin to the News, dated to-day, says that last night about dusk the stage, carrying the mail and eleven passengers, of whom three were ladies, was stopped about twenty-three miles from here by three armed men, who cut the front horses*

*from the traces and took all the passengers' money and jewelry,
and broke open their trunks, and gutted the mail bags, taking
off one of them. Among the passengers were Bishop Gregg, and
Mr. Breckenridge, President of the National Bank of San Antonio, from whom they took $1,000. They secured about $3,000 from
the passengers. The stage was a regular four-horse stage from San
Antonio to Austin, and did not reach Austin until 4 o'clock this
morning.*

The response to the robbery, which threatened to damage the
public's trust in a crucial component of Western infrastructure,
was swift and decisive. A $3,000 bounty was offered by the gover-
nor of Texas, another $3,000 reward was added to that from the
United States mail agent, and Sam T. Scott, senior partner at S. T.
Scott & Co., the owner of the stage line, threw in another $1,000
bounty to boot, all so "this most daring and outrageous crime may
be ferreted out." True, entanglements with the law and with dangerous men were certainly nothing new to Jim Reed. But this time,
something was different, and it must have dawned on him, with a
full *$7,000* bounty hovering over his head from this crime alone,
that he finally might have gone too far. For that kind of money,
men would do anything—even turn on friends and kin. Ironically,
Rosa McCommas, his inexperienced young lover, may have been
the first to realize the true size of the hornet's nest Jim had just
kicked. While Reed and his accomplices went into hiding, she fled
San Antonio for Dallas, surely horrified by the scope of what had
occurred—only to get picked up by authorities and sent straight
to Austin for questioning. She was released on a $1,000 bond, and
eventually charges were dropped, as there was no evidence she participated in the robbery. However, it appears that in her panic at
being examined, she may have dropped the dime on Jim Reed. It's
probably no coincidence that on that same day, authorities received

"positive information" that Reed and his accomplices intended to pass through Dallas before hiding out in Indian Territory.

Yet even with the tip-off, Jim Reed remained slippery. Traps were set, but he somehow managed to evade them. He slipped away from a posse of twenty-five men and several sheriff's deputies who were waiting outside a house Rosa McCommas was believed to be staying at. He would also elude authorities in Indian Territory less than two months later, following a shootout at one of his familiar hideouts—the home of a Cherokee, interestingly enough, by the name of Starr.

With nowhere left to run and running out of accomplices he could trust thanks to a massive bounty that seemed to be growing by the day, Jim Reed returned to Texas. In the scorching heat of high summer, he hid out with one of the few reliable friends he had left—an old drinking buddy and fellow mischief-maker named Henry Russel, who resided just outside the town of Paris. But even in Paris, Texas, as a hunted man who couldn't step out the door without wearing a disguise, Jim Reed longed for one more score—the chance at some extra cash to help fund his life on the run, perhaps to buy a train ticket back to California or passage south to Mexico. Which was why when he was approached by an acquaintance of Rosa McCommas's named John T. Morris, with plans to rob an old man in Arkansas allegedly crawling with gold, Jim Reed didn't have it in him to say no. The temptation was simply too great, and the payoff simply too large. After a final night spent at Henry Russel's, in the coolness of a prairie twilight, he and Morris set off together on horseback toward Arkansas, pistols oiled and primed, the morning star still burning in the east, the faint remainder of the Big Dipper canted toward the Pole Star, pointing the way.

But John T. Morris wasn't just a chance acquaintance of Rosa McCommas. He was a former peace officer and bounty hunter, specially deputized by U.S. marshals, who had been tailing Jim Reed across Texas and Indian Territory for the better part of three months. In fact, it was at the house of John T. Morris where the initial trap involving Rosa McCommas had been set—a trap that sprang too early when a gun was fired by mistake, alerting Jim Reed and allowing him to get away. Now, with the criminal exposed and out in the open, far away from friends and family, Morris finally saw his chance.

But he didn't take it—at least not yet. Morris was a professional, a disciplined and dispassionate killer. And as a Collin County resident himself, he knew exactly how dangerous these ex-guerrilla Missouri boys could be. They were not ones to surrender and definitely not ones to die easy. Rather than risk a gunfight on the open plains, he decided to bide his time and wait for the ideal moment. And that moment came toward midday, when the duo decided to stop for dinner—that being the term used by Upland Southerners for lunch—at the farmhouse of a man named S. M. Harvey, who apparently was willing to offer the travelers a meal. Reed and Morris ate together in the dining room, Morris preternaturally cool as he finished the last of his food. While Reed was still cleaning his plate, Morris excused himself, went back into the main room, and calmly explained to their host, Mr. Harvey, what was about to transpire. He then went out to the horses, retrieved both his own and Reed's weapons, and returned to the dining room, where, upon drawing his pistol, he said: "Jim, throw up your hands." Reed, no doubt surprised, initially complied, sliding back in his chair and raising his arms in surrender—but it was a ruse. In a flash, he flipped up the wooden dining table and used it as a shield while making a lunge for the door. Unfazed, Morris "shot two holes through the table," as he would later report in a coroner's statement, filling the room with hot splinters and sparks. This caused Reed to drop the table, which gave Morris the opening he needed. Raising his pistol again, he blasted away, getting off four rounds and hitting Reed twice, one a "scalping shot in the head" that tore off a sizable chunk of his face, and the other a solid plug right between the ribs.

Even that, however, wasn't enough to stop Jim Reed. Spouting blood and curses in equal measure, almost half of his face gone and his guts ripped apart, he charged at John T. Morris, whose pistol—assuming he carried the ubiquitous six-shot Colt .45 favored by lawmen and outlaws alike—was fresh out of bullets.[1] The crazed and mortally wounded Reed burst through the farmhouse's front door and tackled Morris to the ground, briefly getting the upper hand and showering the man in sputum and gore. It wasn't until Mr. Harvey, the owner of the farmhouse, finally got involved as well, that Reed was pulled off Morris and subdued. Together, they were able to keep the roaring, thrashing outlaw pinned to the dirt until his struggling subsided and he eventually bled out. And if S. M. Harvey had any whiskey stashed away somewhere in a drawer, he and John T. Morris, both of them completely out of breath and covered in grass and blood, almost certainly drank it— unable to believe the thing they had just seen.

ACCORDING TO LEGEND, WHEN Belle was summoned to the town of Paris, Texas, to identify the body of her late husband, she showed no emotion whatsoever and flatly denied that the mangled corpse

---

[1]   In his Paris, Texas, coroner's statement, the wording John T. Morris uses leaves some ambiguity about how many total shots he fired. After Jim Reed drops the table, Morris states that he "shot at him four times," leaving it unclear if four shots were fired in total, or after the initial two while Reed was still holding the table. If he fired six shots in total, his pistol would not have fired because he had expended all his cartridges. If he fired only four shots, then it was an issue of his pistol malfunctioning—which very well may have been the case if he was not using a Colt .45, but an older model of revolver. Guns like the Colt Paterson and the Colt 1851 Navy Revolver were both weaker and more prone to jamming.

lying on the table and collecting flies was her husband. It was a denial made purely out of spite, the story goes, to deny John T. Morris, whom she regarded as the worst kind of traitor, the bounty he was owed. More recent historians and biographers have largely dismissed this story as apocryphal, perhaps in part because the body *was* identified and Morris did collect a bounty for the killing. But much like the horseback wedding story, it was told often enough and by varied enough sources that it's worth considering that there may be at least some truth to it. Belle was a belligerent woman, and she came from belligerent people. And she did have a documented history of not responding particularly well when men close to her were shot to death. In a letter she would send two years later to Jim Reed's family in Missouri, she would express unalloyed hatred for John T. Morris, not to mention a passive-aggressive disappointment in Jim's brother Solomon for not seeking revenge. In her correspondence, she accuses him of "not having the pluck and love for Jim" that she thought he did. She even goes so far as to suggest that she would have offered "Solly" Jim's prized horse Rondo, if only he had come to Texas and "sought revenge." The Reed family may have regarded this a selfish request, given that they had already lost two sons to gun violence. But then again, so had the Shirleys. Belle did live by a code, both the code of the outlaw and the code of the frontier—that is to say, the code of the Appalachian, of the Upland Southerner. To her, John T. Morris was a collaborator and a rat, and the debt he had incurred needed to be answered by blood; it was a brother's duty, first and foremost, to settle the score.

As to why she didn't try to kill Morris herself—something that must have crossed her mind—her position as both a single mother and a woman were the likeliest deterrents. Revenge killings usually meant some stretch of time on the run, wanted by the law. For Belle, not only would this be extremely difficult to do as a mother with two young children to care for, but it was practically impossible to execute as a woman. In that time and place, a female traveling alone and unescorted was exceedingly rare and would have provoked instant scrutiny. Buying a train ticket, checking into a hotel, finding a residence, seeking employment—none of this would have been possible. In the years to come, Belle certainly would acquire enough criminal clout to arrive at the point where she didn't need to run. Like a mob boss, she would have the agency and resources to stay in one place and operate more or less in the open. But that was far in the future.

The very fact that Belle craved revenge at all may come as a surprise, given the manner in which Jim Reed had abandoned her and the children, skating off for San Antonio with his new mistress. But he and Belle had a complicated relationship, and it's likely that her reaction to his killing was equally so. And if the rumors of her own infidelity with Cole Younger had any truth to them, perhaps she accepted his betrayal as a "getting even" of sorts and found it in her heart to forgive him.

Then again, there may also be another, far less romantic origin for the story of her refusing to identify her husband's body. Jim Reed was killed in Northeast Texas, in the sweltering heat of August. Not just killed, but ripped apart, with his face blown open and his innards torn to shreds. And all that exposed flesh and blood, with temperatures skirting a hundred degrees—needless to say, he would not have been a pretty sight or smell by the time his corpse was ridden back to Paris, flopped over the saddle of his own horse. Yet as bad as the stench may have been, it would have been far worse by the time Belle arrived from Scyene for the final viewing the next day. According to one witness: "Reed's body had become very much decomposed, particularly about the head, having been shot just between the nose and right eye. The drayman, in carrying him to the potter's field mistook the place, and in returning, with the breeze to the windward of the corpse, he took sick, and was compelled to abandon it on the roadside." So even if loyalty to her husband and hatred for Morris wasn't enough to deter her from identifying the body, the fact that it had become a bloated, maggot-infested corpse too foul-smelling to even approach may have been.

Whether because Belle refused to claim the body or just because she had no money for a decent burial, on August 8, 1874, Jim Reed, the outlaw who had aspired to achieve wealth and greatness, was carted off instead to an empty field outside the town of McKinney and buried by a retching sheriff, in an unmarked pauper's grave.

IN THE ABSENCE OF Jim Reed, many of the Belle Starr legends, popularized and aggrandized by her early biographers, have the merry widow cavorting around Dallas in full Western regalia, gambling, drinking, playing the piano, and taking the occasional break to race her horse through the town's crowded streets. The reality, however, was far more mundane and far less jubilant. Belle may well have spent time in the saloons of Boggy Bayou, ignoring the stares of the establishments' overwhelmingly masculine clientele, choking back whiskey—photographs of her weathered visage taken later in life do seem to imply that she was no stranger to the drink. But if she did imbibe in saloons, the mood would not have been particularly celebratory. With the possible exception of the year she would later spend in a Detroit prison, the period just after Jim Reed's death was probably the most difficult of her life. In fact, it represents one of the few occasions when her emotional state is not mere conjecture—a letter survived, written on borrowed stationery from the Dallas sheriff's office in Belle's own hand. It was penned to her in-laws in Missouri on August 10, 1876, catching them up on current events and the general well-being of Jim's children. The letter is worth including here in its entirety, because of the insight it provides into Belle's fraught emotional state at this time, but also for the exceedingly rare opportunity it offers the reader to hear Belle in her own voice:

Dear Mother and Brothers and Sisters:—I write you after so long a time to let you know that I am still living. Time has made many changes, and some very sad ones indeed. My poor old father has left this world of care and trouble. He died two months ago today. It seems as if I have more trouble than any person. "Shug" got into trouble here and had to leave; poor Ma is left alone with the exception of little Eddie [James Edwin]. She is going to move away from here in a few days and then I'll be left alone. Eddie will go with her, and I don't know that I shall ever see him again. He is a fine, manly looking boy as you ever seen and is said to resemble Jimmie very much; he is very quick motioned, and I don't think there is a more intelligent boy living. I am going to have his picture taken before he leaves and I will send you one; would like for you to see and know him. I know you would love him for the sake of the dear one that's gone. Eddie has been very sick and looks pale and wan, but I think my boy will soon mend up. Rosie [Rose Lee, aka "Pearl"] is here in Dallas going to school; she has the reputation of being the prettiest little girl in Dallas. She is learning fast. She had been playing on the stage here in the Dallas theatre and gained a world-wide reputation for her prize performance. My people were very much opposed to it but I wanted her to be able to make a living of her own without depending on any one. She is constantly talking of you all, and wanting to visit you, which I intend she shall sometime.

Jno. L. [*sic*] Morris is still in McKinney, at large. It seems as if justice will never be meted out to him. Pete Fisher is in Colin City, where he has always lived. Solly hasn't the pluck and love for Jim I thought he had. I have Jimmie's horse Rondo yet; I was offered $200 for him the other day. If Sol had come to Texas, freely would I have given the horse to him if he had sought revenge.

I think Brocks are in Montague county. I will realize nothing from my farm this year. Brock rented it out in little pieces to first one and another, and none of them tended it well, so I made nothing. I am going to sell it this fall if I can.

I am far from well. I am so nervous this evening from the headache I can scarcely write.

And that's how the letter ended, with no complimentary close, not even a signature. Just a nervous woman who was "far from well," enumerating the sorrows that had been visited upon her during the previous year. In the wake of her husband's death, her own father, John "Judge" Shirley, the pillar of the Shirley clan, had finally passed away, leaving his Confederate disappointments and postwar frustrations behind him forever. Her younger brother Cravens, referred to as Shug, his nickname, in the letter, had followed in the juvenile delinquent footsteps of brother Edwin and was forced to flee Texas to escape a similar fate. Her mother, Eliza, would soon leave Scyene as well, and planned on taking Belle's son Eddie with her, caring for two children at once apparently being a financial burden that a penniless Belle could not shoulder. Her husband's killing was still unavenged, her small farm had gone to seed, and the only bright spot in her darkening life seemed to be her seven-year-old daughter Pearl. Who, interestingly enough, Belle insisted on receiving theatrical training, so that she could support herself one day, without "depending on any one"—which is to say, depending upon a man. It was a lesson Belle had learned the hard way; her entire world was essentially collapsing, with nearly every person she loved either lying in the grave or preparing to move away.

As if all that wasn't enough, less than a month after the letter to her in-laws was sent, news of yet another calamity would reach Belle's ears. There is no solid record of her reaction to the tidings, but word of the arrest would have no doubt spread like prairie fire around the saloons and gambling dens of north Texas. On September 7 of that same year, fate finally caught up with the James-Younger gang, following a string of audacious bank and train robberies that had tempted it at every turn. What began as a run-of-the-mill bank heist in Northfield, Minnesota, quickly went south when enraged townspeople, much to the gang's surprise, sounded the alarm and poured onto the street bearing arms. Cole Younger was outside the bank at the time, standing guard with Jesse James, his brother Jim, and two other gang members named Clell Miller and Bill Stiles. Frank James, Bob Younger, and Charlie Pitts, meanwhile, were inside carrying out the actual stickup. With the gun-toting citizenry of Northfield bearing down upon them, it quickly became apparent to Cole that their carefully laid plan was falling apart. He fired his pistol in the air as a warning, but that seemed only to further provoke the townsfolk, and within seconds, shots were ringing out from every direction, including from inside the bank. Clell Miller received a shotgun blast to the face; Bill Stiles, meanwhile, took a bullet through the heart, knocking him clean off his saddle. Cole himself was shot in the thigh, and his brother Bob's right elbow was completely shattered by a bullet, but the surviving gang members were still able to get on their horses and ride off, with a furious posse of vigilantes in pursuit.

In the end, Frank and Jesse James[2] separated from the group and made it all the way back to Missouri. The Youngers, on the other hand—Cole, Jim, and Bob—did not. They were slowed down by Bob's wound, and unlike the James brothers, who had already hightailed it west, Cole and Jim were unwilling to leave their injured brother behind. The posse caught up to them not long after, and in a wooded ravine just west of Madelia, the three brothers made their last stand, shooting it out until the very end, as if reenacting some horrific guerrilla battle from the war. Fortunately for the Youngers, the Minnesotans apparently had far more mercy than the average Kansas jayhawker or Missouri bushwhacker—they did not kill the three brothers. But they did drill them full of bullets and beat them to a bloody pulp before dragging them off to the county seat of Faribault for trial.

In the end, despite having killed two innocent bystanders during the botched robbery, the Youngers were able to avoid the hangman's noose by confessing to their crimes. But their outlaw days were over. All three brothers were sentenced to life in prison, their epic careers as criminals coming to a close with the final slamming of those iron bars. As for John, the fourth Younger brother, the fugitive who had shot the Texas sheriff in the throat, he'd already gotten his two years earlier, back in Missouri. He took a bullet in a gunfight with a Pinkerton—in the throat, no less, in the darkest kind of poetic justice. His death, however, was not immediate.

---

[2] It's interesting that in Cole Younger's autobiography, the Northfield Raid—which he pleaded guilty to participating in—is the only crime he admits to, despite a career of heists that spanned a full decade. He also refuses to identify Frank and Jesse James as accomplices in the Northfield Raid, instead referring to them as "Howard" and "Woods"—an example of the care he took to avoid implicating fellow outlaws in crimes they were not officially found guilty of, and evidence of his willingness to alter the facts to suit his agenda. It's possible he did the same to protect Belle Starr's reputation—or even his own—when it came to their rumored relationship. Part of the outlaw code was never to implicate oneself or fellow outlaws unless there was already an admission of guilt, and Cole Younger generally abided by it.

Clutching his neck, jets of dark arterial blood squirting out between his fingers, John had used his last seconds among the living to chase the Pinkerton detective into the woods on horseback and gun him down, finding revenge among the shifting shadows of those hickory trees, if not salvation. He swayed and tumbled from his horse only moments later, when his heart had nothing left to pump, dead at the age of twenty-three.

It was often said that the career of a true outlaw ends in either prison or the grave, and so it went for the Younger brothers. Yet while the tumultuous close to their infamy may make for good storytelling, it was almost certainly a last straw of sorts for the already hopeless and heartsick Belle. The symbolism would not have been lost on her: the very last of the old Missouri boys from her girlhood—including her old flame—snuffed out and locked away for good, leaving behind a void; an overwhelming sense that there was nothing left. An unnameable darkness that threatened to swallow her completely.

THE PERIOD FOLLOWING BELLE's desperate letter to her in-laws is something of a black hole—a relative rarity in a life that is otherwise rambunctious and punctuated quite regularly by public scandal. For four full years, a figure known for her violent love affairs and criminal dealings essentially falls off the map. Yes, there are figments of Western lore that have her cavorting with colorful comic book outlaws and being courted by wealthy ranchers who she later beguiles, but these tall tales are precisely that—designed to sell dime novels and nothing more. Most of what transpired during this period is mere conjecture, although a few established details help to paint a picture, murky as it may be, of how she spent these itinerant days.

It is known that she sold off the small landholding given to her by her deceased father. She probably did not receive much for it, but effectively had no choice, scraping by off the dwindling proceeds as she drifted between the homes of friends and relatives. It is also known that she gave up custody of her five-year-old son Eddie, although in the end he did not go to live with Eliza, who had left the farm in Scyene to reside in Dallas, but rather with the Reed in-laws in Rich Hill, Missouri. The decision would save Belle the burden of feeding and clothing another child, but it would haunt her relationship with the boy for years to come. And it is known that Belle had a brief but tragic love affair with yet another Missourian named Bruce Younger, a tinhorn gambler and part-time criminal who was a half brother of Cole Younger's father. There is considerable anecdotal evidence that the couple cohabitated briefly in the hardscrabble mining town of Galena, Kansas, in the latter months of 1879. The duo was known about town and frequently sighted together at the saloons of "Redhot Street," although whatever form their relationship took, it ended disastrously—as almost everything in Belle's life seemed to during this period. They were together for only months before things began falling apart, and a doomed last-minute marriage, which occurred in Labette County, Kansas, on May 15 of the year 1880, would last less than three weeks. There is a story about that as well, recorded in her earliest biography, Richard K. Fox's *Bella Starr, the Bandit Queen, or the Female Jesse James*, that has her forcing Bruce Younger to marry her at gunpoint—a shotgun wedding in the most literal sense of the word—with a terrified Bruce running out on her shortly thereafter. While that may be pure invention, there is a small detail on her marriage certificate, preserved on microfilm from the Kansas County Marriages, 1855–1911 archive, that's worth noting: Belle lied about her date of birth. The thirty-two-year-old widow and mother of two children gave her age as twenty-three before the probate judge, an oversight of almost a decade, and it's entirely possible that the twenty-seven-year-old Bruce Younger walked out on her upon discovering her true age.

For Belle, a widow now well into her thirties at a time when thirty was considered middle-aged and unmarried women had few financial options, the situation was dire and no doubt frustrating. Beyond her education, which was considerable and often commented upon, she did have a valuable Western skill set. Having grown up on a stock farm, she was an expert in the breeding and raising of horses, and as a man, could have easily acquired employment on a similar stock farm nearby. Indeed, as a man, she could have secured a bank loan with her landholdings as collateral and started a stock farm of her own, becoming the successful entrepreneur and pillar of the community that her father had been back in Carthage. But as a woman, and a widowed one at that, her options were extremely limited. She could have turned to destitute alcoholism, staggering around town as a laughingstock, washing dishes for free meals the way Calamity Jane did in Deadwood. She could have turned to sex work in a brothel, or simply shacked up with some itinerant gunfighter to secure room and board, the way Big Nose Kate did in Tombstone. Or she could have just surrendered completely, cladding herself in a widow's black lace and spending the rest of her life hidden away in monastic celibacy, right alongside her mother Eliza in Dallas. Effectively, in the male-dominated, Anglo-Celtic society of the Western frontier, those were her options—there was nowhere else to go.

Which was precisely when Belle decided she'd had just about enough. She didn't want any of those things. And on the fifth day of June, in the year 1880, she did something remarkable, something nobody saw coming, something that would shunt her destiny toward the myth it was meant to be:

She left behind the world of the White Man forever.

PART II

AMONG THE CHEROKEE

CHAPTER 5

Where Women Can Be Warriors

THERE IS NO EASY English translation for the Cherokee word *Ghigau*. Literally, it means something close to "beloved woman," although that fails to capture the term's historical and spiritual weight. Traditionally, Ghigau was an honorary title bestowed on Cherokee women who had distinguished themselves in battle and proven a selfless devotion to their clan in times of danger and strife. The designation came with tremendous respect, as well as responsibilities. It was believed among the Cherokee that a Ghigau was a direct conduit to Unetlanvhi, the Great Spirit, serving as its earthly representative and voice, and thus was given a place at the head of the Women's Council as well as a seat among the Council of Chiefs.[1] Part priestess, part chieftain, part warrior, part judge, the role was sacred and complex, and possessed no cultural counterpart in the politics or cosmology of the European American world.

Many notable Ghigau figures grace Cherokee history, but the most famous of all was likely Nanye'hi, a Cherokee woman of the Wolf Clan whose name was later anglicized to Nancy Ward. In

---

[1] It may be worth noting that while the role of the Ghigau is described here in the past tense—the position became obsolete when the Cherokee transitioned toward a more representative form of government in the early 1800s—the smaller Eastern Band of Cherokee still do honor the title as something both official and sacred. Descended from tribal members who avoided the Trail of Tears by hiding from federal troops during forced removal, the Eastern Band, still residing in their traditional Appalachian hills, have preserved a number of cultural and political practices that were generally lost following the rest of the Cherokee Nation's relocation to Indian Territory in present-day Oklahoma.

the year 1755, at the age of just eighteen, she first distinguished herself at the Battle of Taliwa, a tribal conflict with the ancestral enemy of the Cherokee, the Muscogee Creek, fought in the hills of northern Georgia. She acted initially as a second to her husband, readying the young warrior's powder horn and shot pouch between each volley of gunfire. And as he reloaded his musket, she chewed on the bullets, making the edges sharp and jagged so they would do more damage to the flesh of their foes. When he was struck down by a Creek gunman, however, Nanye'hi did not run or seek cover. Instead, she picked up her dead husband's weapon and charged the enemy, rallying her people and leading them to a resounding victory over the Creek. Following this act of valor, she was rewarded with the title of Ghigau: she would serve on the Council of Chiefs as a tribal leader, and eventually become a critical ambassador and negotiator for the Cherokee in their dealings with the U.S. government.

In 1781, Nanye'hi met with a delegation led by the politician John Sevier, one of the founding fathers of Tennessee. Her objective was to try to stem the influx of Anglo-American settlers that had begun pouring into Appalachia following the Declaration of Independence—the Cherokee had aligned themselves with the British during the conflict in exchange for military assistance against the Choctaw and the Creek, further complicating what were already difficult relations. And upon meeting with the American delegation, she expressed surprise and dismay at the fact that they had no women representatives among their ranks. It was reported that Nanye'hi spoke the following famous lines to Sevier:

You know that women are always looked upon as nothing; but we are your mothers; you are our sons. Our cry is all for peace; let it continue. This peace must last forever. Let your women's sons be ours; our sons be yours. Let your women hear our words.

Her stirring speech did leave an impression on Sevier, but western expansion in the wake of American independence was not a tide to be easily stopped. Despite her efforts to slow white settlement of their traditional lands, it became clear to Nanye'hi that the steady flow of newcomers could not be halted, diplomatically or militarily. Instead, she used her influence as Ghigau to negotiate treaties and to lead her people in adapting to their new economic and political reality without assimilating completely. During her tenure, she helped her tribe navigate a delicate balance between physical and cultural survival, at a time when Indigenous societies were collapsing all around her. Nanye'hi would live well into her eighties and die a hero to the Cherokee people, their "beloved woman" in every sense of the term: a ferocious warrior whose genius for leadership and diplomacy very well may have ensured the survival of her tribe.

There is no way to be sure that Belle learned of the traditional role of the Ghigau, or of Nanye'hi, the most legendary Ghigau of all. We can't be certain that the tales of her chewing on bullets and charging into a hail of Creek gunfire ever made it to Belle's ears. Such stories may have been passed on, or they may have been forgotten. More likely than not, however, Belle *was* familiar with the life of Nanye'hi. Not just because of the woman's legendary status when it came to the history and survival of the Cherokee people, but because the Cherokee themselves are a matrilineal society, in which clan membership is passed down solely from the mother and recollected accordingly. And as it just so happened, the heads of the Cherokee family who would adopt her could claim Nancy Ward—that is to say, Nanye'hi—as a great-great-grandmother. Belle didn't just become part of a society in which women warriors were celebrated and remembered; she became part of a family directly descended from the greatest female warrior of all.

YEARS LATER, IN A biographical sketch provided to John Foster Wheeler of the *Fort Smith Elevator*, Belle would give the following simple reasoning behind her decision to leave the white world behind and live instead among the Cherokee:

> *After a more adventurous life than generally falls to the lot of woman, I settled permanently in the Indian Territory, selecting a place of picturesque beauty on the Canadian River. There, far from society, I hoped to pass the remainder of my life in peace and quietude.*

She would follow that remark up, however, in classic Belle fashion, by mentioning that "So long had I been estranged from the society of women (whom I thoroughly detest) that I thought I would find it irksome to live in their midst." Her postscript, though full of her signature feistiness, is understandable in its sentiment. Effectively, a fed-up Belle is declaring in no uncertain terms her independence from the expectations imposed upon her by a patriarchal society. A society, as it were, that had spent the first two decades of her life instructing her to act like a prim and proper Southern lady, and the decade after that telling her it was her womanly duty to let her husband take her for granted and treat her like the proverbial doormat. The "society of women" she refers to is the all-encircling, all-encompassing prison of those very expectations. It's the life she would have had in Dallas alongside her genteel widowed mother, or perhaps her life in Missouri had she married another embittered ex-guerrilla who saw little use for her beyond housekeeping and breeding. Among the Cherokee, she found an appealing alternative. And for a brief moment—before that dark and inevitable hunger returned once again—she even found peace.

This may explain the why behind her departure from white frontier society, what she was fleeing from and what she found instead. But it doesn't necessarily explain the how. Belle wasn't adopted by just any Cherokee family. She left her old life behind to go and live with the Starrs, a powerful clan of political rebels, smugglers, and gangsters feared throughout Indian Territory and beyond. The family's patriarch, Thomas Starr, was a seasoned killer and marauder whom many white settlers in the region still regarded as worse than "the devil himself." The transition is remarkable and seemingly inexplicable: less than three weeks after her disastrous marriage to a small-time gambler in a mining camp in Kansas, she was suddenly the honored guest of a Cherokee warlord in Indian Territory, in modern-day Oklahoma. How did this happen? How did someone from the seemingly opposite end of the frontier cultural spectrum come to be welcomed by the Starrs and even embraced?

The only way to make sense of the connection that Belle shared with her Cherokee hosts is to understand the history of their respective families. Because in some ways, the Shirleys and the Starrs were not nearly as different as one might expect. Both had origins in Appalachia; both had passed through the Ozarks before finally putting down roots on the edge of the Southern Plains. Both had a cultural attachment to the Upland South, including a sympathy for the Confederate cause and an abiding hatred for the federal government. And neither clan was shy about using guns as a form of conflict resolution. There was, however, a profound difference as well: The Starrs had not been pulled out of their Appalachian hollows by the promise of free land—they had been pushed. And their family had been shattered by not just one civil war, but two.

ONE OF THE MOST glaring flaws of colonial narratives—aside from the fact they've almost unanimously been authored by the colonizers themselves—is in the simplistic way they have depicted the colonized. Historically, portrayals of native peoples have tended to veer between two opposing extremes: villainization or victimization. The former usually prevails when Indigenous inhabitants pose an existential threat to the efforts of the colonizers, and the latter, when the efforts of the colonizers pose an existential threat to the inhabitants. This drastic shift is a feature of empire building that's as old as the concept of empire itself. The ancient Romans did this in their depictions of the Gauls (compare Julius Caesar's accounts of human sacrifice in *The Gallic Wars* to the romantic courage of *The Dying Gaul*), the British with the Scottish Highlanders (examine the teeth-baring savagery of *An Incident in the Rebellion of 1745* alongside the honorable swashbuckling of Walter Scott's *Rob Roy*), and it has been a reliable feature of European colonialism in the Americas as well, starting with Bernal Díaz's *The Conquest of New Spain*, going all the way up to *Dances with Wolves*. Whether the colonized are portrayed negatively as bloodthirsty savages or positively as noble savages, they are nonetheless presented as fundamentally "savage." That is to say, "primitive," and thus incompatible with the modern, "civilized" world of the colonizer. In short: they're destined to lose. The Pilgrims arrive and the Wampanoags scatter; the Osage move out so that John Shirley can move in.

This approach is problematic for a number of reasons. For one, it distills a vast and exceedingly diverse array of cultures, civilizations, and experiences into a common and simplistic historical trope—at times, a caricature even, without regard to the enormous differences that marked Indigenous societies, specifically in regards to how they interacted, traded, and negotiated power with the colonial presence. To wit, the reason pioneer families like the Shirleys were generally discouraged from settling west of the Appalachians prior to American independence was because of the conditions that the Indigenous Five Nations had imposed upon the British, in return for their help defeating the French. Beyond that, the approach also disregards the importance of the many hybrid identities that emerged from contact between the Old World and the New. Métis, mestizo, Black Seminole, Red River Bungi—history is rife with examples. Quanah Parker, the last great Comanche war chief to take on the whites, was the son of the very same Cynthia Ann Parker who had been kidnapped by a raiding party just ninety miles south of the Shirleys' farm in Scyene—she was adopted by the Comanche and assimilated completely. Relying on a facile dichotomy to explain the colonial experience would seem to negate the very existence of such individuals, not to mention the foundational role they have played within the American experience itself.

The foremost reason this notion of "primitiveness" is problematic, however, is the most basic of all: because it's simply not true. The prevailing narratives of "advanced" Europeans clashing with "primitive" Native peoples, be they sympathetic toward the latter or not, casually gloss over certain undeniable facts. Namely, that the Aztec capital of Tenochtitlan was four times larger than London; that the diplomatic complexity of the Iroquois Confederacy would have humbled the Habsburgs; that the 2,500-mile reach of the Inca empire rivaled that of the Romans; that Native Hawaiians possessed maritime technology that would have baffled Magellan; that the Inuit developed Arctic survival strategies a century's worth of disastrous British and American polar expeditions failed to comprehend. Prevailing colonial narratives gloss over such facts because they don't serve the embedded notion of inherent European superiority that props up both the villainization and victimization story lines alike. Exceedingly rare is the European or European American account willing to concede that the similarities between the two civilizations far outweigh the differences. To admit this would be to grant a sort of human equality and cultural parity that even the best-intentioned of historians and storytellers have seldom been willing to fully acknowledge or explore.

Furthermore, such attitudes about the historic inevitability of colonial conquest elide over an even more important fact: in many instances, Native peoples succeeded quite admirably in repelling colonial advances. From the Pueblo Revolt of 1680, to Pontiac's Rebellion of 1763, to the Caste War of Yucatán beginning in 1847, to the aforementioned campaigns of Comanche raids that kept Spaniards, Mexicans, and Anglo-Americans out of central Texas for nearly two centuries, it is not difficult to find instances of successful Indigenous rebellions in the history of the Americas. One could even argue that the revolutions that reshaped Latin America in the nineteenth and twentieth centuries constituted some of the most successful Indigenous rebellions of all. After all, Pancho Villa and Emiliano Zapata were definitely not Spanish criollos, nor were the vast majority of men and women who fought alongside them. In anglicized North America, colonial power structures have long embraced a kind of James Fenimore Cooper version of Native American history, one in which their beloved "Last of the Mohicans" put up a noble fight, but in the end must vanish proudly yet defeatedly into the twilit pages of the nation's past, making way for a new age of white modernity. Yet somewhat ironically, those same power structures have struggled to embrace the fact that thanks largely to Mesoamerican migration patterns, the borders of the United States of America in the twenty-first century contain far more people of Indigenous ancestry than they did in 1492—that the overarching story of Native peoples in the Americas is not one of disappearance, but *perseverance*.

But if that is the case, and all the above true, it does raise the question: Why do the resistance stories of so many Indigenous societies, especially in North America, seem to end in a similar way? With rebellions crushed, treaties broken, and lands stolen, resulting in some kind of allotment or reservation, usually in a barren place farther west than the original combatants could have ever imagined? Again, the prevailing argument has been that of European advantage; a kind of technological edge coupled with an avaricious genius for territorial gain. And while one could devote an entire book—and some have—to enumerating and debating the various things Europeans had at their disposal that Native Americans did not, there is truly only one that made the loss of Indigenous hegemony in the Americas possible, if not inevitable: an immune system primed to combat Old World diseases.

IT'S VIRTUALLY IMPOSSIBLE TO comprehend the enormity of the apocalypse that was visited upon Native civilizations when illnesses like smallpox, measles, cholera, typhus, and influenza arrived from across the Atlantic. This is not because Western medicine has mastered disease, but simply because nothing in our modern understanding of pathogens and mortality can begin to compare. Exact figures are unknown, but scientific and historical studies have consistently reached the conclusion that around 90 percent of the total Indigenous population of the Americas died from Eurasian diseases in the decades that followed first contact. So profound was the demographic collapse that it actually appears to have altered global weather patterns as millions of acres of Native farmland went untended and returned to forest, cooling the planet and giving birth to the Little Ice Age of the seventeenth century. It's almost too horrific to contemplate, that the quaint Dutch paintings of townsfolk skating across frozen canals during the century's uncharacteristically cold winters were made possible by the excruciating deaths of more than 50 million Indigenous Americans an ocean away. Some of this holocaust was witnessed by colonists, but the vast majority of it was not. Because disease vectors usually far outpaced European exploration, the bulk of these epidemics occurred ahead of any efforts at conquest, well beyond the colonial purview. For centuries, chroniclers have marveled at the feat of 168 mounted and armored Spaniards conquering an Inca empire protected by thousands of warriors. They attribute the Spanish victory to the horses or the steel or Francisco Pizarro's dark and covetous canniness. What they usually fail to mention, however, is that smallpox had arrived in the Andes just prior to Pizarro, completely devastating the Inca capital, killing the emperor Huayna Capac along with his entire line of succession, and throwing the imperial government into chaos with a resultant civil war. The story of European colonial conquest in the Americas overall is not one of fearless conquistadors relying on their superior technology and culture to best a more impassioned but less "advanced" enemy. More often than not, it's the story of completely oblivious soldiers taking on the scattered remnants of civilizations that had already all but collapsed under multiple waves of apocalyptic plagues. Given the generational damage that Eurasian diseases inflicted upon Native populations, the fact that so many were still able to engage European nations in both outright warfare and complex diplomacy while maintaining their independence is beyond admirable—it's simply astounding. Even if that independence was frequently short-lived.

In America's Eastern Woodlands, however, there was one tribe that managed to do precisely that for the better part of an entire century: the Cherokee. An Iroquoian group that had migrated from the Great Lakes to southern Appalachia in ancient times, they engaged in a mixture of hunting and agriculture and lived in compact villages scattered across the mountainous portions of Tennessee, the Carolinas, Georgia, and Alabama. Cherokee society was clan-based and governed by councils held at both a local and tribal level. According to Cherokee oral traditions, the old system of governance and social hierarchy in place for centuries involved a hereditary priestly class composed of representatives from all seven Cherokee clans, complemented by a separate warrior class with unique wartime duties—essentially, a society that bore a striking resemblance to medieval Europe, albeit with the hereditary powers belonging to the ritual-oriented church, rather than the spear-wielding feudal nobility. And while their settlement patterns and economies may have been similar, the Cherokee had considerable linguistic and cultural differences from their southeastern tribal neighbors: the Choctaw, the Chickasaw, the Muscogee Creek, and the Seminoles. Differences that frequently resulted in large-scale warfare, with the Creek in particular.

One thing all these groups had in common, however, was a vulnerability to the diseases that first appeared in tribal lands in the sixteenth century. The Spanish expedition to the Carolinas led by Hernando de Soto in 1540 was the first to introduce smallpox and measles to the region, doing untold damage to Indigenous communities. No Spaniards stayed behind to chronicle the epidemics that followed in their wake, but it was almost certainly catastrophic, shaking Cherokee society to its foundations. A second wave of disease would again sweep through the southern Appalachian region between 1738 and 1739, in the form of a smallpox epidemic likely brought by British slave traders from Charlestown. And unlike that first Spanish outbreak, the true scale of this catastrophe is known. Among the Cherokee, who previously could boast of a robust tribal population of 16,000 members, living across sixty-four towns and villages, protected by some 6,000 warriors, one witness to the outbreak put the mortality rate at close to 50 percent—roughly half the entire tribe died from the virus in a single year. Which was terrible timing, because the Cherokee people were shortly to be forced into a series of disastrous wars with the French, the Creek, and the Americans, all with a fighting force that had been halved and civic institutions that had been left in shambles, thanks to a horrific, disfiguring disease.

Which also goes a long way in explaining the Cherokee alliance with the British government throughout much of the eighteenth century. In the British, whose presence west of the Appalachian frontier was relatively nonintrusive, they saw a lucrative trading partner, as well as an ally against the Creek and the American colonists, both of whom had a penchant for encroaching on their hunting grounds. Their Iroquois cousins to the north had forged a similar alliance, using it to crush Algonquin and French rivals while monopolizing the fur trade, and with few exceptions, the Cherokee followed a similar model. This partnership served them well for several decades, up until the outbreak of the American Revolution—a conflict that proved a boon for colonists itching for western expansion, but a catastrophe for Native peoples who lived beyond the Appalachian frontier. Essentially, the Cherokee sided with a loser, which meant that after the American victory, there was nobody to stop land-hungry and openly hostile American settlers from pouring into their traditional lands. Cherokee delegations, like that led by the Ghigau Nanye'hi, did their best to negotiate treaties with the Americans and establish borders, but the treaties were seldom respected by the successive waves of white homesteaders.

As one might expect, the ensuing friction would eventually ignite a powder keg of violence. Specifically, the Chickamauga Wars, a series of raids and ambushes in the aftermath of the American Revolution conducted by a faction of Cherokee led by the war chief Dragging Canoe. The conflict also represented one of the first—though certainly not the last—major cleavings of Cherokee solidarity in the face of European American expansion. While some Cherokee, like Nanye'hi, favored a policy of negotiation and partial assimilation as the only means of ensuring their sur-

vival as a tribe, others, like Dragging Canoe—who happened to
be Nanye'hi's cousin—flatly refused anything short of total adherence to Cherokee culture and full-scale rebellion. Ultimately,
Dragging Canoe saw no way to reconcile his differences with the
American government or with the opposing factions of Cherokee.
He led some 500 like-minded Cherokee westward, beyond the
reach of white settlement, to continue his guerrilla campaign and
gather other Native peoples to his cause. And he did experience
some success in his aim—only to suffer a heart attack before it
could be fully realized. After an entire night of ritual dancing to
celebrate a new alliance with sympathetic Creek and Choctaw warriors, both Dragging Canoe and his rebellion breathed their last
and died.

One of the great ironies for the Cherokee who chose to stay in
their traditional lands and negotiate with the new American government was that they were regarded by whites as one of the "Civilized Tribes"—a designation applied to them only because they
had been forced to adopt so many elements of European American culture in order to exist peacefully in American society. For
leaders like Nanye'hi, this was a conscious choice. It represented
a necessary survival strategy for a people who had suffered catastrophic demographic loss and near-total civic collapse during decades of disease and warfare. Essentially, the Cherokee had done
what was necessary to stay alive, which often included marriage
outside the tribe, the adoption of European American dress and
family structures, the creation of a Cherokee writing system, and a
partial conversion to Christianity. Even African chattel slavery was
borrowed as an agrarian labor practice, replacing the older, more
kinship-aligned forms of slavery that had served for centuries as a
means of incorporating war prisoners into tribal society. Living on
cattle farms, going to church, wearing wool dresses and linen trade
shirts, oftentimes speaking English—by the first decades of the

1800s, the physical lifestyle of many tribal members was beginning to bear a closer resemblance to that of their white neighbors than to that of their own Cherokee predecessors. In 1827, the Cherokee even formally established their own constitution, inspired by that of the United States, to delineate their borders and establish themselves as a sovereign nation. But in the end, even that wouldn't be enough to be treated as such.

When President Andrew Jackson signed the Indian Removal Act of 1830, any hopes of retaining ancestral lands uncontested instantly collapsed. For the Cherokee, it was no longer a question of if the U.S. government would attempt to relocate them to Indian Territory west of the Mississippi, but how and when. Again, the tribal leadership split into two camps: the Treaty Party, led by the Cherokee Council clerk, John Ridge, which accepted removal as inevitable and believed negotiating with the American government could secure the tribe a better allotment of land across the Mississippi, and the National Party, led by the tribe's principal chief, John Ross, which advocated for resisting removal at all costs. Once again, survival came down to the question of negotiation or resistance, only this time, unlike in the era of Nanye'hi and Dragging Canoe, the Cherokee had a far better idea of exactly who they were dealing with. Neither faction harbored any illusions about the designs of the U.S. government; both factions ultimately wanted what was best for their people. They simply had different interpretations of what real autonomy meant for the tribe, and how best to ensure its future. A truly heartrending speech, given in the Cherokee Council House by Major Ridge, John Ridge's elderly father and a founder of the Treaty Party, provides some insight into the mindset of those who saw negotiation as the only means of tribal survival:

> *I am one of the native sons of these wild woods. I have hunted the*
> *deer and turkey here, more than fifty years. I have fought your*

battles, have defended your truth and honesty, and fair trading. I have always been the friend of honest white men. . . . I know the Indians have an older title than theirs. We obtained the land from the living God above. They got their title from the British. Yet they are strong and we are weak. We are few, they are many. We cannot remain here in safety and comfort. I know we love the graves of our fathers, who have gone before to the happy hunting grounds of the Great Spirit—the eternal land, where the deer, the turkey and the buffalo will never give out. We can never forget these homes, I know, but an unbending, iron necessity tells us we must leave them. I would willingly die to preserve them, but any forcible effort to keep them will cost us our lands, our lives and the lives of our children. There is but one path of safety, one road to future existence as a Nation. That path is open before you. Make a treaty of cession. Give up these lands and go over beyond the great Father of Waters.

MAJOR RIDGE'S INTERPRETATION OF land sovereignty, as expressed in his moving speech at the Cherokee Council House, did gloss over certain historical facts. The title to the Cherokee lands in northern Georgia of which he spoke may well have been a gift from "the living God above," but it also came at the bloody expense of a great number of Muscogee Creek, the rival tribe that the Ghigau Nanye'hi had once fought, and who believed with equal conviction that same living God had given it to them. Such was the nature of tribal warfare. However, his oratory speaks quite accurately to a painful and inevitable truth: the depleted woodland tribes of the East, Cherokee and Creek included, were collectively facing a vicious onslaught of western expansion against which, by the year 1835, they could no longer defend themselves. This wasn't a matter of keeping scattered settlers or isolated armies at bay, as they had throughout most of the eighteenth century. By the middle decades of the nineteenth century, they were up against the merciless steamroller of Manifest Destiny itself. Committed idealists like John Ross may have decided to make a stand on principle, but tribal leaders like Major and John Ridge, who considered themselves realists, believed that resistance at this point was tantamount to tribal suicide.

The Cherokee Nation may have been split, but when it came to the negotiation of actual Indian removal, the U.S. government was not. It knew exactly which faction it wanted to deal with. The state of Georgia, whose northern hills were the site of the Cherokee Nation's governing bodies, was already disregarding the federal government completely and auctioning off Cherokee lands to farmers and gold prospectors—actions that should have enraged President Jackson but did not. He wanted the Cherokee gone as well, and he needed the state of Georgia more generally on his side to further his own political ambitions. And on December 29, 1835, his representatives met with John Ridge and twenty other prominent members of the Treaty Party in the Cherokee capital of New Echota, to negotiate the financial and territorial compensation that tribal members would receive in exchange for forfeiting their traditional lands for good. The principal chief John Ross, upon learning what had occurred behind his back, was outraged, as was a sizable majority of the Cherokee population, many of whom viewed the Ridge faction as nothing more than a band of economic opportunists and "mixed bloods" who had sold out their nation. The Treaty Party themselves may have considered their actions legitimate, even necessary—a way of avoiding a genocidal war. But to John Ross and his supporters, who valued Cherokee sovereignty at all costs, the Treaty Party hadn't just committed treason—they'd committed the greatest sin of all, the crime explicitly labeled a capital offense by written

Cherokee law: they had sold tribal lands to whites without tribal consent. In essence, it wasn't just a treaty they had signed; it was a declaration of civil war, not to mention their own death warrants.

That civil war would have to wait. Realizing they were no longer safe in Eastern lands and recognizing the horrors of forced removal if they stayed, John Ridge and his supporters left the eastern Cherokee Nation with their families voluntarily between 1836 and 1837, receiving federal protection during the voyage as part of their deal. They originally resettled west of the Mississippi in what is today Arkansas, where a small community of relocated Cherokee known as the Old Settlers had been living for the last two decades.

Among the Ridge supporters who voluntarily left for Indian Territory was another tribal leader by the name of James Starr. A prominent statesman of mixed Cherokee and white ancestry, he had been present at New Echota and had personally signed the treaty—meaning he, too, was essentially marked for death by the Cherokee government of the East. But while he may have been on the National Party's hit list, he was also the great-grandson of the legendary Ghigau, Nanye'hi, on his mother's side—and he already had kin among the small band of Western Cherokee who remembered him well. He, along with the rest of the Ridge supporters, were generally embraced by the Old Settlers and welcomed into the western branch of the tribe, as they all did their best to rebuild west of the Mississippi what they had lost in their ancestral eastern hills.

Which was precisely when the tribal civil war they had tried to avoid came right to their doorstep, in the form of John Ross and the nearly 10,000 Eastern Cherokee who had just completed the 800-mile Trail of Tears under far more brutal circumstances than their Treaty Party predecessors. According to a missionary doctor who accompanied the Cherokee during the ordeal, as many as 4,000 people, somewhere between a fifth and a quarter of the tribe's total population, died between 1838 and 1839 on the trail. True to Major Ridge's word, John Ross had been unable to stop the federal government's campaign of Cherokee removal—he and the other holdouts had been forced from their homes effectively at gunpoint. And after a sweltering summer spent in disease-ridden internment camps and following a frigid winter death march and boat ride that had killed his own wife, the principal chief of a freshly relocated Cherokee Nation was not in a forgiving mood upon his arrival in Indian Territory in the bitter spring of 1839. It would be here, among their own kind, far from any federal interference, that the true bloodshed would begin.

Major Ridge and his son John, the leaders of the Treaty Party, were hit first. It's not known if John Ross personally approved the assassination or not, but regardless, on June 22, 1839, a posse of his supporters killed the architects of the Treaty of New Echota. But far from resolving anything, the assassinations—or executions, depending on one's perspective—were just the first volley in a brutal confrontation that had been building for years. On the surface, the Cherokee civil war was a blood feud between Treaty Party supporters and National Party supporters—that is to say, those who chose to negotiate with the U.S. government regarding the terms of removal and those who flatly refused to entertain the notion of removal at all. On a more symbolic level, it was a battle to determine who would claim the mantle of leadership over the new, united tribe west of the Mississippi: the Western Old Settler government, which had already been in Indian Territory for years and was led by their own principal chief, first John Jolly and later John Rogers, or the Eastern Band of new arrivals, who saw themselves as the only legitimate Cherokee government and who continued in their allegiance to principal chief John Ross. And the violence that ensued, that the *colonial* violence of forced removal had in fact unleashed, was hauntingly atavistic.

War paint, ritualistic torture, scalp taking, blood vengeance—they would all make a vicious comeback in the years ahead.

James Starr dodged the first waves of reprisal killings, in part by hiding out at nearby Fort Gibson any time members of the Ross faction were in the area. His luck ran out, however, on November 9, 1845, when a gang of thirty-two mounted and painted warriors, under direct orders from principal chief John Ross, ambushed his home and gunned him down on his front porch, killing him instantly while also mortally wounding his disabled fourteen-year-old son Buck in the process. Suel Rider, a cousin of the Starrs who lived down the road, and Washington Starr, another of James's sons, were attacked by the same war party just minutes later and fared little better. A gut-shot Suel gurgled out his final breath as a Ross henchman leaped from his horse and put a knife through his heart; Washington was shot multiple times but was able to escape into the woods, leaking blood through the dead autumn leaves and screaming for help.

At the funerals for James, Buck, and Suel, only the women of the Starr family dared to show their faces. A sweeping death sentence had been passed, an edict of eradication against James Starr and his sons, as final payback for what had happened in New Echota and as wartime retribution for what they had done since. What the Ross faction hadn't counted on, however, was that one of James Starr's sons in particular would pass a far more effective death sentence upon them.

All of them.

To ENUMERATE THE MASCULINE relationships that entered Belle Starr's short but fiery orbit is to chart a veritable solar system of dangerous men. *Hard* men. Scalp takers, bone crushers, individuals for whom violence wasn't a last resort, but a quotidian tool, a way of life. Men who gave no quarter and killed their enemies without hesitation or mercy. And if there's a standout from among their blood-soaked, powder-burned ranks, at least before Belle's arrival in Indian Territory, it's probably Cole Younger, an outlaw and skilled gunslinger who cut his teeth with Quantrill's Raiders and only sharpened them further during an epic career rustling cattle and robbing banks. But if there was one man who crossed Belle's path and who made Mr. Younger look like a veritable choir-boy in comparison, it was Thomas "Ta-Ka-Tos" Starr, the second eldest of James Starr's sons, who was just thirty-two at the time of his father's murder. The hit on the elder Starr that principal chief John Ross authorized had been intended as a calculated message to the entire Starr clan, a means of cowing their rebellious nature and getting them in line with the new Eastern Cherokee leader-ship. What he hadn't factored into that calculation, though, was that James Starr would have a son like Tom.

Even prior to the assassination of his father, Tom Starr had a reputation as a brigand and an outlaw, wreaking havoc on white settlers and rival Cherokee alike. To the Treaty Party faction, he was something of a folk hero, throwing lawmen off his trail by nailing his horse's shoes on backward, leaping into rivers and hold-ing his breath until danger had finally passed. As a champion for their cause, he was almost perfect: incredibly strong, unusually tall, good with any weapon, and impossible to outsmart. A letter penned by John Rollin Ridge, the son of the late John Ridge, in Fayetteville, Arkansas, on April 17, 1846, provides some sense of how the younger Starr was regarded by his supporters:

> I saw a man this morning from Boonsboro who had seen Tom
> Starr and Sam'l McDaniels they were in fine health and spirits.
> Those fellows, especially Tom Starr, are talked of frequently and
> with wonderment about here. He is considered a second Rinaldo

Rinaldina.[2] Robberies, House-trimmings, and all sorts of romantic deeds are attributed to this fellow, and the white people in town and around say they had rather meet the devil himself than Tom Starr!

Of course, this is from the perspective of someone belonging to the same Cherokee faction as the Starrs, not to mention the son of the Treaty of New Echota's primary architect. The rival Cherokee and white homesteaders that Tom Starr raided and put to the gun would have surely seen nothing "romantic" in his deeds. There are stories of Tom Starr wearing a rawhide necklace of dried earlobes taken from the men he killed, of putting the farmhouses of his enemies to the torch and burning entire families alive, children included. And it's hard to say how many of them are true. What is known, however, is that rather than submit to John Ross and his government, the flint-eyed six-and-a-half-foot Cherokee swore a blood oath to hunt down all thirty-two of the men who had been party to the slaying of his father and end their days as painfully as possible. And this was a promise that Tom Starr evidently did an impeccable job of keeping. He didn't just go on the warpath—he went on the rampage, assembling his own private army from the ranks of Starr supporters and becoming the horror and bane of the Ross regime, as by pistol, by knife, by tomahawk, or by his own two bare hands, he took them out one after the other.

One of his first victims was the Ross henchman who had stabbed his cousin Suel Rider through the heart—he paid him back in kind. The rest he hunted down methodically and killed at his leisure. A longtime neighbor of Tom Starr's, who spoke to him often in later years, would recall Tom saying the following: "You know there was thirty-two men that slipped up and killed my daddy—well, I got

---

[2] Rinaldo Rinaldini was a heroic, swashbuckling character in *Rinaldo Rinaldini, the Robber Captain*, a penny dreadful by Christian August Vulpius first published in 1797.

most of them except a few that got sick and died in bed before I could get to them." Identifying each of his victims would be an all-but-impossible task in a time before detailed death or burial records were kept, but his vendetta campaign was both prolific enough and egregious enough to warrant an indirect mention in the formal peace accord that was finally signed, under intense pressure from President James Polk, the following year. Polk had threatened to split the Cherokee Nation into three separate entities by force if they didn't end the conflict, and the warring political factions, realizing such a schism would effectively ruin the tribe, at last complied. According to a February 4, 1847 article that appeared in the *Cherokee Advocate*, the clause in the treaty that had granted amnesty for individual crimes committed during the Cherokee Civil War was specifically "aimed at the pardon of the Starrs, particularly Tom Starr," for the rage-fueled campaign of blood vengeance he had unleashed upon the Ross faction of the tribe. So fierce had been the vendetta of James Starr's warlord son, when it came to negotiating a truce, he had practically become a nation unto himself.

Relative peace and unity had come at last to the Cherokee Nation following the peace accord and its subsequent pardons. But the United States of America was coming apart at the seams. With Tom Starr's thirst for revenge temporarily slaked, he settled farther south, establishing a homestead with his wife Catherine and his brood of twelve children on the banks of the South Canadian River in present-day Oklahoma. This portion of Indian Territory had been designated for the Cherokee, right alongside parcels allotted to their old "Civilized Tribe" neighbors from back east: the Choctaw, the Chickasaw, the Seminole, and the Muscogee Creek. However, the region's patchwork of displaced tribes, mostly forgotten by the federal government following their "removal," gained a sudden strategic importance with the outbreak of the American Civil War on April 12, 1861. The eastern half of Indian Territory lay squarely between the Confederate strongholds of Texas and Arkansas, and the federally controlled states of Kansas and Missouri. With Union and Confederate troops encroaching on their lands from all angles, the Cherokee found themselves forced to pick sides. And while some, like John Ross and other "Pin Indians,"[3] eventually chose to fight on the side of the federal government, a substantial portion of the Cherokee, led by the Ross rival and old Treaty Party member Stand Watie, aligned themselves with the Confederate cause.

Long-standing animosities toward both the U.S. government and the Ross faction surely influenced the Cherokee-Confederate alliance, but one of the most significant factors was slavery itself. African chattel slavery had been present in Cherokee society since the eighteenth century, when tribal members in Southern states first began to adopt the antebellum culture and agrarian customs of their white neighbors. Some tribal elites, like the principal chief John Jolly of the Western Band of Cherokee, had even owned sprawling plantations before removal, embracing the lifestyles of wealthy Southern planters, despite continuing to speak the Cherokee language and adhering to traditional Cherokee attire. And in one of the sad and tragic ironies of history, when such individuals were forcibly removed from their traditional lands in the southeast to walk the Trail of Tears, many brought their African American and mixed-race slaves along with them, viewing their ownership as a symbol of prestige, just as white slave owners like John Shirley did farther north in Missouri.

In fact, there are several interesting parallels between Missouri and the Cherokee Nation during the American Civil War. Both

---

[3] "Pin Indians" was a derogatory term applied by Treaty Party Cherokees to hostile, pro-Union Cherokee, Creek, and Seminole during the Civil War. The animosities that flared up between tribal members during the conflict often had their roots in the divisions that had first appeared during the era of forced relocation to Indian Territory.

were geographic and political "border states" sandwiched between assembling armies. Both allowed slavery, although they were not economically dependent on it. And both were ideologically cloven by the idea of pledging allegiance to the federal government. For the Cherokee Nation, lingering animosities from the removal era were sometimes overshadowed by the simple fact that many Cherokee relied on the protection offered by federal forts to stay clear of Kiowa arrows and Comanche lances. To the raiding parties of Plains tribes who made frequent forays into lands held by the "Five Civilized Tribes," the Cherokee farms and ranches of present-day Oklahoma were considered just as invasive and just as viable targets as Anglo-American homesteads in Central Texas. And given what Kiowa arrows and Comanche lances could do, delivered via lightning strike from a thundering mounted cavalry, siding with the federal government surely felt to some Cherokee like the lesser of two evils. The Cherokee's relocated "Civilized Tribe" neighbors, the Chickasaws, suffered terribly from Comanche raids throughout the year of 1861, forcing many to leave Indian Territory altogether and relocate to Kansas, where there was a stronger federal presence. Creek and Choctaw communities experienced attacks that year as well. However, it would be the Tonkawa Massacre of 1862,[4] a raid in which

---

[4]   As masters of the Southern Plains, the Comanche had contentious relations with most neighboring tribes, with the possible exception of the Kiowa. However, few of these tribes seemed to provoke their ire like the Tonkawa, a relatively small and unimposing band that posed no threat to Comanche hegemony. One reason for their animosity, however, very well may have been the Tonkawa penchant for cannibalism, a practice most Plains tribes regarded with disdain. If a Comanche war party did in fact burn alive and eat their Tonkawa victims in 1862, it was likely eye-for-an-eye blood-vengeance for a previous incident of cannibalism. In the attack described by Herman Lehmann just over ten years later, the wrath of the Comanche war party resulted from discovering the charred leg of a missing Comanche youth in a Tonkawa cooking fire. However, despite being nearly exterminated as a tribe by the Comanches, the handful of Tonkawas who survived the massacres would eventually get their revenge, by volunteering as federal Indian Scouts in the brutal U.S. military campaigns of the 1870s—campaigns that would end Comanche resistance for good.

Comanches slaughtered, and according to some accounts, roasted alive and cannibalized nearly half of the 300-member Tonkawa tribe while they sheltered at an understaffed Confederate fort, that would provide the most viscerally unsettling example of what could happen on the open plains without strong federal protection. And while such grotesque details could easily be dismissed as fanciful wartime exaggerations, they are strongly supported by recollections of an *actual* adopted Comanche and full-fledged warrior named Herman Lehmann,[5] who participated in a very similar attack against the tribe just over a decade later. The defenseless Tonkawas would once again experience the full wrath of a Comanche war party, as Lehmann himself would unapologetically recall:

> *A great many of the dying enemy were gasping for water, but we heeded not their pleadings. We scalped them, amputated their arms, cut off their legs, cut out their tongues, and threw their mangled bodies and limbs upon their own campfire, put on more brushwood and piled the living, dying and dead Tonkaways on the fire. Some of them were able to flinch and work as a worm, and some were able to speak and plead for mercy. We piled them up, put on more wood, and danced around in great glee as we saw*

---

5 *Nine Years Among the Indians, 1870–1879*, the memoir of Herman Lehmann, a German American settler who was kidnapped by Apaches as a child, only to flee and join their blood enemies the Comanches, is considered one of the most revelatory captivity narratives of the era. Despite being taken from his birth family against his will, Herman Lehmann, much like Cynthia Ann Parker, was fully assimilated into Apache and Comanche society, and only reluctantly rejoined the world of the whites; he criticized Anglo-American civilization relentlessly and defended his Native hosts to the last. He was even adopted by the great Comanche war chief Quanah Parker and later given an allotment of land on the Kiowa-Comanche reservation. He did eventually readapt to white society, but would occasionally participate in county fairs and Wild West shows, entertaining audiences by chasing a calf around an arena on horseback, killing it with arrows, and jumping from his mount to eat its liver raw—a technique he had mastered hunting bison on the open plains with his Comanche brothers, many years before.

the grease and blood run from their bodies, and were delighted to
see them swell up and hear the hide pop as it would burst in the
fire.

Granted, the Cherokee were ferocious guerrilla warriors in their
own right. And they were no strangers to torture. They, like most
Eastern Woodland tribes, had a long tradition of exacting excruciating punishments upon those who threatened their people, and
they had come to anticipate such treatment from their enemies in
return. There is even a story from the Seneca tribe, recorded in
1883 by the Smithsonian ethnographer Jeremiah Curtin, that re-
counts how a pair of tattooed Cherokee Ghigaus sentenced a captured warrior to death by having his feet held to flames until they
were badly burned, slicing open the blisters on his soles, inserting
dry corn kernels under the skin, and chasing him barefoot with
clubs until he expired. Agonizing punishments like these were not
historically uncommon for male prisoners of war among Eastern
tribes, and though they were brutal, there was a logic behind them:
warriors were expected to fight to the death, and showing bravery,
like singing a "death song" while enduring torture, was a way for
captured prisoners to salvage their honor. The fact that women,
many of whom would have lost male relatives in the preceding warfare, were frequently involved in dictating the torture also served
a social function. The practice was ritualized, it was personalized,
and it did possess a larger spiritual, even sacrificial significance to
tribal participants.

The mounted Comanche, however, with their blitzkrieg raids
and their scorched-earth policy, were unlike anything the Cherokee had ever seen back east—a galloping nightmare almost beyond
reckoning, willing to wipe entire tribes off the face of the earth.
And to more than a few Cherokee, the idea of fighting alongside
the very same federal soldiers who had forced them at gunpoint

from their lands and death-marched them west, while certainly not ideal, was preferable to seeing entire families get flayed alive and slow-roasted over a fire, as was the case with the Tonkawas. The Cherokee Nation was not a typical target of the plains-dwelling Comanche, but the highly mobile horse tribe had already shown its willingness, if not enthusiasm, for attacking their "Civilized Tribe" neighbors just a short ride away, and an official federal presence was known to be a far better deterrent than a disorganized Confederate one.

Perhaps that should have made things simple, but it didn't. Because complicating matters even further was the fact that the Osage, traditional enemies of the western Old Settler Cherokee in Arkansas, had already decided to fight on behalf of that very same federal government. Animosities between the two tribes went back to 1817, when a war party of freshly arrived Cherokee, considered unwelcome invaders by the Osage and thusly harassed, had executed a revenge attack on one of their villages. Most of the Osage men were away on a buffalo hunt at the time of the assault, which killed sixty-nine women and children and triggered yet another vicious cycle of blood vengeance. The violence between the two tribes did subside somewhat in the 1820s, and by 1839, most of the Osage had relocated to a reservation in Kansas, leaving what is today northwestern Arkansas and northeastern Oklahoma to the Cherokee newcomers. However, at the onset of the Civil War in 1861, the bloody conflict would have still been within living memory for many members of both tribes, and the idea of fighting alongside one another would have been unsettling at the very least. Essentially, a hundred years of forced relocations and the existential warfare that resulted had left the Cherokee with copious enemies, and choosing allies in the brewing American conflict was fraught with complications.

All of this explains why the Cherokee Nation, much like Missouri, initially hesitated when it came to solidifying its alignment, preferring to remain neutral. And just like Missouri, it would eventually be invaded and occupied by Confederate and Union forces alike. Thomas Pegg, acting as chief in the absence of John Ross, who had left for Washington to discuss his tribe's stance with President Lincoln, explained the Cherokee dilemma upon entering the war as follows:

> *Our Government has been paralyzed by the incursion of an over-*
> *whelming force from the army of the Confederate States. . . . Our*
> *legitimate protection, the Government of the United States was*
> *far away. And every channel of communication cut off. Every*
> *Military Post in our vicinity was abandoned or occupied by the*
> *Enemy. We were perplexed and Embarrassed. Our wisest men*
> *knew not what to do.*

The vacillating, the uncertainty, the fear of the wrong choice bringing destruction and ruin—it sounds very much like Mark Twain's description of Missouri wringing its collective hands at the storm on the horizon. And as in Missouri, that storm's eventual arrival would resurrect grievances from decades prior, fanning the old embers of the Cherokee civil war back into full flames, just as the animosities of the Bleeding Kansas period had been given new life when the Union invaded.

Not surprisingly, the end result was a brutal guerrilla war that closely echoed, and eventually spilled into, that of Missouri. Midnight raids, lynchings, barn burnings—many Cherokee men of fighting age joined partisan guerrilla bands aligned with the cause they supported and went on the offensive, attacking white and Native American settlements alike, in gangs that mirrored the jayhawkers and bushwhackers of Missouri to the north. And while a fair portion were driven by ideological conviction, Tom

Starr seems to have gotten in on the action simply because pillaging was the one thing he was exceptionally good at and possibly even enjoyed. Much like with the Shirleys, internecine violence had transformed the Starrs over time from a respectable family of community leaders and statesmen into a clan of guerrilla fighters and warlords, with Tom Starr serving as its principal commander. There's even some evidence he raided on behalf of the federals at the war's onset. Morris Sheppard, the slave of a Cherokee farmer in the Webbers Falls area, would recall in an interview how Union-aligned Pin Indians raided his master's farm in 1861: "They would come in the night and hamstring the horses and maybe set fire to the barn. . . . Joab Scarrel and Tom Starr killed my pappy one night just before the war broke out." Far greater opportunities for pillaging and mayhem were soon to present themselves from the Confederate side, though, particularly in the form of William Quantrill and his band of Confederate guerrillas. Tom Starr joined the 1st Regiment of the Cherokee Mounted Volunteers, serving as a scout under tribal leader Stand Watie, and through his Confederate military service came to know the members of Quantrill's Raiders quite well, even teaching them a thing or two about Cherokee-style guerrilla warfare tactics in the process.

This was when two seemingly disparate family histories—that of a European American family called the Shirleys and that of a Native American family called the Starrs—began to overlap. Because also fighting with Quantrill's Raiders were the Missouri boys Cole Younger and Jim Reed. And when Quantrill's Confederate guerrilla band fled south into Indian Territory following their bloodiest campaigns in Kansas and Missouri, it was among the Confederate-aligned Starr clan that they found sanctuary. The tribute system that Belle Starr would later exploit—allowing outlaws to find shelter at her compound on the South Canadian River in exchange for a cut of their plunder—was first begun by Tom

Starr, who offered Cole Younger and Jim Reed a safe hideout from pursuing federal troops, and probably helped them fence stolen horses and cattle as part of the deal. As Belle told a journalist for the *Fort Smith Elevator* years later, "My home became famous as an outlaw's ranch long before I was visited by any of the boys who were friends of mine." Even prior to Belle's arrival in Indian Territory, the Starrs had already established what was in effect a protection racket—one of the central pillars of organized crime—backed up by a private army of Starr foot soldiers, all joined together by a shared loyalty to a single family. A Cherokee mafia, if you will.

Cole Younger and Jim Reed didn't give up their illicit ways with the surrender at Appomattox, and neither did Tom Starr. After the war, he continued to offer sanctuary to bandits fleeing the law in exchange for tribute, he continued to fence horses and cattle, and he even added some whiskey smuggling into the mix, likely dealing directly with Jim Reed and the Fisher gang. And *this* is how Belle became acquainted with the Starrs. It is known that Jim Reed sought refuge with the Starrs following his San Antonio stagecoach heist—a crime that Belle was not present for—and it seems almost certain that he was also staying with Tom Starr at the time of the massive Watt Grayson theft—a crime that Belle *was* involved in. The Grayson ranch was just across the South Canadian River, only a few miles from the Starr compound in the neighboring Cherokee Nation. In retrospect, it's not at all unlikely that the tip-off came from Tom Starr himself. It seems dubious that Jim Reed, a non-Native outsider, would have known which leaders of rival tribes were rumored to have vast sums of gold hidden away. Tom Starr, however, the local strongman and mafia don with informants on his payroll, would have. Contracting the job out to a crew of Anglo-American criminals in exchange for a cut of the loot was a smart way to deflect the blame and avoid what could have escalated into intertribal warfare. It is known from Belle's own testimony that she was waiting in the woods just outside the Grayson ranch during the theft, and that she joined her husband and his accomplices shortly thereafter, to divide the gold and make their getaway. She and Jim Reed almost certainly roomed with the Starrs while planning the caper, and it was probably then that she met for the first time the man that she would one day build a criminal empire with, not to mention marry: Tom Starr's son, Samuel. At the time of the Grayson heist, however, Sam was only thirteen, and any romantic sparks seem unlikely. But they would come later.

It stands to reason that Belle revisited the Starrs at some point in the years between the Grayson robbery and her short marriage to Bruce Younger. This very well may have occurred while she was traveling north from Texas to visit her son Eddie and her in-laws in Missouri. Tom's compound would have served as a convenient way station and allowed Belle to exchange gossip about some of her old Missouri friends, many of whom still used Tom Starr's place as a hideout following a crime spree.

It also could have occurred later, perhaps even while she was in a relationship with Bruce. The original Richard K. Fox biography contains an outlandish story of Belle forcing Bruce to marry her at gunpoint in Indian Territory, while staying with Cherokee acquaintances. This is demonstrably false—their actual marriage certificate is clearly from Kansas—although the tale may contain a kernel of truth. Perhaps Belle took Bruce Younger with her, just prior to their marriage, to visit friends and relatives in Texas—after all, her mother did still reside in Dallas. It's not unlikely that she would have stopped at Tom Starr's along the way, to find safe lodging and to catch up with Cherokee acquaintances. Only on this visit, his son Sam Starr would have been a handsome dark-haired twenty-three-year-old man. True, even as an adult, Sam was of slightly lesser stature than his father Tom, both in terms of physical size and outlaw reputation, but he was a courageous gunslinger in his own right, something he would later prove to lethal effect. Like his father, he wore his hair long, in the traditional Cherokee fashion, and like his father, he was not above a little raffish adornment, although he eschewed the necklace of human earlobes and fox-skin cap for a slightly more sophisticated red silk hair ribbon and broad-brimmed black hat. *This* was the Sam Starr that Belle would have met upon her later visit to the Starr compound, and this time around, there very well may have been flirtatious glances exchanged in the glow of the hearth fire. Indeed, there must have been, to a certain extent; otherwise it would be all but impossible to explain how their relationship came to pass. As to whether these feelings were acted upon at that time, during some short and sweaty interval in Bruce Younger's absence, that's less certain.

What is known, however, is that upon the collapse of her ill-advised and catastrophically short marriage to Bruce Younger back in Kansas, Belle made a beeline straight to the Cherokee Nation and into the arms of Samuel Starr. And on the fifth day of June, in the year 1880, they were married. She entered the timber courthouse of Cherokee district judge Abe Woodall as the widow Belle Reed—that was the name she gave for the marriage certificate—but she walked out with a new name, one that twanged like a bullet off spit-shined brass:

Belle Starr.

CHAPTER 6

The Black Widow of Younger's Bend

W HEN BELLE MARRIED SAM Starr, officially becoming part of the most notorious crime family in all of Indian Territory, more changed than just her name. Her entire outlook, her approach to life, transformed with it. Unlike Belle Reed, *Belle Starr* refused to play second fiddle to any man; to ever again submit meekly to any husband or lover. No, those days were over. Among the Cherokee, in a traditionally matriarchal culture where the idea of a female warrior had long been cherished, and where clan membership, house ownership, and the custody of children were all considered proprietary to women, she would come into her own, destined to not only join the crime syndicate established by her father-in-law Tom Starr as a full-on gangster, but to one day practically run it—to become a Cherokee mafia don in her own right.

But aside from assigning her a new name, the very timing of the marriage was cathartic as well. Belle probably did not know it beforehand, but the weeks of midsummer are of great religious significance for the Cherokee. It's the time of the Green Corn Ceremony, or Busk, a New Year's ritual in which the first of the ripened corn shoots are burned, as a sacrificial offering to ensure a bountiful harvest later. The Busk is a time of new spiritual beginnings; a moment in which the sins and mistakes of the previous year are absolved, swept away and carried skyward by chanted invocations and billowing smoke. The corn sacrifice is usually accompanied by communal feasts, as well as stomp dances, rituals in which tribal members circle around a sacred fire to the beat of a drum, reciting prayers of purification and gratitude.

Back in the cooler hills of Appalachia, ancestral home of both the Starrs and the Shirleys, the ceremony typically took place in late July or August. In the warmer climate of Oklahoma, however, the corn ripened sooner, and the sacrifice and its attendant feasts usually began several weeks before that. Given the timing of Belle and Sam's wedding, it's not unlikely that their marriage celebrations carried right into the Green Corn Ceremony festivities. It's easy to imagine the newlywed and newly christened Belle Starr watching in wonder as her in-laws sang their holy songs of atonement and danced counterclockwise around a sacred flame. As a new citizen of the Cherokee Nation through marriage, she may have even joined in, learning the steps if not the words, shuffling in her skirts through the purifying smoke and the rising dust of the dance ground, her sins erased, her mistakes forgiven, her spirit cleansed and born anew.

ONCE THE FEASTING WAS over, however, and the sacred smoke and the dust died down, there was work to be done. On paper, the transformation of the widow Belle Reed into the matriarchal Bandit Queen Belle Starr may have occurred with a simple "I do" and the slash of Judge Woodall's pen. But in real life, despite her new outlook, Belle would need time to ease into her new identity and inhabit it completely.

First, she and her new husband would have to establish a home base. In the Cherokee Nation, land was communally owned and doled out by the tribal government for personal use over the course of a lifetime, which posed obvious complications given the Starrs' violent history with precisely that same government. Second, she would need to prove herself to both the local community and her new criminal family. Ingratiating herself with her Cherokee and Choctaw neighbors, while also instilling some measure of respect and even fear in them, was no easy feat. And third, she would have to reunite her own fractured family, a task complicated by half a decade of rootless wandering, not to mention a sizable amount of parental neglect. At the time of her marriage to Sam Starr, Belle had only intermittent custody of her daughter Pearl, leaving her for weeks on end with distant friends and relatives, and she'd barely seen her son Eddie for five years. Such were the challenges Belle had before her upon her arrival in the Cherokee Nation.

FOR THE FIRST FEW months following their marriage, Sam and Belle had limited options when it came to living quarters, as Cherokee tribal law contained strict regulations about the ownership and transfer of land titles. As a remedy to the ancestral problem of Cherokee territory being chiseled away piecemeal by individual land sales to encroaching white settlers, the tribal constitution now barred private ownership of land—it was all retained and managed by the Cherokee Nation. Any tribal citizen could be granted a land permit, generally lasting the course of a single lifetime, as long as a parcel was available and the government approved of it. Ordinarily, this was no great hurdle—at least not for most Cherokee families. The Starrs, however, were not like most Cherokee families. James Starr, the first to come west, was still considered, even long after his death, the ultimate traitor by many in the tribal government for his role in orchestrating and signing the Treaty of New Echota. His son Tom Starr, who had raised his own private army and nearly brought that same tribal government to its knees as revenge for his father's killing, was still regarded by his enemies—who were legion among Cherokee leadership—as a dangerous pariah, if not an existential threat. Sam Starr didn't have any major strikes against him personally, aside from perhaps a reputation as a whiskey smuggler who assisted in his father's criminal organization, but his family's reputation certainly didn't help his bid. Which was probably why he and Belle spent the first few months following their marriage living in a tiny shack just south of what is today Porum, Oklahoma.

But out of sheer serendipitous coincidence, a parcel opened up. A log house situated on sixty-two acres of forested hills, right at a bulbous bend in the South Canadian River. Its former tenant, an elderly Cherokee hermit named Big Head, had apparently expired. As to why the tribal government finally agreed to give Sam and Belle Starr the allotment, it's hard to say. Possibly a bribe was involved; it's also conceivable that the fact that all the surrounding holdings were occupied by Starr family members meant that no other Cherokee candidates were willing to live in their decidedly dangerous midst. But it's also possible that with its dense woods, rocky hills, and inaccessible trails, the allotment was considered all but useless for any substantive form of agriculture—that the Cherokee government believed they were giving the newlywed Starrs the equivalent of swampland in Florida. What they didn't factor in, however, is that those same dense woods and rocky hillsides that made much of the acreage useless as pasture or farmland would render it a perfect hideout for fleeing outlaws and an ideal headquarters from which to run a criminal enterprise. There are varying accounts to explain the name bestowed upon Belle Starr's compound. Some say it was christened as such by Tom Starr in honor of his favorite member of Quantrill's Raiders; others claim it received its appellation from Belle herself, in nostalgic tribute to her first true love. Regardless, the stronghold from which she would oversee her crime syndicate, shelter her outlaw friends, and deal extensively in smuggled whiskey and stolen horseflesh would come to be known as Younger's Bend.

The legend of Belle Starr first gained traction outside of Indian Territory thanks to Richard K. Fox, publisher of the *National Police Gazette*, a true-crime tabloid based in New York City. Fox provided coverage of some of her early criminal exploits, and he released a sensationalized Belle Starr biography shortly after her death in 1889, securing her a place in the Wild West pantheon. (*Courtesy of the Library of Congress*)

The Battle of Carthage, fought on July 5, 1861, was one of the first armed confrontations of the American Civil War, and the first real taste of violence for the Shirley family, marking the beginning of their transition from community leaders to renegade outlaws. A teenage Belle would support her older brother Bud in his Confederate guerrilla activities by conducting reconnaissance missions and gathering intelligence. (*Courtesy of the Library of Congress*)

A portrait created from a tintype of a young Belle, probably taken just after the end of the Civil War. The Shirley family, like many Missourians, fled their ravaged state as war refugees, seeking to start a new life in Texas. Belle's "lost generation" of displaced guerrilla fighters would drift toward banditry on a lawless frontier, feeding the myth of the Wild West outlaw. (*Courtesy of the Oklahoma Historical Society, Edna Mae Couch Collection*)

An ambrotype believed to depict John Allison Shirley—better known as "Bud"—while fighting for the Confederate cause in Missouri. Bud's death at the hands of a Union militia would send an enraged Belle into town with a brace of pistols, vowing revenge. The experience of losing her beloved older brother would scar Belle for life and bring her one step closer to the way of the outlaw. (*Courtesy of the Library of Congress*)

A photograph of Belle taken shortly after her family's resettlement to a farm just outside the wild frontier town of Dallas, Texas. In this portrait, Belle's transformation is complete, from an educated Southern lady to a true character of the Western frontier. This style of dress would have been extremely unusual for a woman at the time, but Belle was never one to follow convention. *(Courtesy of the Thomas Gilcrease Institute of American History and Art)*

Jim Reed, Belle's first husband, was a Confederate guerrilla from Rich Hill, Missouri, who reinvented himself upon arriving in Texas as a bandit of the Western stamp. His biggest score, the infamous Grayson heist of 1873, should have set the young couple up for life, but instead he squandered their share of the gold on horse races and whiskey. Jim Reed's days of outlawry would come to an end, however, when a bounty hunter and acquaintance named John T. Morris lured him into a trap and shot him with his revolver.

This mugshot of Cole Younger, taken following his arrest for the failed Northfield, Minnesota, bank robbery of 1876, shows how intimidating the man was in his full, outlaw prime. A far more successful criminal than Belle's husband Jim Reed, Cole was long rumored to have been her lover—something that he steadfastly denied, although he did acknowledge her infatuation with him. *(Courtesy of the Minnesota Historical Society, Gale Family Library)*

A rare photograph alleged to depict the core members of the James-Younger gang in their outlaw heyday, with Jesse and Frank James seated, and Cole and Bob Younger standing behind them. Together they would commit a string of bank, train, and stagecoach robberies unmatched by virtually any other criminals of the era. *(Courtesy of the Library of Congress)*

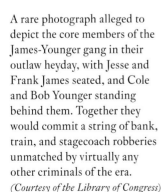

Many have remarked on the resemblance between this photograph of Cole Younger in his later year and this portrait believed to depict Belle's daughter Pearl, adding significant fuel to the rumors of their love affair. Regardless of the veracity of such stories, Belle obviously had a lifelong fondness for Cole, and she may have even named her Younger's Bend outlaw ranch after him. *(Courtesy of Heritage Auctions Archive, HA.com)*

Depiction of a Cherokee delegation sent to England in 1762. The Cherokees clashed with American settlers across the Southern frontier following the American Revolution, when waves of homesteaders, no longer constrained by British policy, began pouring over the Appalachian crest, hungry for land. After being decimated by decades of disease, warfare, and overhunting, many tribal members saw negotiation and partial assimilation as the only means of ensuring their survival, although others insisted on unbending resistance. This ideological divide first revealed itself in the days of Nanye'hi and Dragging Canoe, and it would explode into violence during the Cherokee civil war that followed the Trail of Tears. *(Courtesy of the Smithsonian Institute, National Anthropological Archives)*

Belle Starr's original cabin at Younger's Bend, along with some of the maple trees she planted. This frontier homestead would serve Belle as both headquarters and hideout in her new role as a gang leader and Starr family associate. Together with her husband Sam Starr, she would run one of the largest banditry and smuggling rings in all of Indian Territory, becoming the bane of both the Cherokee tribal police and the U.S. marshals in Fort Smith. *(Courtesy of the Oklahoma Historical Society, Frederick S. Barde Collection)*

In the Cherokee Nation, Belle Starr came into her own as an outlaw queen, always dressing the part of a Wild West gangster on her frequent trips into nearby Fort Smith—and garnering far more attention from federal authorities than many Cherokee wanted.

To some in Indian Territory, Tom Starr was a hero and a freedom fighter; to others, he was a criminal and a warlord. All parties, however, respected and feared the six-and-a-half-foot Cherokee warrior, who in his later years would control much of the whiskey smuggling and livestock rustling in the Cherokee Nation. As Belle's father-in-law, he initially welcomed her into both his family and his criminal organization, although the unwanted attention she would bring from the U.S. marshals in Fort Smith would become a sticking point and end in a prison sentence for the aging patriarch. *(Courtesy of True West Magazine Archive)*

The original 1882 arrest warrant for Belle and Sam Starr, charging them with larceny following the theft of two horses in the Cherokee Nation. The outlaw couple would flee from authorities and attempt to escape north into Osage territory, only to be captured right on the border. *(Courtesy of the National Archives and Records Administration)*

One of Belle's first visitors to Younger's Bend was none other than the outlaw Jesse James, who used her ranch briefly as a hideout in 1881. His presence and patronage helped to establish her as a bona fide gangster and earn her the respect of the Starr family. In this 1864 portrait from the Civil War, a very young Jesse James can be seen brandishing three pistols and his trademark sneer. *(Courtesy of the Library of Congress)*

The only known surviving photograph of Frank West, the Cherokee tribal police officer and mortal enemy of Sam Starr. In revenge for wounding him and killing his wife's favorite horse, Sam would challenge Frank to a gun duel, a decision that would prove fatal for both men in the end, leaving Belle a widow for the second time. *(Courtesy of the West family, private photo collection)*

The Detroit House of Correction, where Belle and Sam Starr would serve their prison sentences upon being convicted of horse theft. This photograph, taken circa 1880, shows the stark contrast between the industrial world of stone and iron where Belle would do hard time, and her frontier home in the Cherokee Nation nearly a thousand miles away. *(Courtesy of the New York Public Library, Miriam and Ira D. Wallach Division of Art, Prints and Photographs)*

John West, later in life, standing between two other tribal members of local law enforcement. His testimony against Belle and Sam Starr ignited the feud that would end in his younger brother Frank's untimely death. John West, however, would go on to have a long and storied career, helping to keep the peace in the Cherokee and Creek nations.

When Belle Starr turned herself in to federal authorities in 1886, facing charges related to armed robbery and horse theft, she refused to play it coy or tone down her criminal persona. Instead, she went shopping for pistols, posed for photographs, and gave scandalous interviews, fully embracing her identity as a "friend to any brave and gallant outlaw."

Part of Belle Starr's 1886 criminal PR campaign included lending moral support to a Cherokee outlaw named Blue Duck, who was charged with murder for the drunken slaying of a local farmer. Blue Duck was rumored to be both a Starr family foot soldier and one of Belle Starr's many lovers, although such claims are difficult to prove.

Eddie Reed, Belle Starr's son, pictured far right. This photograph was taken in the town of Claremore, not long before his death there in 1896. After numerous run-ins with the law and a short stint in prison, Eddie made an attempt to go straight, even serving briefly in law enforcement—only to get gunned down in a saloon altercation, the details of which are often disputed. *(Courtesy of the Denton, Texas, Public Library)*

Some have claimed that the man in this photograph—alleged to be the troublesome Florida cane farmer Edgar J. Watson—is in fact the same Edgar A. Watson who got into a lease dispute with Belle Starr and possibly murdered her. Watson was briefly detained in Fort Smith but never formally charged with the crime, due to a lack of evidence, as well as eyewitness testimony that was deemed exculpatory. The Floridian left Indian Territory for good shortly after his release, fearing for his life, only to be arrested several months later for stealing horses in Little Rock, Arkansas, as part of a desperate bid to fund his family's escape. What happened to Edgar A. Watson after that has been the subject of much historical debate, although Everglades folklore has long insisted that he returned to Florida, changed his middle name, and managed to commit a number of heinous crimes before finally getting himself killed by a posse of angry swamp folk. How much of this is true is difficult to say, although if there is any substance to such stories, then it could nudge the needle of suspicion back in Watson's direction. *(Courtesy of Smallwood Store Museum Archive)*

Belle Starr's famous tombstone at Younger's Bend, showing the epitaph poem that her daughter Pearl had engraved upon it. The mystery of Belle's 1889 murder has never been definitively solved, although various suspects have faced scrutiny over the years, running the gamut from resentful sharecroppers to scorned lovers to her own embittered children. It is a mystery that is likely to endure—just like her legend. *(Courtesy of the Oklahoma Historical Society, Frederick S. Barde Collection)*

In folklore, and in the dime-novel accounts that embraced and perpetuated it, Younger's Bend has frequently been depicted as an almost cartoonishly rugged Wild West robber's roost, surrounded by treacherous canyons, towering lookout ridges, secret treasure caves, and even lethal quicksand. In fact, Younger's Bend still exists today, a quick stop off Oklahoma State Highway 71, just before the Eufaula Dam. And aside from a redirection of the Canadian River thanks to said dam and the loss of much of the old-growth forest that would have been prevalent in Belle's day, its fundamental geography and character have remained very much unchanged. If anything, the first sight of her new home likely provoked in Belle's heart a pang of nostalgia, reminding her of her family's original pioneer stock farm outside of Medoc, on the outer rim of the Missouri Ozarks—the place where she had first learned to ride and to shoot, under the tutelage of her beloved older brother John Allison. Younger's Bend was and is a bucolic place of layered, undulant hills and wide, meandering waters. In Belle's time, when the region was sparsely populated, it would have stunned any new arrivals with pristine river vistas interrupted only very occasionally by the gently smoking clay chimney of a Cherokee log house; the hollows and hillsides would have abounded in wild game and been marked by the almost preternatural silence of cathedral groves of towering cedars. After the years Belle had spent on the desolate plains of North Texas, it's easy to see how Younger's Bend would have felt like home to a girl of Appalachian extraction, born and raised on the western edge of the Ozark plateau.

As for the domicile itself—also described in fanciful accounts as some kind of frontier fortress of pine palisades—it was nothing more than a sturdily built cabin of cedar logs, with a main room about fourteen feet in length, augmented by an exterior kitchen lean-to in the back and a porch that covered most of the front. Belle evidently did what she could to add a bit of warmth and charm to the log house's crude interior; an account published in 1898, less than ten years after her death, would provide the following description of her cabin at Younger's Bend:

> *The home . . . was not a palace, nor was it furnished in regal style; it was superior however, to any of its class in that part of the country; its puncheon floor was laid as straight as the axemen could lay it, and the interior walls were covered with bright hued calico, which was renewed as often as was necessary to prevent its showing too plainly the stains of age. Buffalo horns and the antlers of prairie deer occupied prominent places above the rough but tasty mantel and at other places, and at times sprigs of cedar with clusters of mistletoe festooned the walls, while photographs or life sized portraits of her friends occupied commanding positions here and there tastefully arranged by herself . . . altogether the place bore the aspect of a home, such as is seldom found on the frontier. Whatever was needful to the warmth and comfort of the inmates were not lacking and books, of a kind too as are seen in the best libraries, were there in plenty.*

Assuming that this account is an honest one, it is revealing in that even after years spent among her cadre of rowdy outlaw friends and rough Western characters, Belle preserved some of the social graces and Southern charm passed down to her from her parents, John and Eliza. In her collection of leather-bound books, in her unfailing hospitality, and in the piano, which would be added later to facilitate her musical passions, perhaps Belle was even re-creating the old Shirley House hotel in miniature. She would even go on to build two other smaller cabins to accommodate her guests—although unlike her father, who had catered to traveling appellate judges and visiting statesmen back in Carthage, Belle would become host to some of the most dangerous outlaws operating in the territory. And where her father had maintained a blacksmith shop and a livery stable constructed to service the mounts of his boarders, Belle would build a grapevine corral, hidden back in a ravine, where the stolen horses she and her husband so frequently trafficked in could be kept in secret.

Granted, it wasn't *all* outlaw exploits and criminal cunning at Younger's Bend. The place was a functioning frontier homestead, after all. And while protection rackets, whiskey smuggling, and horse theft would significantly augment Belle Starr's personal finances, daily life still involved a fair amount of pioneer labor. Cows required milking, corn patches needed hoeing, hams had to be smoked, and hunting and fishing would have been quotidian chores. None of which would have been new to Belle, having grown up on a very similar farm, reliant on a very similar form of subsistence agriculture. Apparently, she even enjoyed it. By her own account, she found great pleasure in her new life, living "very happily" with her new husband "on the Canadian River . . . far from society." After the instability and restlessness that had marked most of her adult life, not to mention the toxic relationships she had endured over its troubled course, she had achieved something more grounded. Her marriage to Sam Starr, which was evidently a loving one—surprisingly so, in fact—had at last given her a sense of stability. And with the establishment of Younger's Bend as her new home base, she had acquired a solid foothold in both the Starr family and the Cherokee Nation.

A physical foothold, anyway. Belle may have won over Sam Starr with her well-documented charms, that tangy, contrasting blend of buttery Southern refinement and Bowie-sharp frontier wit. But winning over his Indigenous warlord parents would have certainly posed a unique set of challenges. Years later, the *Fort Worth Daily Gazette* would remark that Tom Starr "had his day and made a record that has never yet been equaled for bloodshed and desperate deeds." This doesn't seem to be hyperbole. Letters, journals, and newspaper articles of the day all seem to reach the same conclusion: Tom Starr and his kin were among the most violent and ruthless criminals in the Indian Territory, possibly in the West, and maybe even in the country. If there was ever a case of having to please difficult in-laws, this was it. There is even a story, conceivably true although impossible to validate, that some tribal elders recognized the dark potential of this newcomer to their nation and urged Tom Starr to kill her before it was too late. One early version of the anecdote, recorded by the Oklahoma sheriff and Belle Starr chronicler Burton Rascoe, has an elderly Cherokee chief pleading with Tom Starr:

> *Uncle Tom, I'm warning you that this woman will be the ruin of your boys. If you don't kill her, she will ensnare them and bring them to destruction. She is wicked and poisonous. She will make them do her bidding and will lead them into outlawry. When that happens it is only a short way to Judge Parker and to Hangman Maledon with his rope at Fort Smith.*

According to Rascoe, Tom Starr simply "shook his head and said that he could not harm a woman," deciding to let Belle live after all. This story, though prescient in some of its predictions, is suspect for several reasons, one of which is that Tom's boys certainly didn't need Belle to lead them into "outlawry"—they had their own father for that—and another being that based on his own lengthy record of indiscriminate killing, Tom Starr would likely not have had his hand stayed by Belle's gender if he'd felt she posed a threat to his family. However, it makes sense that many within the Cherokee Nation and perhaps within the Starr clan itself would have harbored considerable misgivings, if not resentment, toward the newcomer.

But the remarkable thing: not only did Tom Starr decline to slit Belle's throat in the night and sink her corpse in the Canadian River—as some members of the community, if the story is to be believed, urged him to do—but he involved her directly in his family's criminal dealings. And if her ensuing federal rap sheet is anything to go by, he involved her quite rapidly. As to why Belle was welcomed into the inner circle of his crime family, her own frontier magnetism likely played some role, as did the same feisty independent streak that had her racing her horse across enemy lines as a teenage spy back in Carthage. But the most probable reason is also the most practical: it was good for business. After all, Belle had an expertise that would have come in extremely handy for a criminal enterprise whose primary source of income, going back to Tom's raiding days in Arkansas, was the stewardship of stolen horseflesh. In fact, the Starr family's close relationship with the horse probably went back much farther than that.

As a woodland tribe of the Southeast, the Cherokee had never embraced an equestrian lifestyle to the same extent as the nomadic buffalo-hunting tribes of the Great Plains, but they were early adopters and advocates of the horse nonetheless. Prior to the Yamasee War of 1715, a horrific conflict between southeastern tribes and English settlers that killed off roughly 70 percent of South Carolina's entire colonial population, horses had been regarded by the Cherokee primarily as exotic prestige items. They were used by tribal leaders as outward signs of wealth and power, and little more. In the wake of the bloody conflict, however, horses gained a far more utilitarian significance due to the rise of a new exportable commodity: buckskins. The war's closure may have temporarily ended hostilities between the Cherokee and colonists, but it permanently ended the Indigenous slave trade. No longer could Cherokee bands sell off their Native prisoners of war to English planters in exchange for guns and other coveted goods. Suddenly, another export was needed. The Cherokee found it in the form of buckskins, used by colonists for clothing and furnishings. And they found a reliable means of transporting the heavy bundles of deer hides from their woodland villages to colonial settlements, in the form of the horse.

However, one inevitable by-product of this new trade network, made possible by European horses, was an enhanced proximity to the European American world, as intermarriage and a certain amount of cultural assimilation ensued. Whereas many Plains tribes would garner nearly a century and a half of unbroken independence from—at times, even dominion over—the European colonial world by deploying the horse as a weapon of war, Southern Woodland tribes like the Cherokee inadvertently gained a sizable amount of societal contiguity by employing it instead as a tool of commerce. Even Nanye'hi, the great Cherokee Ghigau and matriarchal ancestor of the Starrs, ended up marrying a visiting Anglo-Irish buckskin trader named Bryant Ward shortly after the death of her first husband at the Battle of Taliwa in 1755, becoming Nancy Ward and learning to speak English in the process.

On a tribal level, that same proximity would of course prove disastrous in the decades that followed, bringing with it smallpox epidemics, environmental destruction caused by overhunting, and an endless series of wars with unwelcome settlers who always wanted just a little bit more. However, it would serve Cherokee horse traders—especially the illicit ones—exceedingly well a century later in places like Oklahoma, simply because they were well situated, from both a geographic and cultural perspective, to act as go-betweens. The "Five Civilized Tribes" who had been forcibly removed to Indian Territory did serve by design as a buffer of sorts, between the Plains tribes and Anglo outlaws that frequently raided frontier homesteads and the larger towns and cities that clustered along the frontier's edge. But that buffering position also made them extremely effective as middlemen—as *traders*. Because just as a Comanche warrior in full scalp-trimmed buckskins would have had great difficulty walking into a livestock auction in Dallas without getting shot, a Stetson-wearing stockman from Fort Worth would have had an equally difficult time strolling through the buffalo lodges of a Comanche horse swap without getting riddled with arrows.

Enter tribes like the Cherokee, who were Native but at the same time familiar with European American customs. Previously, when Texas had been part of Spain, a class of mixed-race traders known as Comancheros had served the role of commercial intermediaries, taking freshly raided horses off the hands of Southern Plains tribes, usually in exchange for European iron and steel— something they needed for their arrowheads and lances, to hunt buffalo and wage war. In the Anglo-American era, following the Indian Removal Act, relocated Eastern tribes like the Cherokee, as well as local "reservation" tribes like the Wichita and Osage, often filled that gap. And families like the Starrs, who had few moral qualms with larceny, were the ideal fences for stolen horse-flesh, catering to the Plains tribes and Anglo-American outlaws alike. When not stealing horses on their own, such dealers would happily acquire them from either source. Given his relationship with Tom Starr, forged during their shared participation in the Confederate guerrilla campaigns of the Civil War, it's probable that Cole Younger himself unloaded some of his stolen horses and rustled cattle from Texas upon the Starr clan, who in turn would have been just as comfortable selling them to a passing band of Osage as to a family of German grain farmers. Effective criminals tend to neither ask questions when buying nor discriminate when selling if there's good money to be made. And as a Cherokee gangster stationed in Indian Territory, smack-dab between the lawless Southern Plains and the more law-abiding agrarian north, Tom Starr was in a position to make money, indeed.

Assuming, of course, he had an expert on hand capable of judging the quality and negotiating the price of all that stolen horseflesh. Which was exactly what Belle Starr was. Growing up on a stock and stud farm, she had an unparalleled understanding of all things equine. And as the daughter of a horse *breeder* with deep cultural roots in the equestrian traditions of Kentucky and Virginia, she was the custodian of a precious store of knowledge that was not accessible to just any horse trader. Beyond the Comanche, who truly were expert horse breeders, relatively few Native American tribes ever mastered the delicate art of strategic gelding and selective breeding necessary for producing masterful horses. Belle, however, knew all of this. From breech-birthing foals, to saddle-breaking mustangs, to line-breeding quarter horses, she was an equestrian authority. These skills had gone long underused and underappreciated in the male-dominated world of the Anglo-American frontier, where there was simply no place for a woman to be seen arguing over stud fees or castrating stallions. But to a clan of Cherokee outlaw warlords whose criminal enterprise was all but founded upon raiding, stealing, and dealing in horses, Belle Starr was practically worth her weight in gold. She had the soft skills, too: riding, shooting, and a deep familiarity with the kind of gunslinging desperadoes with whom the Starrs so often did their business.

Which leads to Belle's other major selling point: she was practically a walking Wild West–era Rolodex of potential clients. Nearly two decades of running with some of the most dangerous outlaws in the West—the James brothers, the Youngers, the Reeds, the Fishers—had given her a bona fide reputation as an outlaw herself, as well as an extensive list of criminal contacts. It's worth remembering that the Starrs were familiar with Belle from her marriage to Jim Reed. She likely had even been staying with them at the time of the epic Grayson robbery, one of the biggest heists in Indian Territory to date, which had probably netted Tom Starr a considerable amount of money, assuming he was paid for the tip-off and subsequent protection. Belle had connections, and the Starrs knew it. They would have also known that bringing her into the fold meant gaining access to an even wider network of outlaws looking to take advantage of their other main racket besides horse theft: *protection fees*. Tom Starr had made a name for himself by first offering a refuge in Indian Territory to Confederate guerrillas looking to flee their Union pursuers, and later, to wanted criminals looking to escape local sheriffs and federal marshals in surrounding states. All of which required a significant fee. With Belle's criminal accomplices added to the roster, he would have anticipated a visible uptick in profits, as a new wave of high-profile bandits chose Younger's Bend as their hideout. After all, at the time of Belle's marriage to Sam Starr in 1880, Tom would have been nearly seventy years old, hardly a young man. With his own influence and list of criminal contacts waning, and with a desire to see his son continue to flourish in the family business after he was gone, it stands to reason that he would have seen Belle as a good match—perhaps even a Ghigau of sorts, albeit it one with some rather notorious friends who promised to bring some much-desired gold to the table.

If Tom Starr took a calculated risk in incorporating Belle into the family business, it was a risk that paid off in spades—at least during her initial few years at Younger's Bend. Because not only did she manage to secure a significant protection deal with a wanted criminal; she came to personally shelter perhaps the most wanted criminal in America at that time. Her first "client," so to speak—the first outlaw to seek her out and pay for her protection—was none other than Jesse James.

Rumors and their ensuing folklore had long maintained that Belle Starr had harbored the more famous of the James brothers, which would have been easy to dismiss as just that, if it weren't for a surprising fact: Belle Starr confessed to it. Not in any formal legal proceeding, but rather in the same biographical sketch she would later provide to the journalist John F. Weaver of the *Fort Smith Elevator*. Worth noting, however, is her careful wording of her involvement. Just like Cole Younger, Belle Starr followed the outlaw code of never implicating herself or any living friend, relative, or fellow miscreant in a crime. In fact, her dissociative tone is all but identical to that of Cole Younger's autobiography, almost comically devoid of any sense of personal responsibility:

> *My home became famous as an outlaw's ranch long before I was visited by any of the boys who were friends of mine. Indeed, I never corresponded with any of my old associates and was desirous my whereabouts should be unknown to them. Through rumor they learned of it.*
>
> *Jesse James first came in and remained several weeks. He was unknown to my husband, and he never knew till long afterwards that our home had been honored by James' presence. I introduced Jesse as one Mr. Williams from Texas.*

The fact that the Starrs' collected abodes had served as an "outlaw's ranch" prior to her arrival is probably the only detail that's correct. The idea that an extremely calculating—and by that point world-famous—outlaw would not only randomly show up at Belle's door but also go unrecognized by her criminally inclined spouse and ex-Confederate father-in-law is borderline absurd. She almost certainly invented those details to avoid implicating either herself or her husband in the crime of harboring a fugitive. If anything, the Starrs, Sam and Tom both, would have been delighted at the prospect of offering safe haven to a former bushwhacker who was seen as nothing short of a Confederate Robin Hood by Southern sympathizers, many of whom followed his exploits in local papers practically as a form of serialized entertainment. There have long been stories of Belle using a cave at the top of Hi Early Mountain, one of the timbered hills that girdled her property, as her hideout for wanted outlaws. This could have been the case, or she may have simply sheltered them in one of her log cabins. Regardless, it's a spaghetti Western–worthy image too tempting not to evoke: Jesse James, Tom Starr, Sam Starr, and Belle, seated around the dying embers of a campfire deep in the cavern, sharing wincing swigs from a jug of raw Cherokee whiskey and reminiscing on the legendary heists they each had been party to, while below the cave's mouth—far below—a pack of red wolves herald with their howls a rising moon that's already throwing flickering scales of silver across the ever-churning waters of the South Canadian River . . .

Such a scene only begs the question: Which of his many heists had Jesse James just committed upon seeking out Belle Starr and hiding at Younger's Bend? The combined James-Younger gang had ceased to exist by necessity following the disastrous Northfield bank robbery of 1876—Frank and Jesse had opted to peel off and make it back to their familiar safe houses in Missouri, while Cole and Jim Younger had decided to stay with their wounded brother Bob, only to be captured after an epic shootout. No doubt shaken by the failure of the raid, Frank and Jesse would try to lie low by posing as farmers in Tennessee for the next three years. The old itch, however, was too strong, for Jesse in particular. Fed up with farming, he recruited some new outlaws to join his gang, to fill the missing slots left behind by the Youngers, and turned his attention to robbing trains, stagecoaches, and stores—no more banks. This new iteration of the James Gang was involved in several such heists during the first two years of Belle Starr's tenure as the rustic chatelaine of Younger's Bend.

But given the fact that Belle seems well-established at her new homestead at the time of Jesse's arrival and that he showed up without his brother Frank, it seems likely that the visit occurred shortly after the famous Blue Cut robbery of September 7, 1881—the date being significant, as the caper was designed to commemorate the five-year anniversary of the failed Northfield Raid, as a tribute to the imprisoned Youngers. The James brothers, along with a team of relatively inexperienced and unproven new recruits, donned their masks and held up a train from the Chicago and Alton Railroad outside of Glendale, Missouri. The robbery went relatively smoothly, although the bandits took to lifting cash off individual passengers, as the train's safe held little in terms of treasure. All in all, the gang made off with some $3,000—not insignificant, although certainly not a major score when split six ways between the members of the gang. Frank James evidently took this as a sign. He'd enjoyed civilian life far more than his brother Jesse, and he had displayed some reluctance about getting back into organized crime. Disappointed by the size of the payoff and perhaps spooked by the fact that so many of his fellow gang members had already been captured or killed, he decided to split ways with his brother in the aftermath of the robbery and give up the desperado life for good.

This was almost certainly the moment that Jesse James, alone and on the run with a fresh $5,000 bounty on his head, chose to head south into Indian Territory and seek shelter with Belle Starr. A former member of Quantrill's Raiders, James would have been no stranger to hiding out in Indian Territory, and the fact that Belle, whom he knew quite well through Cole Younger and Jim Reed, was already there, would only have sweetened the deal. With such a sizable price on his head, he would have been aware that virtually anyone might turn against him, and that Myra Maybelle from old Jasper County was someone he could trust. According to Belle's own account, he "remained several weeks," just long enough for the heat to die down, before giving his hostess her cut for taking him in and returning to his familiar haunts in Missouri to live under the alias of Thomas Howard and begin planning his next heist with what remained of his gang.

It was propitious that Belle Starr's first criminal guest—the one that likely established her as a force to be reckoned with among the Cherokee and secured her place in the Starr crime family—was Jesse James. Because while it may have been his first visit to Younger's Bend, the Blue Cut robbery would also prove to be his last. Like so many of the young men who figured prominently in Belle Starr's life, Jesse James too found himself on the wrong side of a gun barrel shortly thereafter. On April 3, 1882, while standing on a chair and dusting off a framed picture in his own parlor in St. Joseph, Missouri, the thirty-five-year-old James was shot in the back of the head. His killer was not some Pinkerton or criminal rival, but twenty-year-old Robert Ford, a member of Jesse's gang who had sold out his leader for a chance at the reward money and the promise of a pardon. Evidently he'd struck a deal with the Missouri governor himself. The crack of a revolver, the snap of a chair leg, a fantail of crimson across paisley wallpaper, and just like that, another legendary outlaw had fallen. The owner of the rented house where Jesse James and his wife Zerelda had been staying would later run tours of the premises and sell blood-soaked splinters prized from the floorboards for twenty-five cents apiece. Robert Ford would receive both a portion of the reward money and the pardon he sought, but would forever be branded in saying and song as "that dirty little coward that shot Mr. Howard." And ironically, in the end, he would meet a similar fate. Ten years later, while working at the tent saloon he owned in the mining camp of Creede, Colorado, he would be mowed down for no apparent reason at all by a shotgun-wielding sociopath named Edward O'Kelley—who in turn would be gunned down twelve years after that while assaulting a police officer in Oklahoma City, somehow managing to set the officer's clothing on fire and bite chunks out of both of his ears before the lawman finally wrestled his gun free and put a bullet through his brain. A daisy chain of senseless killing, almost too bleak to be even called karma—it's just the way things were in the West.

THE YEAR 1882 MAY have marked the end of Jesse James's career as a gangster, but for Belle Starr, it was just the beginning. James's visit had solidified Belle's reputation as a legitimate criminal—someone with real underworld contacts, a person who was not to be trifled with. And her role within the Starr crime family appears to have grown in importance accordingly. Being organized criminals, they kept no damning diaries or ledgers; what happened at Younger's Bend in the following years occurred largely in the shadows. However, from the recorded testimonies of victims—more will be said about that later—a rough picture of Belle's criminal involvement can be gleaned. She was definitely involved in horse theft—this is fact. She also continued to participate in the family's long-standing protection racket, offering shelter at Younger's Bend to a variety of wanted criminals, including the horse thief John Middleton and the stickup artist Jack Spaniard, to name a few. She very likely participated in stickups herself, while disguised as a man, although she would never be found guilty of the crime. And she almost certainly smuggled whiskey on the side. Fencing stolen goods, planning armed robberies, smuggling controlled substances—by dint of her marriage to

Samuel and her subsequent entry into the Starr clan's illicit en-
terprises, Belle had finally become a full-on gangster. Gone were
her days as a tagalong, a sidekick, someone to hold the horses
during a heist. Belle Starr was now the genuine article.

It was a role she took to wholeheartedly. She dressed the part,
especially when she rode into nearby towns like Fort Smith or Eufaula, reaffirming her position as someone of means, to be both
respected and feared—an *uomo d'onore*, as she would have been
known in the Sicilian Mafia, if only she had been a man. An account of one of her visits to Fort Smith, published in the *Dallas
Morning News* under the subtitle "Belle Starr, Girl Who Shelters
Outlaws," describes Belle as attracting "considerable attention
wherever she goes, being a dashing horse-woman, and exceedingly graceful in the saddle." The article mentions her fondness for
sporting "a fine pair of 45-calibre revolvers, latest pattern," as well
as a "broadbrimmed white man's hat, surmounted by a wide black
plush band, with feathers and ornaments, which is very becoming
to her." It concludes that she is "of medium size, well formed, a
dark brunette, with bright and intelligent eyes." Such a description
could easily be passed off as romantic exaggeration or an example of some journalistic creative liberty, if it weren't for one simple fact—there are pictures of Belle Starr dressed exactly in this
fashion. Perhaps the most famous, taken in Fort Smith, Arkansas,
on May 23, 1886, shows a woman fully at ease with her Western
gangland persona. In it, a glaring, steely-eyed Belle sits poised and
confident atop her prized mare Venus, on an elaborately-tooled
custom-made sidesaddle, with a quirt dangling from a leather-
gloved hand. She is dressed in an all-black velvet riding habit, with
a pinned and plumed Stetson angled across her brow and a massive
holstered revolver hanging menacingly off her hip. This kind of
presentation wasn't just unusual for a woman on the frontier—it
was unusual for anyone not looking to get "their ticket punched,"

to use the verbiage of the times. Simply put, nobody in their right mind would ride into a blood-and-guts border town like Fort Smith, dressed and armed in such a clamant fashion, unless fully prepared to back up that strut. It was an intimidation tactic as well as a calibrated message: Belle Starr was the cock of the walk, a force to be reckoned with. And anyone looking to engage in organized criminal activity in that corner of Indian Territory would need to go through her first.

As to whether Belle found the need to resort to violence, that's harder to say. It's well established from witnesses that she had no qualms pulling those pistols when she felt threatened or disrespected. As to whether she ever pulled the triggers and took a life—once again, organized crime is by nature a murky business, and it's difficult to know what went on in the shadows. An account from S. W. Harman's *Hell on the Border*, written less than a decade after her death by someone intimately familiar with Oklahoma outlaws, would claim the following:

> *Her ideas of outlawry seemed to have been more for the wild plea-sure of the chase than for any desire to take human life, and it is claimed that it was only when angered beyond control by some act of betrayal or when driven to a corner, that she committed the crime of murder. Love of money, horses and books was with her a ruling passion, and she would go to almost any ends to procure the former; it was on that account that she confined the greater part of her efforts, while on the scout, to directing raids that should result in available plunder.*

It appears even a few years after her death, even in Oklahoma, nobody was quite certain if Belle ever found call to carve notches into her pistol. Although it's also quite possible that she never needed to—that as a high-ranking member of an organized crime family, she had underlings and button men to do the dirty work for her.

Or perhaps she never used *pistol* notches at all. In an article published in the *Dallas Morning News* on July 28, 1929, Fred E. Sutton, a journalist who claimed to have known Belle Starr personally, had the following to say about her famous Winchester rifle: "On one side of the stock is Belle Starr's name, and on the other side a brass star. Instead of being notched as is some-times the case, there are seven brass tacks driven into the front end of the stock. What do they mean? Who knows. Perhaps nothing. Perhaps . . ." His insinuation is of course purely speculative—the brass tacks could have been decorative and nothing more—but given the penchant of Western gunslingers to somehow mark their lethal tally on their weapon of choice, it at least warrants consideration. Maybe seven was just a lucky number or the brass felt good to the touch. Or maybe each tack *did* represent a rival gangster who found their end in a shallow grave at Younger's Bend or at the cold bottom of the South Canadian River. It's one of several Belle Starr mysteries that will likely never be solved.

By the spring of 1882, in eastern Indian Territory and in the environs of Fort Smith, she had made her point clear: there was a new gangster in town. She had aligned herself with the Starr family's crime syndicate and established herself, alongside her husband, as a local power player in the Cherokee underworld. This "career success," if one can call it that, was augmented by the fact that in Sam Starr, she seemed to have finally found a true partner, both in love and in business. They supported each other and defended each other, and when the situation called for it, they were willing to kill for each other. Which isn't to say there weren't complications. Much as with her marriage to Jim Reed, rumors of infidelity circulated, involving Belle and Sam Starr both. In the case of Belle, there is at least some evidence to support their veracity. In spite of whatever conflicts or distractions appeared in their marriage, though, Belle was, in her own words, passing the days "very happily" with her new husband at Younger's Bend. Together, she and Sam had laid the foundations for a home. All that remained for Belle was to build—or rather, *re*build—her family.

It's unclear if Belle's then eleven-year-old daughter Pearl was living with her mother when she moved in with Sam Starr in the summer of 1880. Technically, Pearl was in her custody, although Belle had a habit of leaving her little girl with friends and relatives for extended stretches any time she went off on one of her sprees or took up with a new man. That Belle Starr cared deeply for her daughter is beyond dispute—letters written to Pearl and about Pearl attest to that fact, and more than a few witnesses commented on her devotion. But Belle was an imperfect mother, to say the least. Which was perhaps why she felt compelled to so often leave Pearl with more responsible, upright kin, limiting her daughter's exposure, to the extent that she could, to her own sordid milieu of gamblers, cutthroats, and thieves. Saloons, dance halls, bawdy houses, gambling parlors—this was the world that Belle Starr knew, and it was a world she seemed to have made at least some effort to shield her daughter from. It is known, however, that Pearl was definitely residing full time with her mother by the time she moved into Younger's Bend. Belle even took to calling her daughter "Canadian Lilly," after the broad, turbid river that meandered around her land. It was a chance for Belle to expose Pearl, long accustomed to being shuffled through the cheap hotels and boardinghouses of frontier towns, to an environment as bucolic as the stock farm of Belle's girlhood on the outskirts of Medoc. And Belle almost certainly schooled her daughter in the same skills her older brother had once taught her there: to ride, to shoot, to fish, to hunt. When not engaged in such outdoorsy pursuits, Belle would have spent time reading and singing with Pearl, doing her best to instill in the girl the same love for books and music that had blossomed for her in the parlor of her parents' hotel. According to some accounts, Belle and Pearl even tamed two wild fawns, keeping them as pets they could play with, together in the garden. They became a family once again at Younger's Bend, with Belle's new marriage and new homestead providing the stability that had been lacking for so long.

All that was missing was her son. James Edwin Reed, "Eddie," the boy whose custody she had surrendered to her in-laws in Rich Hill, Missouri, six years before. Whether it was out of economic necessity, concerns regarding her lifestyle, or some combination of both is hard to say, but while Belle had at least made a nominal effort at raising her daughter Pearl, when it came to her son Eddie, she'd made no effort at all, beyond an occasional visit when she went north to Missouri. At Younger's Bend, however, by the year 1882, with a reliable husband and an established abode, Belle was at last ready to make up for lost time—to finally call her only son, now almost twelve years old, back home and to make her family, scattered in the tumult that followed the bloody death of her first husband, whole again.

It was a beautiful dream, bringing her only son home to Younger's Bend, but unfortunately for Belle, it would not come to pass—not then, anyway. Because the townspeople and assorted ruffians of Fort Smith weren't the only ones to notice that a new outlaw was in town. And while federal marshals and tribal police had both long done their best to avoid any sort of armed confrontation with the Starrs, by the spring of 1882, some in the law enforcement community were coming to the realization that they had no choice. The article from the *Dallas Morning News* that mentioned the brass tacks in Belle's rifle stock also described the following incident, as recounted by the Fort Smith portrait photographer who witnessed it:

> *One day I heard a big racket in the street, and upon looking out, I saw Belle on her favorite saddle mare, Venus, with a forty-five in her belt and a rifle across her lap, cussing out a bunch of policemen, and daring them to try and arrest her. I knew her well and stayed in my studio until the storm blew over. While it was at its height, I sneaked up to the window and snapped a picture of her. This is the one I lost, and the only other one I know of was made for Dr. W. F. Carver, who was greatly smitten with the outlaw queen.*

Both Belle and the Starrs would have been known to federal and tribal authorities as outlaws. The U.S. marshals had been dealing with Belle and her problematic male companions for nearly two decades—she was familiar to authorities in Fort Smith due to Jim Reed's involvement in the Shannon-Fisher feud, and she had even been questioned in Dallas by U.S. Commissioner Long and Deputy Marshal W. H. Anderson regarding her participation in the historic Grayson robbery. And when it came to the Cherokee tribal police, as an organization, they were directly descended from the very same posses of Lighthorsemen who had gone to war with the Starr clan and their Treaty Party supporters decades earlier. Both law enforcement bodies had compelling reasons for wanting to get Belle and Sam Starr behind bars, yet both knew that doing so came with considerable risks. Cherokee warlords were generally not the sort of folk one wanted to anger, after all. The vendettas of old Tom Starr were still spoken of with fear and awe in western Arkansas and the Indian Territory, and the relative calm that had prevailed during the preceding decades was largely the result of the elder Starr agreeing to tone down his criminal activities so long as authorities agreed to grant him considerable berth. However, with Belle Starr's growing reputation as a local power player, and with her open flaunting of tribal and federal authority, it was becoming increasing clear that something had to be done. She and her husband had gone too far.

All that was missing was a prosecutable crime that could be pinned upon the outlaw couple—a deceptively hard thing to find. Crimes committed between Cherokees were handled uniquely by the tribal courts, while crimes committed between whites were the domain of the federal court in Fort Smith. The fact that Belle was a white woman living in the Cherokee Nation complicated the matter considerably. This ambiguity was in part why so many white outlaws had historically sought refuge from prosecution in Indian Territory. Among the sovereign Indian nations, they occupied a somewhat nebulous legal space where they were slightly beyond the reach of tribal and federal courts alike. For an airtight case to be made against Belle and Sam both, authorities needed an attestable crime that involved both a white and a Cherokee victim, each of which was willing to testify against the outlaw couple. It was the best way to guarantee that the charges would stick in the relevant courts, but also an exceedingly unlikely scenario.

Then in the summer of 1882, after two long years of watching Belle Starr and wringing their hands, the U.S. marshals in Fort Smith received a tip from local Cherokee lawmen. Finally they had found their case. On July 21, after examining the evidence presented before him, Cassius M. Barnes, the chief deputy U.S. marshal at Fort Smith, signed a writ in the presence of U.S. Commissioner Stephen Wheeler for the apprehension of Belle Starr and Sam Starr. Orders were passed on to L. W. Marks, the deputy marshal assigned to the district that encompassed the Starrs' holdings, to take the couple into custody. Guns were oiled, horses were saddled, and prayers were no doubt muttered as a team of marshals prepared to ride into Younger's Bend. Knowing Belle's reputation, not to mention the violent history of the Starr family, the lawmen expected resistance. This was no time for a "knock and announce," but rather for a surprise door-kicking raid.

Luck may have been on the side of the federal marshals when they arrived at Younger's Bend to serve the writ, but the element of surprise was certainly not. Deputy Marshal Marks and his men did make it out of the Bend alive, but they also did so without Sam and Belle in their custody. They probably never even needed to kick in the door—it had essentially been left wide open. Belle and Sam, almost certainly tipped off by one of their paid informants in Fort Smith, knew the arrest was coming and had already fled.

The chase was on, and the tracks were fresh. The couple was headed north, which to Deputy Marshal Marks would have meant only one thing: Belle Starr was making a break for the Osage Nation, a place where even federal marshals were reluctant to set foot.

The Osage Nation Reservation in present-day Oklahoma was unique in that the land had been purchased in 1872 from the Cherokee by the Osage themselves, using funds from the sale of their previous federal allotment in Kansas. Old grievances against their traditional tribal enemy had been set aside in the interest of besting an even more threatening adversary: the U.S. government, which had broken any number of treaties with Native peoples in the fever of Western expansion that followed the Civil War. It was an exceedingly prescient move on the part of the Osage, as they ended up retaining considerably more sovereignty and self-governance than the many other tribes that existed solely on U.S. handouts. This general lack of federal intervention made the Osage Nation a favorite hideout for wanted criminals looking to escape from the law. Additionally, the Osage had a reputation as being crucial middlemen in the frontier horse trade, both legal and otherwise, taking in herds from the rest of Indian Territory and the Southern

Plains and funneling them into the rural and urban markets of their old homelands in Missouri. It's likely that the Starr family had dealings with the Osage that went back years, as a convenient outlet for their own stolen horses. Among the tribe, Belle and Sam Starr probably had both business associates and friends to help hide them, which was why stopping the couple before they reached the borders of the Osage Nation would have been a priority for the team of U.S. marshals that was hot on their trail.

However, that very trail took them first to Catoosa, a Cherokee cow town roughly eighty miles north of Younger's Bend, known as a haven for cattle rustlers and horse thieves. Belle and Sam Starr had accomplices here as well who were ready to offer them sanctuary, including the Cherokee outlaw Sha-con-gah, known colloquially as Blue Duck. In addition to being a rumored lover of Belle's from the wild years of widowhood that preceded her relationship with Bruce Younger, he was also a ruthless gunman and was thought to have served as something of a foot soldier in the Starr family's criminal enterprise. If he did come to Belle's aid, it would make historical sense, as several years later, Belle, ever the good gang leader, would repay him by supporting his appeal following a Fort Smith murder trial. Regardless of whether they sought out Blue Duck or not, the town of Catoosa would have had plenty of fellow outlaws who owed Belle and Sam money, a favor, or both.

After Catoosa, the trail became harder to follow. Marshal Marks questioned locals but received conflicting reports about the party and its intended direction. Some claimed they had seen a man and a boy traveling north, others recalled seeing a man and a woman—evidence, perhaps, of Belle's alleged penchant for disguising herself in male garb to hide her identity. The days were turning into weeks, and each hour that was lost brought the fugitive couple one step closer to the relative safety of the Osage Nation. The border was fast approaching—after Catoosa, it was just a thirty-mile sprint—and time was running out. Given the town's proximity, Marks surely grappled with the possibility that he had already lost them. Exhausted, frustrated, and probably close to giving up, he ordered his men to make camp for the night on the banks of Bird Creek, a sluggish, tea-colored river that snaked its way along the very edge of the Osage land, less than a mile from the reservation's borders. Which was precisely when the element of surprise that had eluded the lawmen back at Younger's Bend was suddenly and unwittingly on their side. Completely oblivious to what awaited them, Sam Starr and a young African American man sharing the couple's campsite came down through the brush, leading their horses to water. Sam had walked right into a trap, one that the U.S. marshals themselves had not even known that they were setting. Outnumbered, caught off guard, Sam gave up without a fight—he had no choice. He raised his hands above his head and let the federal marshals take his weapons, putting up no protest as they chained him to a tree. His wife, however, waiting back at the campsite, would not go down *quite* so easily.

CHAPTER 7

A Queen Dethroned

FOR MYRA MAYBELLE SHIRLEY, the daughter of slave-owning parents, born and raised in the Confederate stronghold of Jasper County, Missouri, the idea of making camp and breaking bread alongside a family of Black migrants making their way west would have been all but unthinkable. For Belle Starr of Younger's Bend, however, the notion apparently posed no problem whatsoever. Indian Territory was a place of dynamic racial identities and intense creolization. It was a multicultural melting pot where prosperous Choctaws often rented out their lands to poor white sharecroppers; where Cherokee Freedmen, the descendants of African American slaves who had walked the Trail of Tears, spoke Cherokee as a first language and considered themselves part of the tribe. It wouldn't have been uncommon to find relatives of mixed European, Native American, and West African ancestry in any tribal family tree—and with the Starrs, Belle had married into just such a family.

It's impossible to know what was said and shared between Belle Starr and her traveling companions on that twilit evening of September 21, 1882, just a stone's throw away from the banks of Bird Creek. Perhaps she helped them bake supper over the coals in a Dutch oven—corn pone was a special favorite of hers. Or maybe they whiled away the hours together in song—old hymns and mountain ballads were said to be Belle's preferred material, and she was known to sing "Jesus, Lover of My Soul" and "There Is a Fountain Filled with Blood" while strumming away on a guitar. Or maybe they just talked quietly around the campfire, with Belle happy to share the remembrances of her own family's migration to the Western frontier almost two decades earlier, trundling toward Texas in a pair of covered wagons.

Regardless of what they were doing, the travelers were surely caught by surprise when the son who had gone down to water the horses with Sam came scrambling back up from the banks of Bird Creek, panting in fear and wide-eyed with terror, begging for Belle to come quickly—her husband needed her. Belle obliged, gathering her skirts and racing after him through the brush, down the narrow path that led to water. Of course, there was no way for her to know that it was all a ruse; no way for her to guess that the U.S. marshals had held a pistol to the young man's head only minutes before, threatening him with death if he didn't cooperate.

Maybe she broke through the briars and saw Sam chained to the tree. Maybe it all happened so quickly she didn't have the chance. If she did catch a warning glimpse of her husband, however, it didn't make a difference. It was already too late. Federal marshals sprang on Belle from both sides of the path, eager to subdue her in case she had a weapon—and as it turned out, she was armed to the teeth. While the two men lunged for her arms, she made a grab for her six-shooter, which was hidden "under the drapery of a pannier overskirt." They did succeed in wrestling away the revolver from the furious woman, who "fought like a tiger" and "threatened to kill the officers," only to discover an unpleasant surprise: Belle also had two small derringer pistols "concealed in the bosom of her dress." Despite a valiant struggle, the well-armed fugitive was eventually pinned to the ground and disarmed completely, no doubt leaving the two sweat-soaked marshals, chests heaving, wondering how in the *hell* such a small woman could put up such a fight.[1]

If they thought they had her bested, however, they were soon to

---

[1]   It is worth noting that while this detailed account of Belle Starr's arrest came courtesy of the widow of Deputy Marshal L. W. Marks, and not from the lawman himself, it was later confirmed by a former Fort Smith deputy marshal named Elias Rector, who actually participated in the manhunt for the Starrs. The only major discrepancy in his version: in addition to the hidden .45 revolver beneath her skirt, he remembered Belle having only one derringer pistol tucked into her bodice, not two.

stand corrected. According to an interview conducted years later with Fannie Blythe Marks, the wife of the deputy marshal charged with arresting the outlaw couple, "Belle Starr was the most exasperating prisoner that the marshals ever dealt with." Her behavior may have even earned her what would be considered police brutality by modern standards. As Fannie Blythe Marks would also recount: "Because of her sex the officers were as considerate and forbearing as possible, until patience ceased to be a virtue." Reading between the lines, one can easily imagine the rough treatment that a frontier marshal might have inflicted upon a spitting, cussing, fugitive outlaw who refused to submit to their authority. A backhanded smack if they were lucky, a pistol-whipping if they were not.

Whatever they subjected her to, it wasn't enough. At some point during the long, slow journey back to Fort Smith, not far from the Muskogee fairground, the bulk of the marshals decided to leave Belle under guard while they left camp to serve a writ for another wanted criminal rumored to be nearby. When they returned for dinner, however, they "heard a shot and saw Belle running around the tent, a smoking revolver in her hand, in hot pursuit of the guard." As Fannie Blythe Marks recalled:

> She had been alone in her tent eating her dinner when the side blew up, disclosing the guard seated on the outside, his pistol in his scabbard, with his back toward her. It was but the work of an instant for her to seize the pistol; she intended to kill the guard, liberate the other prisoners, her husband and herself. Unfortunately for the success of her plans . . . the timely arrival of the officers saved the day.

Had the other marshals arrived only minutes later, the biography of Belle Starr might have assumed an entirely different trajectory, with Belle killing the guard, freeing her husband, and galloping away with him on a pair of stolen horses, to live out their lives as fugitive bandits among the Osage. Instead, she found herself staring down the gun barrels of who knows how many furious lawmen. She was swiftly disarmed, and for the remainder of the journey, kept in chains.

Upon their arrival and subsequent detention at Fort Smith, Belle and Sam hired a local law firm to defend them—only to fare poorly at a preliminary hearing before Commissioner Stephen Wheeler in the second week of October. The couple was scheduled to appear before a grand jury the following month, and bail was set at $1,000. Tom Starr, the "Godfather" himself, came to their assistance, posting their bail by using seventy head of cattle, ten horses, and one hundred and sixty sheep as collateral. This allowed them to return to Younger's Bend and work with their lawyers to plan their initial defense. However, the grand jury proved just as disastrous for the couple as the preliminary hearing, and Belle and Sam both received a bill of indictment for larceny, standing accused of being horse thieves. A trial date was set for February 15, 1883, to be presided over by Isaac "Hanging Judge" Parker—so named for his manifest fondness of the noose. Over the course of Judge Parker's gavel-smashing Fort Smith career, he sentenced 160 criminals to hang.

NEARLY AS LONG AS the legend of Belle Starr has circulated throughout the American consciousness, there have also been naysayers and detractors who have sought to diminish her criminal reputation. Skeptical historians, incredulous biographers, men— and they are almost exclusively men—who have been unwilling to accept the possibility, let alone legitimacy, of a female outlaw in the Wild West. In the eyes of these cynics, she is nothing but a "dissolute woman," as the journalist Frederick S. Barde once labeled her, a lost soul who was "unfortunate in her early life, and in her later years merely a companion of thieves and outlaws." Devoid of any talent, deprived of all agency—such descriptions diminish Belle down to something sad, pathetic even: a lonely middle-aged woman, a societal castoff. Certainly not someone to be respected or feared.

However—if one were to select just one episode, just one allegation, from a historical record absolutely rife with evidence strongly to the contrary, in order to put the issue to rest once and for all, it would probably be Belle's first arrest and subsequent trial by the federal court in Fort Smith. Sending a full team of U.S. marshals on a weeks-long manhunt—in Indian Territory, no less—was no small act. A criminal had to do something to deserve that level of "heat." Jim Reed, Belle Starr's first husband, certainly earned the distinction, but it was only after getting directly involved in the frontier mafia war that was the Shannon-Fisher feud and assassinating two men in broad daylight as part of a massive, and very public, mob-style hit. And the fact that Belle's specific case was based on evidence first brought forth by *tribal* authorities only further proves the point—with the Trail of Tears still within living memory, the idea of inviting federal gunmen onto reservation lands to arrest citizens of their nation would not have been one the Cherokee government broached casually.

Then there is the issue of the significant costs associated with the various hearings and trial itself. The U.S. District Court at Fort Smith handled cases from across the entire Western District of Arkansas and Indian Territory as well, a swath of land positively swimming in outlaws and brigands. Needless to say, they had a full docket and would not have wasted precious space in their jail or valuable resources in their courthouse to prosecute some minor hoodlum or miscreant. To put it simply, the notion that tribal and federal authorities would have colluded and gone through this much trouble to apprehend a "dissolute woman" who was little more than an occasional "companion of thieves and outlaws" is downright preposterous. True, the case against her involved the stealing of just two horses, but it's worth remembering that Belle Starr was involved in an organized crime racket well versed at hiding its tracks, and these were the charges her prosecutors were confident they could get to stick. There was no RICO Act in the 1880s, no convenient way to convict a specific defendant of large-scale criminal conspiracy. Law enforcement had to work with what it could get, and just as the violent reign of Al Capone came to an end thanks to an eleven-year sentence for mere tax evasion, the federal marshals at Fort Smith sought to bring down Belle Starr with a relatively basic conviction for horse theft. And because they had both a white and Cherokee victim willing to testify against her, as well as the tacit compliance of Cherokee tribal authorities, they were confident that the apparatus would be in place to put her husband Sam behind bars as well. In effect, Belle Starr had broken— perhaps inadvertently—the fragile truce that had existed between the Cherokee Nation and the Starr family since 1846. Gone were the days when authorities, both tribal and federal, were willing to look the other way when it came to the Starrs' criminal dealings. Trotting stridently through the dusty streets of Fort Smith wearing her plumed hat and gun belt, Belle Starr had in effect dared the authorities to go ahead and arrest her. And finally they had.

If this kind of historical deduction alone isn't enough to convince the skeptic of Belle Starr's criminal legitimacy, however, her trial's coverage by the press should be. It wasn't mentioned by the large Eastern publications—her reputation wouldn't spread that far until after her death—but it did receive considerable ink in local papers, the following article from the February 22, 1883, edition of the *Fort Smith New Era* included:

In the U.S. district court last week the case [was held] of Sam Starr and Belle Starr, his wife, of the Cherokee Nation, charged with the larceny of two horses on the 20th of April, 1882. . . . The very idea of a woman being charged with an offense of this kind and that she was the leader of a band of horse thieves and wielding power over them as their queen and guiding spirit, was sufficient to fill the courtroom with spectators. . . .

As an equestrian, Belle Starr is without rival, is said to be an expert marksman with the pistol, and it is claimed that she was at one time the wife of Bruce Younger, the notorious horse thief and desperado, and while she could not be considered even a good-looking woman, her appearance is of that kind as would be sure to attract the attention of wild and desperate characters. . . .

[S]he would frequently hand notes to her attorneys, and it was subject of remark that they paid strict attention to the contents. A devil-may-care expression rested on her countenance . . . and at no time did she give sign of weakening before the mass of testimony that was raised against her.

Early biographers very well may have embroidered Belle Starr's posthumous legacy with invented yarns and concocted adventures. But articles like this speak directly to how her contemporaries viewed her. In her own time, among the residents of Fort Smith, she certainly was regarded as an imposing woman adept at both riding and gunplay, the ruthless leader of a criminal gang. And it appears to be very much common knowledge that she "wielded power over them as their queen and guiding spirit." Seated confidently in the courtroom during witness testimony, writing orders on slips of paper and passing them casually to her attorneys with a "devil-may-care" expression on her face—this Belle Starr bears a far closer resemblance to a mafia don on trial for racketeering than a wayward woman who occasionally shacked up with unsavory characters. If there ever was a Belle Starr who tagged along with minor hoodlums and took orders from petty thieves, she vanished for good at the borders of the Cherokee Nation. The Belle Starr of Younger's Bend didn't take orders from anyone, she gave them. And she wasn't just a gangster—she was a gang*lord*.

The trial took place in a bustling Fort Smith courtroom, presided over by Judge Isaac Parker and filled to capacity with milling, murmuring spectators who, as the *New Era* described, were eager for a peek at the notorious female bandit they had all heard so much about. Such trials were usually lively affairs, attended by outraged neighbors and aggrieved kin, and when it came to maintaining order in the court, Judge Parker would have had his work cut out for him, although his demeanor and reputation no doubt helped. Hard wooden benches, steamed-up windowpanes, the smell of sweat and unwashed wool—the atmosphere would have been anything but pleasant, but Belle appears to have done an impeccable job of maintaining her composure.

As for the facts of the case itself, as laid out in *United States v. Sam and Belle Starr*, they are fairly straightforward. According to prosecutors, Belle and Sam were responsible for the theft of two horses, one belonging to a white man residing in the Cherokee Nation named Andrew Crane and the other to a Cherokee individual named Samuel Campbell. After briefly penning the stolen horses as part of a small herd with a neighbor named John West—who would end up testifying against the couple—Belle and an accomplice named Childs rode south to the town of McAlester, in the neighboring Choctaw Nation, presumably to sell the entire herd, stolen horses included. The testimonies of the two victims, Crane and Campbell, paint a picture of Belle Starr as the clear ringleader, and an intimidating one at that.

When Crane began to suspect that the Starrs had stolen his horse, he approached Belle—not Sam—with a threat to go to the authorities. Belle's initial reaction was to offer him a small payoff of thirty dollars, with the understanding that he "must not claim it as hush money." When Crane refused, she told him that if he did press charges, she and her husband would "not be a bit too good to waylay [his] road." Essentially, she threatened to try to kill him if he went to the authorities. And it was evidently a threat that she kept. Crane would later testify to that effect, telling the court: "someone waylaid my road while I was hunting my horse and I thought they burst a cap at me." Perhaps the anonymous gunshot was an intimidation tactic, or perhaps it was intended to kill but missed—regardless, it was precisely the kind of approach one would expect from an organized crime syndicate seeking to silence a witness. Belle would go on to threaten other witnesses as well, attacking a Mr. Alfred L. Harper, who claimed she met him with "a tirade of abuse," promising that "if she ever got out of this she would make it hot for us fellows up at Briartown," while also labeling Crane "a damned old Arkansas hoosier" who couldn't keep his mouth shut. And when the time had come to unload the stolen horses, it was once again Belle, not Sam, who had taken them to McAlester accompanied by her underling Childs.

If anything, from the court records and articles surrounding the trial, Sam comes off as hesitant, even timid at times, compared to his bold and fiery wife. In the testimony of their neighbor, John West, he claims that Sam Starr asked him for advice about what he should do to appease Crane and Campbell. When West suggested he take the horses back, Sam replied that "he was afraid to go . . . afraid they would kill him." According to West, Sam then went on to ask what he thought about "his wife going off with that man," referring to Childs, who had accompanied Belle to McAlester to sell the horses—evidently Sam was confident they were having an affair. When West asked for Sam's own thoughts on the matter, Sam answered that "he just thought she was laying around with him," indicating Belle's interest in Childs was purely sexual. Granted, this should be seen within the context of Cherokee culture, which traditionally allowed for plural marriage and had very different sexual mores from the Judeo-Christian world—Sam was rumored to have lovers as well. But still, it does seem to indicate that Belle had a habit of making her own rules when it came to both crime and love, and she, not her husband, was running the show.

Regardless of Belle's wandering eye, however, there is also evidence of her strong feelings for Sam, her ready devotion. One of the few moments during the trial that a cool-countenanced Belle Starr ever showed any emotion at all was when Sam, whose first language was probably Cherokee and not English, became visibly confused by legal jargon while taking the stand and was subsequently mocked by the district attorney. This enraged Belle, and according to the *New Era* reporter who witnessed the episode, "If looks had been killing, the prosecutor would have dropped in his tracks." Belle may have been an imperfect wife and occasionally an absentee partner, but no one—*no one*—ridiculed her husband or her adopted people. Not if she had anything to say about it.

Even the couple's defense strategy would portray Belle as the more able of the two. As an alibi, their attorney made the claim, supported by Tom Starr on the stand, that Sam had been bedridden with the measles and that Belle had been by his side caring for him at the time of the alleged horse theft. Under cross-examination, however, the precise timing of their alibi came apart due to the fact that, according to Tom Starr: "Indians don't keep the day of the month like white people. We keep it by the moon." As to whether this was the truth or a clever ploy on the part of Tom Starr to avoid perjuring himself in front of an aggressive district attorney is hard to say. But either way, the defense's inability to offer proof of Sam and Belle Starr's whereabouts when the horses disappeared seriously hurt their case.

Complicating matters further was the ethnic identity of the two victims. Campbell, like Sam Starr, was unambiguously a Cherokee, which meant that the U.S. District Court at Fort Smith had no punitive authority there as far as Sam was concerned—it would be left up to tribal authorities, if they chose to prosecute the theft of Campbell's horse. Debate raged, however, whether Crane was actually in fact white. Although he did not vote in the Cherokee Nation, there were claims that the young man had Cherokee blood on his mother's side, which could have canceled out the district court's authority there as well. But in the end, it was determined that Crane was indeed living in the Cherokee Nation as a white man. Which was bad news for the outlaw couple when the guilty verdict was read, because it meant both Sam and Belle would be held accountable for the theft of *his* horse. The jury found Sam guilty on one count of larceny, as it pertained to Crane, and it found Belle guilty on two counts, for Crane and Campbell both. The pair were brought before the court for sentencing on March 8, 1883, and while a defeated Sam stared blankly ahead, a defiant Belle looked "Hanging Judge" Parker right in the eyes, "bold and fearless," as reported in the *Fort Smith New Era*. Being condemned to the gallows for simple horse theft, with no murder attached, was extremely unlikely. But a heavy sentence was still to be expected. Judge Parker cleared his throat as even more spectators crowded into the courtroom, standing on their boot tips for a glimpse of this new outlaw queen, holding their breath in tense anticipation.

One year for Sam and two consecutive six-month terms for Belle, to be served at the House of Correction in Detroit, Michigan—one of the only penitentiaries that accepted female felons. It's hard to believe the defendants and their collected supporters in the crowd rejoiced at their sentences, but they almost certainly would have felt some relief. Their punishments were relatively lenient, perhaps because it had been their first conviction. Judge Parker could have thrown the book at them if he had so chosen; stealing a family's horse, which was their livelihood on a hostile frontier, was generally regarded as a grave offense. Vigilante posses often killed horse thieves—that is, after all, how Belle's own brother Edwin Benton lost his life—and judges had no qualms doling out sentences of five, even ten years if the suspected thieves were brought in alive. Had Sam and Belle possessed prior convictions, perhaps he would have. But Judge Parker went relatively easy on them. It's possible Belle's charms, or simply her identity as a woman, had something to do with it, too—maybe Judge Parker, like so many of her later skeptics, refused to believe wholeheartedly in an outlaw queen.

If there was one individual in the jostling gallery of onlookers who did not feel any relief, however, who perhaps even fumed with indignation at the light sentence, it was thirty-year-old Franklin Pierce West. Ironically, Frank West was Sam's cousin—the West and the Starr families were related, and they lived in close vicinity to one another, scattered around the banks and bends of the South Canadian River. He was also the younger brother of John West, the neighbor who had testified against Sam and Belle during the trial. But Frank was tribal police, an Indian deputy marshal, and as such, had a deep and abiding hatred for his relatives' recalcitrant ways. The Starrs and the Wests may have shared bloodlines, but they had very different relationships to tribal government. While both families had initially supported the Treaty Party—Frank's father had even been exiled from the Cherokee Nation for killing a National Party judge named Isaac Bushyhead during the tribal elections of 1843—the Wests had eventually fallen in line and integrated themselves into tribal politics and law enforcement. To fall back on an old trope, the Wests became cops and the Starrs became robbers. In fact, it was Frank and his brother John who had tipped off the U.S. marshals in Fort Smith, in part, no doubt, because of their limited authority as tribal police to apprehend a white woman like Belle Starr. For them, it was simply a practical move, a way of cutting out a cancer that they believed posed a threat to their community. To Sam and Belle Starr, however, it was the ultimate betrayal—being ratted out to the federal government not by some paid stool pigeon, but by actual *kin*.

This transgression was the beginning of a blood feud that would have grave consequences in the years to come. However, their mutual vendettas would have to be set aside for the time being. A prison cell—or more accurately, two prison cells—were waiting for the outlaw couple in Detroit.

THERE'S NO WAY TO know what Belle Starr was thinking as she sat in that railroad prison car on March 19, 1883, shackled and swaying among nineteen other prisoners—all men. For a first-time convict, the idea of the Detroit House of Correction must have posed a novel kind of horror. True, Belle had spent a few weeks in a Fort Smith jail cell following her arrest by the U.S. marshals, and she *may* have even spent a few nights behind bars during those troubled times that followed the death of Jim Reed. There are stories of her being arrested twice in Texas—once for arson and another time for bank robbery—and subsequently being rescued by male admirers, although there's scant evidence to support these tales, and they may be apocryphal. Back-to-back stretches in a grim penitentiary of stone and iron would have been a very different situation, however—a solid year in a place packed to capacity with murderers, rapists, and the criminally insane.

Of course there was also the fact that the prison was located in the heart of Detroit, an unknown city in a totally foreign part of the country, a full *thousand* miles away from her home at Younger's Bend. For a creature of the frontier like Belle, accustomed to log cabins and endless skies, the industrial North must have felt as alien as the surface of the moon. In 1883, Detroit had a population of roughly 120,000, more than half of it foreign-born, representing over forty different nationalities. It was a place of iron foundries, stove factories, shipyards, and pharmaceutical plants, all roaring with machinery and belching smoke into the air. It had electric streetlights, a professional baseball team, tram cars, and even telephone lines. It's hard to imagine how all this would *not* have been terrifying, or at the very least intimidating, to a woman who had never known anything beyond remote frontier towns and Native American reservations. If the train arrived in the evening, instead of a glorious Western sunset or a shimmering Milky Way, she would have seen only the coke flares from the tops of the city's blast furnaces glaring through the smog.

Regret and longing were probably tormenting Belle before the train even pulled into the station. And the one person who would have figured prominently in her thoughts—other than Sam, who was shackled in the prison car right beside her—was her fourteen-year-old daughter Pearl. This can be stated as more than mere conjecture, as a letter penned in Belle's own hand shortly before being transferred to the House of Correction in Detroit, survived and was later transcribed.[2] The missive is addressed to a "Miss Pearl Younger," who had been staying in Kansas for the duration of the trial with Mrs. "Mama Mc" Mclaughlin, an old friend of Belle's from her time spent in Galena. The name itself jumps out—some biographers have suggested that the "Younger" was a remnant of her marriage to Bruce Younger, and a means of hiding her daughter from overzealous prosecutors who might call her to take the

---

[2] Some historians have questioned the authenticity of Belle's famous prison letter, which was first published by S. W. Harman in 1898. Harman claimed to have transcribed the text personally, without ever producing the original document. However, certain details contained in the letter—especially obscure references to individuals who were identified much later—seem to indicate that the text is indeed authentic.

stand against her. This is a possibility but unlikely. Why would she give her daughter the surname of a man who had jilted her after only three weeks of marriage? And why would she have sought to hide her daughter from the district attorney when the verdict had already been issued and testimony was no longer needed?

A far more likely scenario is that the "Younger" was a product of her alleged relationship with Cole Younger—supporting the long-circulating rumors that he was Pearl's true father—and that if there was any subterfuge involved, it likely was to hide her daughter's whereabouts from rival factions within the Cherokee Nation. With Belle and Sam in prison, it probably wasn't safe for their daughter in Indian Territory. Tom Starr was aging and no longer the fighting force he once had been, making Pearl an easy target. Which explains why Belle sent her daughter to live with friends 130 miles away in Kansas, rather than with next-door relatives in the Cherokee Nation. This theory is supported by the overall tone of the letter, which in addition to being wrought with fear for her daughter's well-being, is wracked by an almost tangible sense of heartache and remorse—a rare glimpse of Belle's more vulnerable maternal side, and a far cry from the threats and intimidation tactics of the fearsome gangster depicted in the trial. As Belle wrote from Fort Smith:

Baby Pearl,
My Dear Little One:—It is useless to attempt to conceal my trouble from you and though you are nothing but a child I have confidence that my darling will bear with fortitude what I now write.

I shall be away from you a few months baby, and have only this consolation to offer you, that never again will I be placed in such humiliating circumstances and that in the future your little tender heart shall never more ache, or a blush called to your cheek on your mother's account. Sam and I were tried here, John West the main witness against us. We were found guilty and sentenced to nine months at the house of correction, Detroit, Michigan, for which place we start in the morning. Now Pearl there is a vast difference in that place and a penitentiary; you must bear that in mind and not think of mamma being shut up in a gloomy prison. It is said to be one of the finest institutions in the United States, surrounded by beautiful grounds, with fountains and everything nice. There I can have my education renewed, and I stand sadly in need of it. Sam will have to attend school and I think it the best thing ever happened to him, and now you must not be unhappy and brood over our absence. It won't take the time long to glide by and as we come home we will get you and then we will have such a nice time.

We will get your horse up and I will break him and you can ride John while I am gentling Loco. We will have Eddie with us and will be as gay and happy as the birds we claim at home. Now baby you can either stay with grandma or your Mamma Mc, just as you like and do the best you can until I come back, which won't be long. Tell Eddie that he can go down home with us and have a good time hunting and though I wish not to deprive Marion and ma of him for any length of time yet I must keep him a while. Love to ma and Marion.

Uncle Tom [Starr] has stood by me nobly in our trouble, done everything that one could do. Now baby I will write to you often. You must write to your grandma but don't tell her of this; and to your Aunt Ellen, Mamma Mc, but to no one else. Remember, I don't care who writes to you, you must not answer. I say this because I do not want you to correspond with anyone in the Indian Territory, my baby, my sweet little one, and you must mind me. Except auntie; if you wish to hear from me auntie will let you know. If you should write me, ma would find out where I am and Pearl, you must never let her know. Her head is overburdened with care now and therefore you must keep this carefully guarded from her. Destroy this letter as soon as read. As I told you before, if you wish to stay a while with your Mamma Mc., I am willing. But you must devote your time to your studies. Bye bye, sweet baby mine.

The letter, though relatively short, provides an outsize quantity of insight into what is otherwise a complex and enigmatic persona. For one, it demonstrates quite clearly that Belle did indeed have the classical education and level of refinement so often attributed to her. On a frontier where illiteracy was rampant and many could barely sign their own name, Belle's prose isn't just competent, it's marked by literary flourishes and poetic allusions. She puts emphasis on the positive aspects of the prison's mandatory education programs and ends the letter imploring her daughter to devote her time to her studies. Besides her erudition, the letter also supports the stories of her legendary horsemanship, complete with an offer to break a wild horse that is aptly named Loco. Breaking a mustang required considerable skill; the idea that Belle could do it casually and with great confidence is convincing evidence that she truly was an expert in all things equestrian.

But beyond reinforcing existing notions of the woman's unique skill set, this letter also testifies to the tremendous affection and devotion she had for her children—another frequent observation made by her contemporaries. Writing to her "Dear Little One," Belle's heart-pangs at having to leave her are almost palpable, and her desire, here openly expressed, of having her son Eddie leave his grandmother and his Uncle Marion in Missouri, to come and join her in Indian Territory upon her return, is nothing short of a yearning. She goes out of her way to allay her daughter's concerns by describing the prison as a pleasant place, "surrounded by beautiful grounds," and not the fortress of iron and stone that it actually was. She even downplays her sentence, claiming it to be nine months—the minimum possible under an early release for good behavior—instead of the full year that the judge had given her. These are clearly the words of a woman crushed by the shame of having to be apart from her children, a mother who can't bear the idea of not seeing her offspring for a year.

Present as well is a pervasive sense of fear, one that embroiders her sentences like a dark silk thread. Her tone verges on paranoia at times, especially in her instructions to Pearl: "Remember, I don't care who writes to you, you must not answer. I say this because I do not want you to correspond with anyone in the Indian Territory, my baby, my sweet little one, and you must mind me." Reading these words, one can't help but sense that Belle truly believed her daughter's life was in danger. They may well express the premonitions of a seasoned gangster who has made serious enemies in her recent dealings and who understands that her enemies might seek to harm Pearl as a means of personal retribution. The letter leaves no doubt that Belle viewed her time in prison as a moment of intense vulnerability, for herself and her family alike, and dreaded it accordingly.

Fortunately for Belle, however, the dramas and dangers that plagued her back at Younger's Bend appear not to have followed her inside the prison walls. Belle did her best to keep her head down, mind her own business, and stay out of trouble, serving her time at the Detroit House of Correction with as little friction as possible. Upon her arrival, she was given a cell in the designated women's block, issued a drab uniform to replace her flashy Western attire, and assigned a prison job weaving cane backings at the institution's chair factory. Sam, who had been sentenced to hard labor, was confined to an entirely different wing of the penitentiary, but the two were likely allowed to correspond with written notes—assuming Sam could read them—and perhaps even visit from time to time.

Most accounts, while thin on specific details, portray Belle as a model prisoner who got along well with both the staff and her fellow inmates, winning their admiration with her level of education and genteel Southern manners—the latter of which she seems to have been able to turn on or off, as the situation demanded. Years later, that same woman claiming to be Belle Starr's granddaughter, writing for the *Dallas Morning News* under the pseudonym of Flossie Doe, would make the claim that Belle had even tutored the warden's children in literature, piano, and French, of all things. While it's difficult to know how seriously to take such stories, they might explain claims that a grateful warden gifted her with an unlimited supply of paper and ink, with the stipulation that she write a book of her experiences. If that manuscript ever existed, it has been lost to the ages, but it is a compelling idea: Belle alone in her cell on a cold Michigan night, scribbling away beneath the halo of a single candle, doing her best to capture on paper the illicit thrills of riding across Union lines under the cover of darkness, of fleeing from a posse of enraged Creek warriors on horses laden with stolen gold, of drinking whiskey by firelight with a fugitive Jesse James, of snatching a deputy marshal's pistol when his guard was down and bursting forth from the prisoners' tent, gun blazing . . .

What a book it could have been.

BELLE'S CHARM OFFENSIVE WORKED. Sam's and her twelve-month sentences were commuted to nine months—including jail time served—for good behavior. And in what must have been a moment of jubilation, she was released from the Detroit House of Correction in time to spend Christmas with her daughter Pearl and the rest of the Reeds in Rich Hill. She surely wanted to see Eddie as well, but he had left the Reeds' home and gone to live in Dallas with his grandmother Eliza Shirley, around the time that Pearl had arrived from her temporary lodgings in Oswego, Kansas. Still, the chance to celebrate the festive season with her daughter and her former in-laws, surrounded by familiar faces in her native Missouri, must have been pure bliss for the newly liberated Belle. It's uncertain if Sam stayed with her or went on ahead to make preparations at Younger's Bend, but when Belle left Rich Hill for Indian Territory just after the holidays, she had not just Pearl by her side, but a fifteen-year-old orphan by the name of Mabel Harrison as well. Mabel's mother had been killed in a botched robbery attempt by outlaws not long before, and the girl had been living with the Reeds in the interim. Belle likely took pity on Mabel, and realizing that she owed the Reeds a prodigious debt for fostering both Pearl and Eddie at various times, agreed to take the girl off their hands and care for her until she was of age. Belle herself had just been given a second chance, and her magnanimous new attitude seems to have reflected that.

This feeling of salvation, of beginning life anew, carried through on her return to Younger's Bend. The noticeable gap in Belle's criminal record for the year 1884 suggests that she did make an effort to go straight following her release from the Detroit House of Correction, focusing her energies instead on being a better wife, mother, and member of the community. Tom Starr, ever the dutiful Godfather, had installed a caretaker to watch over the Younger's Bend farmstead in Sam and Belle's absence, but considerable labor was required to get it back into working order—hoeing cornfields, replanting vegetable gardens, repairing fences so that livestock could be returned. Together with Sam, Belle got to work. She also enrolled Pearl and Mabel at the school in nearby Briartown to further their education, and invested more of her own time in building relationships with her Cherokee and Choctaw neighbors. Belle became known for calling upon nearby families and visiting with sick relatives, gaining a reputation for her musical talents as a result. In all likelihood, this was a change in attitude that Tom Starr would have approved of, even if it did mean less criminal income. Belle's unabashed bravado had garnered his family all manner of unwanted attention from the authorities. Having his daughter-in-law close by at Younger's Bend, tending to farm chores and caring for her family, would have surely been preferable to her swaggering past the saloons of Fort Smith in full outlaw regalia, sneering at lawmen and flashing her pistols.

If Belle merited praise for her efforts or some form of karmic reward, in 1884, she got it. Because not long after her return to Younger's Bend and her subsequent renunciation of her old criminal life she received what may well have been the greatest news of her life: Eddie was coming home. The son whom she had hardly seen since the death of her first husband was finally coming to live with her at Younger's Bend. The family that been rent asunder in the chaos that followed Jim Reed's slaying would at last be together under one roof—her mother Eliza even agreed to travel north to Indian Territory from Dallas and deliver the thirteen-year-old boy in person. If Belle had been seeking a moment of redemption, then this was surely it. A chance to fix her mistakes, an opportunity to suture the still-raw wounds that seemed to make up so much of her past. Repapering the interior of the cabin, hauling over an extra bed frame on muleback from a neighbor's, going into Fort Smith to shop for a fresh suit of boy's clothes—as a mother, these preparations must have made Belle nothing short of ecstatic.

There was only one problem. Belle may have been a mother, but she was also a *gangster*. And as many a half-reformed gangster will testify, it's anything but easy to leave that life behind. Like a drug, the thrill of a big score is addictive, and the high of a successful heist is difficult to give up. Jim Reed and Jesse James had learned that the hard way, their careers—and lives—ending because they both wanted just one more big score. Every ounce of Belle's will may have been committed to walking the straight and narrow, but every fiber in her being was still calling for her to try and sate that implacable hunger that had haunted her since girlhood. By the end of 1884, she had held those urges at bay for the better part of a year, but how much longer would her willpower hold up? How much longer could she spend her nights stitching up homespun by the fireside or plucking a wild turkey for supper, instead of running a herd of stolen horses up to Catoosa or donning a bandit's black kerchief and holding up a stage? What good *was* an outlaw queen without a kingdom to rule over?

There is a story—first recorded as something of a folktale by S. W. Harman, although it was later confirmed by the cowboy in question—of an event that took place around this law-abiding juncture in Belle Starr's life. It occurred just outside of Fort Smith, near Skullyville, during a trip into town, perhaps to procure supplies for her son's arrival. A sudden gust of wind blew off Belle's hat and sent it cartwheeling across the prairie grass. A cowboy by the name of Charles William Kayser happened to be coming in the other direction, and she flagged him down, asking him to kindly get off his horse and fetch her windblown Stetson. Kayser, traveling in the wrong direction and in no hurry to go back and dismount, declined—which drew a reaction from Belle that was as violent as it was instinctual. She went for her pistol, clicked back the hammer, and "drew a bead" on the uncooperative young man, repeating her request, only this time with a string of oaths and the following addendum: "The next time a *lady* asks you to get down and pick up her hat, do as she tells you." Needless to say, the cowboy in question obliged, before hurrying on his way.

Belle Starr may have been on her best behavior, motivated by an abiding love for her husband, her daughter, and her half-estranged son, but her outlaw tendencies were itching to get out. And it wouldn't take long for the darkest of those urges to find their own volcanic release.

CHAPTER 8

Back with a Vengeance

O N THE ELEVENTH OF May, 1885, most likely alerted to its presence by a column of circling buzzards that rose high into the
air, a small search party of Choctaws discovered the body of a man
lying on the banks of the Poteau River. The mud-caked corpse was
already in a state of decomposition, its face half eaten away by scav-
engers. He was wearing a tailored cotton dress shirt, together with
a vest and matching pantaloons of twilled black cassimere. A thick
sandy mustache drooped around the corners of his grimacing lips,
while from his throat hung a necklace of dried rattlesnake tails.
And encircling his waist was a fully stocked cartridge belt and two
rather imposing .45 revolvers. The group of Choctaw men, huddled around the reeking corpse, prodding it with sticks, would
have known almost instantly: this was an outlaw. A *gangster.*

Their suspicions had been aroused four days earlier, when a mud-
died horse had been discovered tangled in briars along the riverbank
a few hundred yards upstream, an expensive saddle on its back and
a revolver strapped to its leather. Here, they realized, was the horse's
owner—and he was trouble. Wishing to rid themselves of both the
stench and the potential for criminal entanglements as quickly as
possible, the Choctaws buried the body nearby and washed their
hands of the incident, literally and figuratively. However, being responsible citizens of their nation, they did pass along a description
of the man and his possessions to tribal authorities, who in turn
passed them on to the *Fort Smith Elevator*, hoping that a published
account of the incident might assist in identifying the body.

It did. Because one of the many residents of Fort Smith and the neighboring Indian Territory who read the May 15 article over their morning coffee happened to be John West. The neighbor who had testified against the Starrs was now, just like his brother Frank, working as a deputy for Cherokee tribal police. And the blond mustache, the rattlesnake necklace, the full brace of pistols—these did more than just ring a bell. It was John Middleton. It had to be.

Middleton was as bad as they came, and as slippery, too. The twenty-nine-year-old Arkansan had first become a fugitive from the law at the age of eighteen, after burning down a courthouse, and his most recent act of infamy—a political assassination the year before in Texas involving a newly elected Lamar County sheriff and a shotgun blast to the chest—had set a bounty of close to $1,000 on his head. Following the same course as so many of the region's white outlaws, he had sought refuge in Indian Territory—more specifically, with Belle Starr. Lawmen from Texas had pursued Middleton into the Cherokee Nation, at which point the trail had gone cold. Which was precisely when they turned to the Wests for help. Together with the Texas lawmen, John West had already raided Belle's compound at Younger's Bend once, in a surprise sweep in mid-April that had yielded them nothing but the sight of an enraged Belle, gun belt strapped around her waist, treating them to her usual string of threats and invectives. Wherever she was secreting the outlaw Middleton—perhaps in one of the caves above or at the bottom of a shallow canyon below—it was a place they could not find. The Texans gave up and returned to Lamar County.

John West, on the other hand, had never called it quits. For him and his brother Frank, getting rid of the Starrs, Belle in particular, had become an obsession. That quiet year of 1884, following the couple's release from prison, had been nothing more than the calm before an inevitable storm. And the arrival of Middleton in Indian

Territory just before the New Year had brought Belle's thunder back to Younger's Bend. Rumors were circulating throughout the territory of horses being stolen, of heists being planned, of stick-ups occurring in various Indian nations—some even said that Belle Starr and John Middleton were lovers. As to how many of them were true, John West could not have said. But he was certain she was hiding the fugitive somewhere near Younger's Bend, and he knew that locating Middleton was the key to putting Belle and Sam back behind bars. And now, with the discovery of a body matching Middleton's description, appearing under somewhat suspicious circumstances—needless to say, John West didn't waste a minute in crossing into the Choctaw Nation and having the local authorities take him to the banks of the Poteau, to exhume the mysterious cadaver.

It was indeed John Middleton. John West identified him right away, despite the decomposed state of the corpse. His initial surmise was that the outlaw had simply fallen from his horse and drowned while trying to cross the rain-swollen waters of the Poteau River. West probably felt a tingle of disappointment at having lost the opportunity to apprehend the criminal alive and question him about Belle Starr before handing him over to the Texas authorities. But there was one minor detail—two, actually—that surely gave the Cherokee lawman a glimmer of hope. The saddle and the .45 found on the stray horse both belonged to Belle.

West had seen that very pistol belted to her waist during the April raid at Younger's Bend, and the saddle was one she had recently purchased in Eufaula. And as for the horse—it was stolen, reported as such by a nearby rancher named Albert McCarty. John West may have had nothing definitive linking Belle to any stickups or murders, nothing that would hold up in court. But he *did* have solid evidence linking Belle to yet another horse theft. And with a second conviction for the same crime, Judge Parker would never be so lenient; he'd put her away for years.

John West, surely in the mood to celebrate, likely rushed home to the Cherokee Nation to tell his brother Frank the news: Belle Starr was going *down*.

IF BELLE'S TROUBLES WITH Middleton and the stolen mare were piquing the interest of tribal and federal authorities, Sam's own exploits certainly weren't doing anything to dissuade them. In fact, he had returned to his criminal calling with an alacrity at least the equal of Belle's. In the spring of 1885, he fell back in with a former accomplice, Jack Spaniard, as well as with Felix and Looney Griffin—a couple of Cherokee stickup artists related to the Starrs through marriage. By late June, Sam was already a suspect in a mail robbery; by the end of October, he was wanted for holding up a Choctaw general store. And by mid-January, he was believed to have assisted in a jail break involving both Felix and Looney, only to get in a heated argument with the former and nearly blow his arm off with a shotgun. Realizing Younger's Bend was no longer safe for him in the wake of his crime spree, Sam had decided it best to go on the run and hide out with sympathetic kinfolk and neighbors, leaving Belle to mind the homestead and watch three teenagers without him, tasks she surely did not relish. And in addition to these quotidian chores, she also faced regular harassment from Frank and John West, who never missed an opportunity to inquire into her husband's whereabouts, as well as from the U.S. marshals, who also took to popping up unannounced at Younger's Bend, in the hope that they might catch her husband at home. According to one account, provided by a former Fort Smith U.S. marshal named Elias Rector, their visits became so onerous she decided to extract a modicum of revenge. Feigning hospitality, she offered the lawmen stew on one of their many visits, only to reveal afterward that she'd actually served them rotten "old rattlesnake," and that they ought to "go out and puke it up"—which evidently some of them did.

If the rattlesnake incident is true, while perhaps amusing to Belle, it certainly did nothing to lessen the marshals' desire to put her behind bars. Shortly after Sam went into hiding, she learned through one of her informants that a formal writ for her arrest pertaining to the Middleton affair had indeed been issued by the federal government. Wishing to avoid another desperate flight for the Osage hills, she chose instead to turn herself in. On January 21, 1886, Belle rode into Fort Smith and surrendered to authorities on the charge of horse theft, entering a plea of not guilty. She posted bond shortly thereafter and returned promptly to Younger's Bend, with a September court date hanging over her head, a wanted husband whose whereabouts she refused to divulge, and every white and Cherokee deputy between Fort Smith and Tulsa wanting to take her plumed hat and nail it to their wall as a trophy.

This might be the moment any normal criminal decided to tone things down for a bit and play by the rules, or to at least adopt the demeanor of a law-abiding citizen, for the sake of the upcoming trial if nothing else. By this point, however, Belle Starr was not any normal criminal. She was an outlaw queen, living up to the reputation that the local papers had given her. And far from toning things down, she decided instead to go all the way, committing an alleged act of criminal audacity while awaiting trial that—if true—would have put her not just in the same league as Cole Younger and Jesse James, but in another one entirely.

OF ALL THE CRIMES attributed to Belle Starr over the years, be they backed up by documentary evidence or conjured by the vivid imaginations of inventive storytellers, few have generated as much speculation, controversy, and debate as the Farrill robbery of February 27, 1886.

The heist itself was by no means extraordinary. It was a standard stickup, perpetrated by three armed individuals upon a farmer in the Choctaw Nation named Wilse Farrill. And only a relatively modest amount of treasure was actually stolen from Farrill in the end. What makes the crime stand out, however, even from among the many heists and holdups rumored to have involved the outlaw queen of Younger's Bend, is that this one actually had a material witness who singled out Belle Starr. Lila McGilberry, a young woman who lived at a neighboring farm and saw the outlaws up close, would later attest, as reported in the *Fort Smith Elevator*, to having seen a bandit with "a six-shooter in each hand, wearing pants and overcoat and a kind of white hat," and who she believed was "a woman dressed as a man." John and Frank West both knew that there was only one woman in all of Indian Territory—perhaps in all of America—willing to cross-dress and stage a holdup with a blazing white hat on her head and a pistol in each hand. And even more shocking than the bravado of Belle Starr to do such a thing while out on bond and awaiting trial was the fact that a witness was finally willing to attach Belle's name to a crime more serious than a horse theft.

More shocking still was the fact that the Farrill job didn't seem to be the only heist Belle had been planning. When John West led a posse of tribal police on a raid into Younger's Bend shortly after the robbery, they discovered a gang of nine men, known "cutthroats, robbers and horse thieves," hiding out on the premises, all members, evidently, of Belle Starr's gang. Sam was there as well, although he got away—according to an article that appeared in the *Muskogee Indian Journal*, the wanted fugitive eluded them by "jumping his horse off a bluff over twenty feet high, and swimming the river." Belle herself wasn't present for the fiasco; she very well may have been out acquiring ammo for their next big score. The same article also reported that "Belle Starr went to Eufaula a few days since and bought 100 rounds of cartridges, and from their maneuvers it is certain that they intended making a raid on somebody soon." The gang was assembled, the ammunition was being gathered—all that was missing was Belle.

The posse of lawmen decided to wait for her, though, a strategy that soon paid off. There's an oft-repeated story that one man, the sheriff William Vann, discovered a stolen peddler's pack full of spectacles in Belle's cabin, and as something of a cruel joke, greeted the oblivious Belle mockingly upon her arrival with a drawn weapon and four pairs of the eyeglasses all resting upon his nose. Belle responded with a drawn pistol, although John West was able to pry the revolver from her grip before she could get off a shot. The anecdote may be apocryphal; either way, the tribal police did not arrest Belle Starr in the end. As a white resident, their authority over her was limited, and Sam, the Cherokee citizen they *did* have the authority to apprehend and charge, had slipped through their fingers yet again. However, they passed on the evidence they had to the U.S. marshals in Fort Smith, and a formal warrant for her arrest was issued shortly thereafter, accusing her, in no uncertain terms, of being the "gang leader" in the robbery of Wilse Farrill. When the U.S. marshals returned to Younger's Bend several weeks later, this time around, Belle Starr, though still willing to openly mock them, did not put up a fight. Sam was still in hiding, and Eddie was away as well, but Pearl was present at the compound, and she accompanied her mother on horseback part of the way as deputy marshals Tyner Hughes and Charles Barnhill led their solemn, slow-clopping procession back to Fort Smith.

This moment—being taken yet again to Fort Smith in irons, being thrown yet again into a holding cell, being dragged yet again into the courtroom for a hearing—probably should have evoked in Belle Starr some kind of epiphany, some form of realization that perhaps it was time to put the gangster persona on hold, at least for the time being. But Belle's viability as a prominent earner of the Starr family's crime syndicate was predicated on that reputation, going back to her earlier dealings with Jesse James. And rather than hide or subdue it, the ever-defiant Belle Starr chose to flaunt it in the most public way possible. Upon posting bond a second time—the district court in Fort Smith was surprisingly lenient about such things by today's standards—Belle stayed in town for the last week of May, for a few days of shopping, paying social calls, and waging what in hindsight resembles a brilliant public relations campaign. She very openly bought herself new pistols, a pair of .45s to replace the ones that the deputies had taken off her during their raid, showing the public that she had nothing to hide. She posed for two now-famous photographs, one taken of her upon her horse while sporting an intimidating scowl and an even more intimidating revolver, and another at the side of Blue Duck, her old foot soldier from Catoosa, who was appealing a death sentence handed out by Judge Isaac Parker. And perhaps most important, she agreed to sit for an interview that would appear in the *Dallas Morning News* the following week, one in which she purposefully portrays herself as an outlaw, albeit with a moral code and stringent principles. The interviewer, upon noticing Belle's new revolvers, is treated to the following chestnut: "Next to a fine horse I admire a fine pistol. Don't you think these are beauties?" Following that, she goes on to profess her innocence in the two cases against her, although she does brazenly admit, in her own words:

You can just say that I am a friend to any brave and gallant out-law, but have no use for that sneaking, coward class of thieves who can be found in every locality, and who would betray a friend or comrade for the sake of their own gain. There are three or four jolly, good fellows on the dodge now in my section, and when they come to my home they are welcome, for they are my friends, and would lay down their lives in my defense at any time the occasion demanded it, and go their full length to serve me in any way.

It's an intriguing approach, and from the standpoint of legal strategy, well ahead of its time. Belle suspected that she would ultimately be judged by a jury of her peers, and that her peers were already well aware of her criminal reputation. Attempting to portray herself as an innocent housewife inadvertently sucked into a bad situation would never have convinced them, and more likely than not, would only have served to further invoke their ire. Her only real hope was to persuade the general public that she was a *noble* outlaw, a female Robin Hood, the kind of person who might steal from a faceless institution or a government body, but never from a hardworking frontier family. And likewise for her associates—she admits to being a friend to any "brave and gallant outlaw," but flatly rejects that "sneaking, coward class of thieves." This was very much the strategy Cole Younger and Jesse James had once employed to render their participation in organized crime more palatable for the masses, and it was a lesson that Belle Starr apparently took to heart, but then adapted to suit her own legal needs. Her intention was never to whitewash her reputation or even to deny her inherent criminal nature. Instead, she hoped to coax an acquittal from a panel of jurors who could be surprisingly tolerant of frontier violence, so long as it was unleashed upon mutual enemies and not upon them.

Belle's somewhat unorthodox legal strategy—it's hard to believe that her Fort Smith lawyers, Thomas Marcum and William Cravens, were thrilled at the idea of their client buying revolvers or giving confessional interviews—may have had another unintended consequence as well. Or perhaps it was very much intended, it's hard to say. Regardless, with the exception of the neighbor Lila McGilberry, none of the victims of the Farrill robbery were able or willing to finger Belle as one of the thieves at her hearing several weeks later. McGilberry did stick to her story, claiming: "I seen [the] defendant here yesterday and I knew it was her." Five other witnesses, however, including Wilse Farrill and his son, all claimed ignorance, stating that they were unable to identify any of the three criminals involved, although they believed that they had been robbed at gunpoint by three *men*—no one else recalled a female among them. The fact that McGilberry had stated from the onset that a non-Cherokee woman had been among the thieves, without any prompting or provocation, and that she later, under oath, directly identified Belle as that woman, certainly should have raised a few judicial eyebrows. After all, how often did white women in Indian Territory don men's clothing and execute stick-ups with a pistol in each hand? And then there was the detail of the white hat. Belle was known to wear a "broadbrimmed white man's hat" around town; even journalists had taken note of this unique fashion statement. Nevertheless, the contradictory testimony of the other five witnesses rendered hers all but moot. Lila McGilberry was the only one willing to openly accuse Belle Starr.

Regardless of whether intimidation tactics played a role, in the end, Belle's defense team didn't even need to call any of their witnesses. The Farrill case was dismissed right then and there based on a lack of evidence. And with the charges dropped, Belle was allowed to return to Younger's Bend, with only the September trial regarding the Middleton affair left to worry about. Sam was still on the run, but Pearl and Eddie were waiting at home, and seeing them would have been a priority after spending most of the summer in Fort Smith, defending herself against charges of horse theft and armed robbery. Perhaps a quick and celebratory stop in one of the town's many saloons was called for, after leaving the courthouse and before setting off for the Bend, in which case Belle almost certainly would have availed herself quite liberally of both its whiskey and its piano.

BELLE'S WINNING STREAK WOULD continue on through her larceny trial involving the stolen mare and John Middleton. On September 30, the verdict of not guilty was announced before the court of Judge Isaac Parker. Much like in her first trial for horse theft, it all came down to two decidedly different versions of how the horse in question ended up in her hands. Belle's version was that she and her daughter Pearl had decided to visit friends and relatives in Chickalah, using a covered horse wagon for the journey and agreeing to take their acquaintance John Middleton part of the way out of sheer generosity. Her husband Sam and son Eddie even offered to accompany them for the first part of the trip. At some point during the journey, Middleton decided to separate from the group—a verbal dispute with Pearl may have been to blame—and Belle was kind enough to assist Middleton in purchasing a horse from a local intermediary and in lending him a saddle and a gun. Once he had the necessary supplies, she simply bid him farewell and sent him on his way—a way that would lead him, unfortunately, straight to his death while trying to cross a rain-swollen river. A tragic turn of events, certainly, but nothing nefarious. According to Belle, she had no way of knowing that the mare she and Middleton "purchased" was in fact the stolen property of a local rancher named Albert McCarty.

The version supplied by the U.S. marshals, however, was decidedly different. In their account, Belle used a trip with her daughter in a covered horse wagon as a means of smuggling John Middleton out of Younger's Bend, so that she and Middleton could go about procuring more stolen horseflesh, including the mare upon which he ended up riding—and in doing so, somehow got himself killed. This was the case that the prosecution made, and by the standards of the day, it was a relatively strong one. They knew the horse was stolen, they had a saddle and a gun connecting her to the crime, and they had a prior conviction for horse theft to help support their claim. One key difference, though, between this trial and her previous one, was that in this instance, Belle was able to produce a witness to back up her version of events: a small-time white stock farmer named Fayette Barnett, who claimed she had bought the horse without realizing it was stolen. His testimony was suspect, to say the least, but it, coupled perhaps with Belle's very public insistence that an outlaw queen such as herself would never stoop so low as to steal an old one-eyed nag, was enough to sway the jury. Belle Starr, in the eyes of the law, was innocent. The U.S. marshals and the district attorney simply had nothing left to pin on her, nothing else that could stick. Like the very best of gangsters, she had bested "the feds" and beaten the rap.

This in and of itself must have enraged law enforcement officials, who knew full well exactly the kind of outlaw Belle Starr truly was. But there may have been an even deeper strain to their frustrations this time around, for one simple reason: apparently not everyone believed the death of John Middleton had been accidental. There have long been rumors, perpetuated in part by certain members of Middleton's own family, that it was a shotgun blast to the face, not buzzards, that had made Middleton's corpse all but unrecognizable. And that it was Belle Starr, not any rain-swollen river, that had ended his days—all to get a fortune of almost $20,000 he had allegedly stolen from the Creek Nation's treasury just before fleeing Younger's Bend. As to the veracity of this claim, there's no tangible evidence beyond hearsay to support it, and it very well could be one more strand of colorful fabrication in the tapestry of Belle Starr's legend. But it does beg pause. John Middleton was a seasoned frontiersman and an expert rider. The idea of his falling off his horse and drowning in a frequently traversed river at the very moment Belle was trying to smuggle him out of Younger's Bend as a legal liability, while not impossible, does stretch credulity. Also, the fact that the body was found such a short distance from the "tangled" horse, washed up on the riverbank just a couple of hundred yards downstream, does seem convenient. Then there's the issue of the horse itself. Western outlaws prided themselves on the quality of their mounts—just look at the regard Belle had for her prized horse Venus. The mare found near Middleton's body was branded, one-eyed, and unshod—this was a throwaway horse, probably acquired at the last minute, and certainly not the kind of mount an outlaw wearing a dress shirt and a black cassimere suit would typically have purchased and ridden. And while it does seem likely that the Wests would have been able to differentiate a shotgun wound from the work of buzzards, if the body was decomposed enough or if the killer had taken efforts to disguise their work, it could have gone unnoticed—or even unreported, if the Wests thought that the horse theft charge was more likely to stick than murder.

Granted, these observations are circumstantial at best. However, they do begin to nudge the needle of suspicion closer toward Belle's direction, raising the possibility that the death of John Middleton was in fact a murder, staged to look like an accidental drowning. But would she have actually done such a thing?

True, Belle Starr did have her code, her affinity for protecting "any brave and gallant outlaw." But is that what she considered Middleton to be? The man was an assassin, a murderer for hire

who had executed another man's political opponent for money back
in Texas. Belle's disdain for bounty killers, like the one who had
gunned down her first husband Jim Reed, was well established.
Also, there was the insinuation that Middleton had been involved
in some sort of dispute with Pearl during their journey. Given how
protective Belle was of her children, Pearl in particular, it's easy
to see how any kind of insult or threat directed toward her daughter could have soured her on John Middleton rather quickly. And
if there's any truth to the stories of the stolen Creek fortune jingling in Middleton's saddlebags—well, that would have tempted
a woman who had already seen her share of the $32,000 Watt
Grayson score squandered by her late husband at the racetrack. If
Belle did feel that Middleton owed her money, either for her participation or for her protection, after the hard lessons learned from
the Grayson debacle, she would not have been shy about using any
means at her disposal to collect it.

With all of this in mind, it's difficult to see the circumstances
of John Middleton's death as anything *but* suspicious. Accidental
drowning was simply not a common cause of death for notorious
wanted gangsters in the Wild West. A gunshot to the head, on the
other hand, most definitely was. Finding hard evidence of Middleton's murder, though, was apparently no easier in 1886 than it
is today. A simple charge of horse theft was the only one for which
there was anything resembling solid proof—and unfortunately for
law enforcement, it was a charge that Belle Starr was once again
able to beat in court.

This time around, however, Belle's legal victory was less of a
joyous occasion, for it came at a time of personal drama. In fact,
the trial itself may have been the least of her worries, as she sat
wringing her hands on the stiff wooden chairs of the Fort Smith
courthouse, listening to the district attorney drone on about one-
eyed mares and borrowed saddles. Belle had received a letter less

than two weeks before, with news that surely fractured the cool, dispassionate demeanor she usually put on before the jury. A short dispatch from Fort Smith that appeared in the *Arkansas Gazette* on September 17 divulges the unsettling contents of the missive:

> *Belle Starr, who is here on bond awaiting trial, received a letter today from her home on the Canadian stating that her husband, Sam Starr, who has been dodging the officers for several years, had been badly wounded in a conflict with the Indian police. Belle says her information is that the police wounded Sam and fired on him without demanding his surrender and killed his horse. He fought them some time before surrendering, about fifty shots being fired. Belle has permission from the court to be absent until next Wednesday, and will leave in the morning for her husband's bedside.*

With the trial over and her case won, Belle would have wasted no time in racing back to the Cherokee Nation to care for Sam, who had, despite the incident, still managed to elude capture by tribal police. As to the "conflict with the Indian police" described above, it far more closely resembled the vicious gangland-style hit the Ross faction had orchestrated against his grandfather, James Starr, during the Cherokee civil war than it did an organized raid by tribal authorities. And not surprisingly, at the helm of the attack was Frank West.

West and a posse of Cherokee and Choctaw lawmen had been trailing Sam along the banks of the South Canadian, determined to finally make their nemesis pay. Belle Starr may have been effectively off-limits to tribal persecution, but as a Cherokee, Sam Starr was well within their jurisdiction. After the outlaw son of old Tom Starr had slipped through their grasp time and time again, the tribal authorities—the Wests, more than anyone—had finally had enough. Frank West didn't even pretend to be on a mission to arrest the suspect. He wanted Sam dead, or at the very least, out of commission. Which was why, when he spotted Sam atop Belle's favorite mare Venus, wading across a cornfield in the ambered September twilight, he went in with guns blazing. A fierce firefight ensued, with a barrage of pistol and rifle shots blowing Sam off his horse and stippling the surrounding yellowed stalks with blood. When the Cherokee and Choctaw lawmen approached through the cornrows, crouched low, pistols drawn, they discovered a severely wounded and unconscious Sam, bleeding from bullet wounds to his head and side, lying just feet from the dead body of Venus. In trying to assassinate Sam Starr, Frank West had also killed Belle's favorite horse. West may have wanted to end things right then and there, but cooler heads prevailed—shooting at an armed fugitive wasn't *quite* the same thing as shooting an unconscious man already in police custody—and he and another lawman went off instead to find a farmhouse where they might hold the prisoner for the night, leaving him under the guard of two other members of the posse.

If Frank West had indeed possessed any dark inclination to deliver a coup de grace and finish Sam off in that twilit cornfield, he would soon regret not acting upon it. Sam, as it turns out, had been playing possum. The moment the guards' backs were turned, the "unconscious" Sam sprang to his feet and snatched one of their guns, backed them off, and leaped onto one of the posse's horses. Within seconds, the young Cherokee outlaw, the inheritor of Tom Starr's intractable and blood-drenched legacy, had thundered away, vanishing into the forest he knew better than anyone else, and shouting a final threat: for killing his wife's favorite saddle mare, Frank West would pay.

Sam may have been feigning unconsciousness, but the severity of his wounds was very real. West's .45 had punched a hole in his rib cage and taken a chunk out of his scalp, and it was only thanks to sheer stubborn will that he was able to make it to the home of one of his relatives before tumbling from his mount. Word had an uncanny way of being able to travel both quickly and quietly in Indian Territory, and so when Belle came galloping in from Fort Smith, fresh from her courthouse victory, she knew exactly where to find him. At his bedside, clutching his hand while tending to his wounds, Belle begged him to do the unthinkable: turn himself in. But *not* to the Choctaw or Cherokee authorities, who had already demonstrated the treatment Sam Starr could expect once he was in their custody. There were old hatreds at play, ancestral grudges that went back to the blood feuds following the Trail of Tears. The truce between the Starr clan and the tribal government that had existed for decades was no longer in effect—any member of the family who broke the law was now considered fair game. Belle had already lost one husband to a legally sanctioned assassination, and she was in no rush to lose another.

Sam's only chance, Belle argued, was to surrender to the U.S. marshals in Fort Smith, and be tried for the only *federal* crime he stood accused of: robbing a U.S. post office. This would likely mean getting sent back to Detroit for a few years, but it would also put him well beyond the reach of the tribal authorities—the Wests, in particular. Plus, there was always the chance that her recent lucky streak would hold; that perhaps the charges would be dropped against Sam as well, while still keeping him out of harm's way up until the hearing. Severely wounded and no longer able to make it on the run, Sam faced better odds of survival in a district courthouse or a federal prison. To remain in the Cherokee Nation unprotected after what had transpired with the Wests was to sign his own death warrant.

Belle may not have been the only one pressing for Sam to turn himself in. After decades of generally turning a blind eye to Tom Starr's illicit activities—a tolerable amount of smuggling and rustling was a small price to pay to keep the peace with the aging Cherokee warlord—the U.S. marshals were finally starting to turn up the heat, almost certainly as a result of Belle's courthouse triumph and Sam's refusal to surrender. A number of old outstanding warrants for Tom Starr's arrest, all related to whiskey smuggling, were still on the books, and by the fall of 1886, word was making its way to Indian Territory that the elder Starr's protected status was not to last—the threat of arrest was now looming. Realizing he was cornered and that his family members would only continue to suffer, Sam finally relented, taking Belle's advice and agreeing to turn himself in. On October 4, 1886, Belle negotiated his surrender to the U.S. marshals in nearby Briartown. Three days later, the marshals escorted the outlaw, bandaged and wincing, into Fort Smith. Belle insisted on accompanying them, riding alongside the procession and sporting, as always, her full outlaw regalia, pistols and all.

From there things went smoothly. Sam was arraigned and granted bond to return to Younger's Bend, although the outlaw couple didn't go home right away. The Seventh Annual Fair of Western Arkansas and the Indian Territory was scheduled to begin the following week, and while there's not any substantive documentary evidence to support it, most of the early biographies and oral traditions have Belle agreeing to participate in a sort of Wild West show as part of the festivities. While performing, according to one report, Belle entertained the crowd by "riding a horse bareback at full gallop," and breaking "clay pigeons and glass balls with rifle fire while in motion, varying the performance by leaping from the animal while moving at full speed." Belle's fondness for public spectacle—particularly if it cemented her standing as an outlaw queen—coupled with her known abilities as a markswoman and equestrian do make the account seem credible, although there does not appear to be any mention of her exploits in the local papers. If the stories of her participation are true, however, the show must have been a sight indeed: Belle in her black riding habit and plumed hat, streaking across the arena on her horse, picking off dangling Christmas ornaments with her Winchester, springing from her mount, only to land with catlike assurance on her feet, and blowing a few clay pigeons to bits before springing back onto her horse the next pass, never breaking stride except to curtsy and bow before the delirious crowd.

It is possible, though, that there was more to the story; that perhaps her aspirations were not *strictly* performative. One common feature of such shows was the execution of staged holdups, often involving local celebrities or law enforcement for a touch of ironic humor. In *Hell on the Border*, S. W. Harman makes the claim that during the fair, Belle planned on using her participation in a mock stagecoach robbery to actually assassinate the district attorney, W. H. H. Clayton—a man she had hated ever since he had ridiculed her husband Sam's illiteracy while taking the stand at their first trial. According to Harman, she intended to replace one of her blank cartridges with a live round and shoot the unsuspecting DA during the reenactment. Her plan was foiled, however, when a last-minute roster change prevented Clayton from participating in the mock holdup. There's no documentary evidence to support Harman's claim, and it's certainly possible Belle first told the story as something of a joke—it does match her own dark brand of violent frontier humor. But it's also possible that the U.S. attorney for the Western District of Arkansas and Indian Territory narrowly missed an exceedingly vindictive and well-placed bullet, delivered through a rattling stagecoach window, courtesy of a galloping outlaw queen.

THE COUPLE RETURNED TO Younger's Bend at the conclusion of the festivities, with the knowledge that due to his surrender, Sam Starr was now under the auspices of the federal government, safe from harassment by Cherokee authorities. The trial, originally scheduled to take place in November, was in the end delayed until February, meaning that Sam and Belle could spend the holidays together at home with Eddie and Pearl. Mabel, their orphaned houseguest, had agreed to spend Christmas with the Reeds in Missouri.

December in the Cherokee Nation brought with it a number of much-anticipated social events, none bigger than the annual Christmas dance hosted by the Surratt family, just across the Canadian River. String bands, whiskey punch, crackling fires—it was exactly the kind of spirited musical gathering that Belle adored. And while the shadow of Sam's impending court date definitely loomed over them, she probably saw the occasion as a time to celebrate their relative good fortune. In addition to her own recent legal victories, which effectively cleared her name, her husband seemed to be safe. Her children were by her side, her family at last reunited for the holidays after years of separation.

On the evening of December 17, the four of them crossed the river by ferry to attend the party, in a chill drizzle that slowly, as the darkness set in, changed first to sleet and then to snow. The mood would have been jovial as they pitched through the flakes across the wind-tossed waters; bottles were probably passed, songs were almost certainly sung. The entrance to the Surratts' ranch was graced by a roaring bonfire, while on the hill above, the glow of cabin windows and the keen of country fiddles announced to all who arrived that the festivities had begun.

Wet coats were shed and holiday greetings shared in a warm mixture of Cherokee, Choctaw, and twangy frontier English. Sam, who had been in hiding for the better part of two years, could finally show his face in public, which surely elicited some good-humored jokes from friends and relatives, amid plenty of backslaps and offers of whiskey. Some accounts say it was a pedal organ, others a small, upright piano, but nearly all have Belle taking a seat before the keys and joining in with the band as they fiddled and strummed for the growing assortment of dancers, including Eddie and Pearl, who joined their neighbors on the floor. It must have been euphoric for Belle, almost intoxicating in its intensity, a time to lose herself in the full wonder of the moment—and she probably did. At least, until a whisper reached her ears, one that surely made her fingers go still and turn to wood upon the ivory keys.

Frank West had just arrived at the party. He could be seen from the cabin door, waiting at the base of the hill, in the feverish glow of the bonfire below. The man who had tried to murder her husband; the man who had killed her favorite horse. Some accounts have her telling Sam to "go down and get that son of a bitch." It's also possible he acted on his own initiative, unable to contain his rage. But either way, Samuel Starr, son of the Cherokee warrior Thomas Ta-Ka-Tos Starr, great-great-great-grandson of the bullet-chewing Ghigau Nanye'hi, did not hesitate. He did not waver. As the other revelers looked on, he stepped over the cabin's threshold and into the darkness and damp snow beyond, marching down the hill, panting out plumes of steam, calling out his mortal enemy, his hand already creeping toward the handle of his revolver. Guests began fleeing; the music came to a crashing halt. Threats were exchanged and both men drew their pistols—both men managed to get off just one shot.

Sam's bullet ripped through Frank West's neck, killing him almost instantly. He staggered a few steps and then fell to the ground. West's bullet tore into Sam with such force that it passed through him and struck the jaw of a twelve-year-old boy who had been running for cover behind him. Despite being shot clean through the heart, though, Sam managed to stay on his feet a few seconds longer—just long enough to see his vendetta completed and the blood debt paid. Just long enough to know that he had kept the promise made back in that cornfield. Then he stumbled and fell dead as well, which left two fresh corpses lying still in the firelight.

On the brink of her fortieth year, Belle Starr had become a widow for the second time.

WHEN SAM STARR CHOSE to challenge Frank West to their brief but fateful duel, he did so to satisfy his own thirst for revenge and to defend his wife's honor. He was all but obliged to do so, by the warrior code of the Cherokee and the larger code of the American West. But in doing so, he also deprived his wife of the last vestige of protection and legitimacy she had enjoyed as a guest of the Cherokee Nation. Tom Starr, the patriarchal "Godfather" who had welcomed her initially into the fold and made her part of the family, was already out of the picture, sentenced to a year and a half at the penitentiary in Southern Illinois for smuggling whiskey—federal authorities had finally followed through on their threats, slapping the elder Starr with trumped-up charges, and he was no longer there to defend her. With Sam now gone as well, Belle's honorary status as a citizen of the Cherokee Nation was in danger. The title she had been granted upon marriage was more akin to a modern-day green card or long-stay visa—marriage had allowed her to live in the Cherokee Nation indefinitely, albeit without access to the benefits and rights of a full tribal member. As a white citizen of the United States of America, Belle was still, to an extent, an outsider. She had capitalized on this fact to great effect when it came to dodging tribal police, whose powers to detain or prosecute her were severely curtailed. Few of the tribal leadership sought to invoke the ire of a historically punitive U.S. federal government.

The same written laws and unspoken rules that had previously protected her, however, now worked to her distinct disadvantage. Cherokee headright-based land grants, dispensed by the Cherokee National Council, lasted a lifetime—that is, after all, how Sam had acquired title on Younger's Bend following the death of the homestead's previous tenant, Big Head. But Sam's tribal contract had been rendered null and void the moment Frank West's bullet tore through his chest. Belle herself was obviously not a Cherokee, and she and Sam had produced no children, meaning that her claim on Younger's Bend was now legally up for debate. The Cherokee courts could have leaned in her direction or even granted a special dispensation, but given her criminal history and reputation for troublemaking, there was little chance of that happening. And the principal chief at the time, Dennis Bushyhead—a Princeton-educated elite of mixed European and Cherokee ancestry who had supported the John Ross faction following the Trail of Tears—had no love whatsoever for the Starr family or the dangerous outlaws they sheltered. Belle's Cherokee and Choctaw neighbors may have been extremely fond of her, but tribal leadership wanted her gone. And with Sam's death, they had a simple judicial means of taking her home and deporting her for good, without bloodshed and without provoking the federal government in Fort Smith. Belle's position at Younger's Bend—and thus her position as a resident in Indian Territory—had never been more imperiled. The middle-aged mother of two found herself, with the crack of those two pistol shots on that cold December night, in an extremely vulnerable position. Eviction seemed imminent, and without Younger's Bend, she quite literally had nothing. Her entire life was at stake.

For someone like John West, who had spent years trying to rid the Cherokee Nation of Sam and Belle Starr, *and* who had just lost a brother to the former's vindictive revolver, the just deserts of the moment must have been especially delicious. To see the woman who had paraded through the streets of Eufaula and Fort Smith, flaunting her expensive gangster attire and openly boasting of her criminal deeds, evicted at gunpoint from her home following a futile court battle and left weeping and destitute on the street—it was the next best thing to watching her hang or putting her permanently behind bars. With Tom and Sam Starr both out of the picture, and with foot soldiers like Blue Duck, Jack Spaniard, and the Griffins all locked up or in hiding, Belle was the last piece of the puzzle. She was essentially all that remained of the Starr clan's once-mighty criminal enterprise.

However, if John West and other like-minded tribal police were expecting to see Belle removed from Younger's Bend and ejected from Indian Territory, they were soon to be disappointed. They would get to see neither of these things. What they would get, however, with the advent of the year 1887, was a surprise wedding.

Belle Starr had outmaneuvered them yet again.

THE REASON WHY BELLE Starr came to marry Jim July—soon to be Jim Starr, at Belle's own behest—is not hard to guess. It was a last-ditch yet highly effective tactic to secure her tenure at Younger's Bend. As to *how* she came to marry the part Cherokee, part Creek youth almost fifteen years her junior, that's not quite so easy to say. Most accounts portray Jim July as something of a lost soul who Tom Starr had taken in, after being bounced around the neighboring Indian Nations for most of his life—a fact that was reflected, evidently, in Jim July's fluency in all five languages of the "Civilized Tribes." He may have been a low-ranking foot soldier in the family's crime organization as well, possibly aiding in whiskey smuggling and horse theft operations, although he didn't appear to have any criminal record when he moved into Younger's Bend at Belle's invitation. But regardless of how she came to know the twenty-four-year-old, Belle and Jim became husband and wife under both tribal custom and common law, in an arrangement that was mutually beneficial. Belle Starr was once again married to a tribal citizen, thus renewing her "green card" in Indian Territory and legitimizing her claim on Younger's Bend, and Jim July, a rootless young man with few financial prospects, suddenly had a sprawling homestead to call his own. But there's no reason to believe their relationship was strictly transactional. There was almost certainly a sexual element as well, which would come to cause enormous problems with Belle's children, Eddie in particular, who did not relish the idea of living in the same household as a stepfather just seven years his senior. Beyond that, not a great deal is known about Jim July Starr, aside from the facts that he had at least some education courtesy of local Indian schools; that he wore his hair long in the traditional fashion, sometimes braided with rattlesnake tails; and that like most of the men in Belle's life, he had a predilection for criminal behavior. He doesn't seem to have been any great gunslinger or arch-outlaw, but he was Belle's ticket to keeping her family together at Younger's Bend, and for her, that was enough.

Her teenage children, however, didn't necessarily see it the same way, and in some regards, his presence only drove Belle and her progeny farther apart. There was a tremendous amount of friction in the Starr household through the years of 1887 and 1888, due in large part to the sudden arrival of an obviously young and ill-equipped stepfather, but also simply because of the psychological damage Belle's absenteeism as a parent had inflicted upon her offspring. Belle had seldom been more than half a mother to Pearl, and to Eddie, she'd hardly been a mother at all. After years of the recurring neglect that came with her criminal lifestyle, Belle's two children had grown resentful and unruly. And not surprisingly, teenage rebellion ensued.

For James Edwin, better known as Eddie, his defiance began as a flirtation with exactly the same kind of criminal mischief that had resulted in the death of both of his namesakes. Staying out late, associating with a rough crowd, "borrowing" horses—for Belle, it must have felt like a very unpleasant form of déjà vu, seeing her son engaged in teenage shenanigans so akin to those that had gotten her brother Edwin Benton shot off a stolen horse and her husband Jim Reed literally blown apart by a bounty hunter. And in classic Belle Starr fashion, she did not respond well to it. According to oral traditions, the enraged mother was not above administering "whuppings" to her son with her leather riding quirt when she lost her temper. There's even one account, possibly invented but at the very least worth mentioning, of Belle discovering that her son had pulled a gun on the local postmaster; her response was to train her own pistol on Eddie, pull a bullwhip off the wall, and "literally cut the blood out of her son's back and shoulders." This tale's veracity aside, stories of Belle's harsh discipline appear often. And while corporal punishment, even with switches and belts, was standard fare for most Upland Southerners at the time, a mother thrashing her teenage son with a riding whip would have surely raised eyebrows.

If Belle hoped to quell or cow her delinquent son with such treatment, it did not work. By the spring of 1888, a fully grown and now mustachioed Eddie Reed had begun riding with a number of local troublemakers. On July 11 of that year, one of those troublemakers, an aspiring Creek horse thief and relation to Jim July by the name of Mose Perryman, tricked Eddie into joining him on a horse stealing run, only to shoot him in the head while he was sleeping, the bullet "entering near the nose and coming out at the ear," according to the U.S. marshal that attended to the case. As for the motive, there was never a clear one, although simply cutting him out of the score seemed to be the most plausible.

Miraculously, Eddie survived the shooting and was able to fully recover at Younger's Bend, thanks in no small part to his mother's own nursing. However, upon recuperating from the blast to the face at point-blank range, he was made privy to an unsettling discovery: that very same U.S. marshal who had investigated the shooting had also sworn out a writ for his arrest. Eddie may well have been shot in the head, by a relative of his own stepfather at that, but he had also been in possession of a stolen horse at the time of the shooting. Suddenly he was wanted for larceny, and while Jim July and his Perryman kin initially offered to assist with his defense costs in exchange for not testifying against Mose, that informal deal soon fell apart, creating a rift between Eddie and Jim July that would make the seventeen-year-old's residence at Younger's Bend extremely uncomfortable. Eddie had been close to Sam Starr, even viewing him as a true stepfather, but he had never liked Jim July, who he regarded as more of a hanger-on and gold digger than a legitimate parental figure. Being shot in the face by one of July's Creek kinsmen certainly did nothing to lessen his distaste for the man, and the situation at home that fall and winter, while recovering from a massive head wound and awaiting his court date, must have been extremely tense, if not flat-out contentious.

Pearl's form of teenage rebellion, on the other hand, while less overtly violent, seemed to have enraged Belle even more, if for no other reason than it affected the long-suffering mother in such a personal way. Eddie's misdeeds may have reminded her of her younger brother and dead husband, but Pearl's poor decisions smacked clearly of her own. Pearl had developed a taste early on for socializing, dancing, and riding about the countryside in search of adventure. Mabel Harrison, the teenage orphan from Missouri whom Belle had been caring for, still lived off and on at Younger's Bend, and together, she and Pearl took advantage of

Belle's frequent absences and visits to Fort Smith to sneak out. Much like her mother, Pearl got involved with a young man with limited experience and prospects, and *just* like her mother, became pregnant at a young age. There is an early version, told in glimmering purple prose in S. W. Harman's *Hell on the Border*, that paints that relationship as something of a Shakespearean tragedy, a sort of frontier *Romeo and Juliet*, with a passionate and dreamy-eyed Pearl coming under the spell of a promising but penniless local youth. The new beau is immediately rebuked by Belle for being an insufficient match for her beloved daughter—which results only in secret trysts, an unexpected conception, and a clandestine wedding. A similar version is also repeated in the Flossie Doe article that was published by the *Dallas Morning News* in 1933, an account allegedly written by Belle's actual granddaughter, who had heard secondhand versions of the story:

> *Pearl, at this time, was 17 and in love with a young man two years her senior, a part Cherokee from one of the best families. The young fellows in that community were nice looking, they dressed well, they had average educations and most of them were excellent horsemen. About the only objection Belle could have to Pearl's suitor was that he was a poor boy, but she openly fought the affair. Her consuming desire was for Pearl to marry a rich man—"A man with at least $25,000."*
>
> *So, my mother told me, she and my father went to old Doc Bullard, who married the young people of the community, and were married secretly.*
>
> *One night, in about January 1887, Mabel and Pearl had ridden into Briartown. A Mr. Kraft, a friend, had dropped in to talk to Belle. Belle suggested that they play a joke on the girls by dressing up in sheets and meeting them on the road. Mr. Kraft said, "Can it be, Belle, that you don't know—?"*

And, in this way, my coming was announced to Belle Starr. No one can realize the bitterness that she tasted that night, or picture what this meant to her. Pearl had always been her pride and the center of her ambitions—she wanted Pearl's life to have all the things her own had missed, and in the bright dreams she had held for her daughter, there had been no place for Younger's Bend.

These versions go on to include romanticized details such as a distraught Belle discouraging her daughter's swain with a series of forged letters, a last-minute arranged marriage with a wealthy livery man that doesn't pan out, and a threat to give away her daughter's child, upon its birth, to roving gypsies. How much of these accounts is true is hard to say, although it seems safe to assume a fair amount of scrubbing and embellishment were included to hide a far more prosaic, albeit socially taboo, story. Again, keeping in mind that this was a time and place where the term "shotgun wedding" was not a mere figure of speech, a more probable version is that Pearl, while attending a local dance party with Mabel, met a young man, engaged in a sexual relationship that resulted in an unplanned pregnancy, and was left in the lurch after said young man turned tail and fled, fearing for his life if Belle discovered his identity. One small detail, subtly included in the S. W. Harman version, however, does smack of the truth. While visiting Fort Smith with her mother, Harman claims that "from the privacy of her room Pearl heard others calmly discussing a plan for her to meet a noted Fort Smith physician." Pearl, who objected to the idea, confronts her mother, crying: "Mamma, I have heard all, and I will never consent; *I am afraid.*" When it became apparent that Pearl was unwilling to agree to an abortion, a decision was reached—possibly by Pearl, although given the friction that would ensue, more likely by Belle—that the unmarried and pregnant teen was best off staying with the Reed in-laws of Missouri until the birth of the child, at which point Pearl would give it up for adoption. This arrangement came to pass, and on April 22, 1887, Belle Starr became a grandmother—to a granddaughter the then-thirty-nine-year-old outlaw would never come to know.

Like many engaged in organized crime, Belle wanted a different kind of life for her children—a better life. She may have gloried in her own outlaw reputation, but she was no stranger to the toll the lifestyle took. She had already lost two brothers, two husbands, and who knew how many friends and lovers to outlaw violence, and the thought of losing a son as well was more than she could bear. And as for her daughter, while the possibility of Pearl's dying from a gunshot wound to the head may have been less of a pressing concern, Belle certainly didn't want to see Pearl trapped in a doomed marriage with a feckless ne'er-do-well, sacrificing her ambition and independence in the process—a mistake whose bitter flavor Belle knew all too well.

As good as her intentions may have been, however, her "tough love" approach came at a steep cost. By the summer of 1888, she was barely on speaking terms with either of her children. Ironically, Eddie's gunshot wound may have healed the rift, at least to an extent, and brought the family back together. After more than a year of hiding from her mother and refusing to respond to letters, Pearl, having learned of Eddie's shooting, finally returned to the Cherokee Nation to help care for her brother and aid in his recovery—without her infant daughter, who was still in the care of Reed in-laws and awaiting adoption. The situation, with the entire family living together in the cabin at Younger's Bend once again, each nurturing their own private resentments and feelings of betrayal, must have been awkward, at least at the onset. By the end of the summer, however, things seemed to have improved considerably. Eddie was up walking again, almost fully recovered and beginning to prepare for his October arraignment, and Belle and

Pearl were once again attending social events together. Toward the end of September, they even spent a day at the International Indian Fair held in the Creek Nation, with both mother and daughter participating in the equestrian competition. Belle, never one to shy away from the spotlight, even agreed to be "substituted as the leading attraction," according to an article published the following week in the *Vinita Indian Chieftain*, when a group of much-anticipated "wild Indians" failed to show as advertised.

As to why the so-called "wild Indians" mentioned by the Cherokee publication—that is to say, Native Americans adhering to a traditional precolonial culture and living beyond the reach of federal authority—did not materialize to perform at the fair, there could have been all manner of explanations, although one may have been that by 1888, there just weren't any left. The West that Belle Starr had been born into and lived in most of her life had changed considerably in the preceeding decades. By the end of the 1880s, it was no longer the same uncolonized frontier—the Wild had been draining out of it for years. The buffalo, which had numbered somewhere between 30 and 50 million when a young Belle had first arrived in Texas in 1864, had been slaughtered on a scale that almost defies the powers of human comprehension. By 1888, there were fewer than *a hundred* free-roaming bison left. The Plains tribes, whose nomadic existence relied on those herds, had witnessed an almost total societal collapse as a result, and faced no choice but to surrender to life on federally allotted reservations to avoid mass starvation. Even the dreaded war machine of the Comanche, which had conquered all rival tribes, withstood almost two full centuries of European colonial expansion, and even persisted in a weakened state through several epidemics of Old World diseases, finally crumpled when its sacred fuel, the wild buffalo, vanished from the American plains. Quanah Parker, that last great Comanche war chief, had gathered the remaining bands of Co-

manche holdouts and surrendered to the U.S. Army in 1875, realizing it was the only way to save what was left of his people. By
1888, what had been one of the greatest mounted military forces in
history, a tribe that had numbered 20,000 strong and controlled
an empire that covered roughly 25,000 square miles, was reduced
to just a few thousand survivors living in poverty on a barren patch
of land in what is today southwestern Oklahoma. This program,
this series of federal practices and policies, was not happenstance
or mere side effect. It was deliberate and it was planned. The extirpation of the buffalo served the American colonial project of
Western expansion in two particularly brutal ways: it freed up the
land for agricultural interests, and it kick-started a campaign of
ethnic cleansing that would remove Indigenous resistance from
the equation.

The effects on white colonial civilization were almost immediate. Across the West, grasslands were becoming farmland; the clapboard frontier towns were becoming brick-bound cities, designed
to handle new markets built around the commodities that all that
fresh farmland and grazing land produced. Dallas, the gritty cow
town where Belle had once raced her horses through the streets
and cavorted with famous rustlers, was, by 1888, a thriving cotton-
market metropolis of almost 40,000 people, complete with electric lights, telephone lines, paved streets, and public parks. Simply
put, the West that Belle had known for most of her life, which had
provided the general lawlessness and vacuum of authority enabling
the criminality of her cohort, had by the final years of the 1880s
all but vanished. The invention in 1874 of practical machinery for
mass-producing barbed wire had eliminated much of the need for
cattle drives, as well as for the cowboys who presided over them.
The ensuing rail boom tore down obstacles of distance, bringing
over 2,440 miles of track to Texas alone by 1879, and spelling the
end for stagecoaches in much of the Southern Plains and Ozark

Plateau. And although it was still a year in the offing, the Indian Appropriations Act of 1889, signed by President Grover Cleveland under mounting political pressure, would result in a land rush that flooded Indian Territory with white farmers, fundamentally altering its character and making Oklahoma's eventual statehood all but inevitable.

For Belle Starr, a career gangster of the old Western stripe, the writing was on the wall. Soon there would be no one left to rob, nowhere left to hide. All but gone were the days of masked bandits holding up stagecoaches or rustling herds of cattle, to then flee on horseback into the lands of the Osage or the Cherokee with a posse of lawmen on their tail. No, the *new* breed of Western gangsters weren't gunslingers at all. They were commodities traders, railroad barons, representatives of cattle interests and mining syndicates, and yes, politicians. They didn't defy authority—they *were* the authority. And they had no qualms using their economic and political power to crush anyone or anything that stood in their way. The Osage murders of the 1920s—committed by contract killers at the behest of a wealthy white rancher and corrupt political boss named William K. Hale, in order to steal lucrative oil headrights from tribal members—provide the perfect example of what frontier gangsterism was soon to become. It was no longer a question of a hardscrabble Appalachian migrant or a hard-up Cherokee refugee pulling a six-shooter on the local cowpuncher or bank teller to make off with a few bucks. Instead, it would be the ranchers and the bankers themselves committing highway robbery, sometimes to the tune of millions of dollars, with an army of Pinkertons at their disposal should they be needed. In order to survive in the new West, an old-school outlaw like Belle Starr would have to adapt. Even the days of the horse were coming to a close—the first American-made gas-powered car, designed by the Duryea brothers in Springfield, Massachusetts, was only five years away.

Fortunately for Belle Starr, though, something had happened the previous year that would ease her transition. In late July, in a number of periodicals from across Indian Territory, including the *Muskogee Indian Journal*, the following letter was reprinted, at the request of the United States Indian agent, Robert L. Owen—the official liaison between the federal government and the Cherokee Nation:

Mrs. Belle Starr
Oklahoma, I.T.

Madam: The complaint against you for harboring bad characters has not, in my opinion, been established and is now dismissed.

I hope sincerely that you will faithfully carry out your promise to this office not to let such parties make your place a rendezvous.

Yours Respectfully,
Robert L. Owen
United States Indian Agent

For more than a century, Western historians and Belle Starr biographers have interpreted this letter as an ultimate victory for authorities and as the final nail in the coffin of an exhausted outlaw's fading career. To them, this missive represents the triumph of tribal and federal power over a wayward woman who had at last been "scared straight." According to their version of the story, Belle Starr, beaten into submission after years of harassment and court dates and no longer able to cope with the pressure, has finally given up a life of crime to be a good citizen—and this letter, a sort of passive-aggressive ultimatum, proves it.

With only one problem: it doesn't make any sense. First, there's no reason, by their logic, a United States Indian agent would bother to write such a letter, and second, there's even less of a reason they would seek to have it published in Indian Territory newspapers for the general public to see. *Unless* the letter didn't represent a smirking federal victory at all, but rather a truce of sorts, akin to the peace accord that had been reached between tribal and federal authorities and Tom Starr nearly half a century before. Just as with Tom Starr, Cherokee tribal police together with U.S. marshals had tried to stop Belle Starr's criminal career and had even attempted to remove her from Indian Territory, but had come up short each and every time. After countless investigations and three separate court appearances had failed to result in any meaningful convictions, the district attorney at Fort Smith, W. H. H. Clayton, almost certainly wanted nothing to do with this belligerent black-clad widow who refused to back down. The Cherokee National Council—one of their own tribal police already killed on Belle's behalf, their legal case to remove her from Younger's Bend having crumbled before their eyes—was also surely in no hurry to tangle with her again. Contrary to what many a Wild West chronicler has claimed before, Belle Starr was not the loser in all of this—not by a long stretch. If anything, she was the victor. And this letter, penned by a U.S. Indian agent and purposefully published for the world to see, makes much more sense as a public declaration of *their* surrender. As was the case with the peace treaty involving Tom Starr that ended the Cherokee civil war, as long as Belle Starr, his daughter-in-law, agreed to limit and disguise her illicit activities just enough to provide some plausible deniability, they in turn were willing to turn their heads and look the other way. It simply wasn't worth their while to keep pursuing her; it had already cost them too much time, money, and blood.

As it so happened, the de-wilding of the West and Belle's conditional truce with local authorities coincided nicely with an economic scheme that was increasing in popularity in the Choctaw and Cherokee nations. Officially, white settlers were not permitted in that corner of Indian Territory unless they were in possession of a special permit, which could be obtained through marriage, through some form of adoption, or thanks to professional need—doctors, schoolteachers, and mechanics were especially in demand. The Cherokee National Council in particular was exceptionally careful about managing the influx of white settlers and ensuring that tribal lands could never be privately sold to outside individuals, understandable given the painful lessons they had learned back east. This is why land was communally owned by the tribe, and lifetime land rights were granted based on tribal membership—to ensure that what had happened in Georgia, Tennessee, and North Carolina could not be repeated in their new home west of the Mississippi. This meant that someone like Belle or any of her Choctaw or Cherokee neighbors had no legal way to sell off the land that they had been granted, to tribal citizens or white settlers. It was not theirs to sell.

There was, however, a legal loophole, one that had been on the books since the late 1860s, although not until the 1880s would tribal members begin taking advantage of it en masse. Selling tribal land may have been forbidden, but leasing tribal land to sharecroppers was not. Which meant that Choctaw and Cherokee citizens in possession of tribal landholdings were legally permitted to lease out their land to tenant farmers in exchange for a percentage of the harvested crop, oftentimes with the caveat that the tenant was required to improve the settlement in some constructive way. This arrangement brought a flood of much-needed economic capital into Indian Territory, not to mention cheap labor. But ironically, most of that cheap labor consisted of landless white settlers who were willing to sharecrop for Native American landlords because they had exhausted their other options.

Belle Starr, the educated offspring of a genteel Southern belle and an aspiring Southern gentleman, did *not* like these people. Not that she was an elitist per se—she was more than accustomed to riding with rough characters, and many of her comrades, white and Indigenous both, would certainly have been illiterate. But to Belle, her friends and neighbors had values, a specific moral code; they had their own culture and traditions, not to mention a certain kind of backwoods wit and charm. These new arrivals, she felt, did not. Many of them were impoverished migrants from the Deep South, swamp folk or plantation "crackers," and lacking, at least in her eyes, in the frontier ingenuity and up-country self-reliance she associated with people rooted in Appalachia and the Ozarks. In the biographical sketch that was given to John F. Weaver of the *Fort Smith Elevator*, most likely in the year 1887, she had the following to say regarding her new neighbors:

> *I have considerable ignorance to cope with, consequently my troubles originate mostly in that quarter. Surrounded by a low-down class of shoddy whites who have made the Indian Territory their home to evade paying taxes on their dogs, and who I will not permit to hunt on my premises, I am the constant theme of their slanderous tongues.*

Needless to say, Belle and these tenant farmers were not on the best of terms. She much preferred her Cherokee, Choctaw, and Freedmen neighbors, with whom she generally got along quite well. Even John West's wife, of all people, was friendly with her. But the number of white sharecroppers was growing, their shacks springing up in startling numbers all along the bottomlands of the South Canadian, and by 1888, they were already beginning to outnumber Native residents.

That didn't mean, however, she was wholly against the idea of using them to her advantage. As the days of the gunslinging bandit faded into history and as local authorities offered her a symbolic olive branch so long as she made a nominal effort at disguising any future criminal dealings, transitioning the finances of Younger's Bend to those of a more lawful business model made perfect sense. She needed a legitimate front not just to enable her to appear to be a law-abiding citizen but also to actually augment her income. Bringing in sharecroppers to Younger's Bend was a new and promising racket. Essentially, it meant revenue that she could easily invest in other ventures—perhaps even a stock farm or a hotel, like those of her father, old Judge Shirley. Taking on tenants was potentially the first step in something bigger, while also dangling the possibility of what so many organized criminals have dreamed of since time immemorial: going legitimate. For Belle Starr, at a time when she couldn't even open a bank account in most of America, let alone apply for a business loan without a male relative as a co-signer, the chance to turn Younger's Bend into a profitable and growable enterprise that she alone controlled must have been tantalizing, to say the least. And the opportunity to have a legal front to conceal her activities should she decide to keep a black-gloved hand in the game must have been even more so.

Overall, the plan appears to have served her well. The one kink, however, involved a ruddy transplant from North Florida named Edgar A. Watson, with whom she became involved in a rent dispute over the course of the autumn of 1888. The source of the conflict was Belle's cancelation of their sharecropping contract. Belle had initially agreed to lease a portion of river-bottom land to Watson, but quickly changed her mind and returned the would-be tenant's rent money. As to why she had this change of heart, there have long been rumors that Belle learned from Watson's wife, whom she had befriended, that the Floridian was secretly a fugitive from the law. Remembering the letter from the United States Indian agent, Robert L. Owen, she immediately backed out of the agreement, fearing that associating with criminals might cost her the federal government's good graces. This version of the story could have some merit, and Watson's criminal history may indeed have come up, although it seems unlikely that this was the deciding factor in the revocation of the lease. The fact is, most of the people in Belle's life had criminal histories—members of her own family had trials pending and outstanding warrants against them—and the notion that she would have backed out of a lease agreement based on that alone simply doesn't match her social reality. Belle was a woman of strong convictions and volatile temper, and more likely than not, she simply took a dislike to the man and decided to rent to someone else. But regardless of her reasons—and Watson's somewhat vociferous objections—the initial deposit was returned, and by January of 1889, Watson and his wife had secured a lease from one of Belle's neighbors instead, thus resolving the immediate issue.

The one issue that was not resolved, however—and it relates directly to the members of her own family with criminal histories—was an old charge of horse theft that been hanging over the head of her husband, Jim July Starr, since June of 1887. The allegations dated back to the period when officials, John West in particular, were still engaged in something of a harassment campaign against the Starrs. Jim July had already been arraigned on the charge, but a series of postponements had allowed him to stay out on bond at Younger's Bend for all of 1888. By the beginning of 1889, however, July's luck had run out, and in addition to Eddie's trial, now scheduled for March, Belle would need to escort her husband to Fort Smith in the first week of February to answer to the old charges before the district court. Both cases were relatively weak—Eddie had even secured multiple witnesses to testify that it was Mose Perryman, not he, who had been riding the stolen horse. With decent legal representation, there was a good chance both would result in either not guilty verdicts or a slap on the wrist. And besides, the days of fleeing into the lands of the Osage or hiding out in the wilds of California were more or less gone. This was a transitional phase for the forty-year-old Belle Starr: new opportunities, both legitimate and criminal, were readily available as soon as she wiped her family's slate clean and put her gunslinging past behind her.

ON THE MORNING OF February 2, 1889, Belle departed Younger's Bend with her husband, traveling toward Fort Smith. They were riding separate horses; the weather was chilly and marked by rains that turned the familiar bridle paths to wallows of mud. After crossing the river, they dismounted briefly at a local general store so that Belle could pay an outstanding bill of seventy-five dollars before continuing the journey. When dusk settled in, they stopped to spend the night at the home of friends living on the Sans Bois Creek. At dawn, though, with the weather still gloomy but plagued slightly less by rain, Belle and her husband parted ways, with Jim July continuing on his own toward the courthouse, while she turned back toward Younger's Bend. This may have been the plan all along, or perhaps she was discouraged by the thick mud and foul weather. The fact that she hadn't bothered to pack her pistols suggests the former—a ride into Fort Smith usually involved wearing a pair of Colt .45s. Either way, she re-trod the familiar road alone, perched sidesaddle on her horse, huddled in her shawl against the winter chill. She paused to have lunch at the same general store from the day before, eating with the owner and his wife, lingering at the table to enjoy the warmth of the hearth and the pleasantness of friendly conversation. Her forty-first birthday was just two days away, and it's not unlikely some well-wishes and toasts were shared to cap off the meal. It was still a three-hour ride from the store to Younger's Bend, so Belle took to the road immediately thereafter, doing her best to beat the darkness home.

At around four o'clock in the afternoon, she passed the house of one of her neighbors on the Choctaw side of the Canadian River, Jackson Rowe, and as expected—it was something of a tradition on Sundays—there was a gathering in the yard. Being so close to home, she decided there was no harm in stopping to say hello. Besides, Eddie had been staying with the Rowes for the last few weeks, possibly because of friction at home with his stepfather, Jim July, or perhaps even with Belle herself, and she hoped she might run into him there. Not seeing her son among the crowd, she opted to stay anyway, hitching her horse to the post and minding her step as she approached through the mud. Pones of sour cornbread—Belle's favorite—were being offered, and she gladly accepted, mingling and catching up with the various white tenants and Cherokee and Choctaw locals who had stopped by. She didn't stay long; after two days of riding through foul weather, she was no doubt eager to sit in her own cabin and warm herself by the fire, perhaps even indulging in a sip or two of whiskey while chatting with Pearl. Belle bid her hosts farewell and remounted her horse, taking the trail down toward the Canadian River, back toward her home.

Many books—and many accounts—have tried to portray this moment with a sense of foreboding, to embroider it with dark strands of premonition and impending doom. There is even an old story, repeated often in Belle Starr lore, that she had appeared unusually gloomy and anxious during her lunch at the general store prior, cutting a silk handkerchief in two and giving half to the owner's wife, predicting that they would never see each other again. But while such flourishes may heighten the drama of a story that, in all honesty, is more than dramatic enough in its natural form, there's simply no reason to believe that they're true.

The Belle Starr who rode away from that Sunday gathering, tall in her sidesaddle, rifle sheathed by her side, was anything but a tragic character. She had achieved everything she had ever sought out to. The little girl from the Missouri Ozarks who had once dreamed of high adventure and of seeing something of her world— she had done it. And the woman from Texas who had pined for a life of freedom and glory far from the rigid strictures of Southern frontier society—she had achieved it. Belle Starr had ridden alongside Jim Reed, John Fisher, Jesse James, and Cole Younger, the very cream of Western banditry, and in the end, she had outlasted them all. A criminal mastermind with a clear penchant for gunslinging, she had bested both the tribal and the federal governments that had tried to end her reign, she had secured a solid future for her family at Younger's Bend, and in the process, she had risen to the very highest ranks of a Cherokee organized crime family. Arguably, with the incarceration of Tom Starr in Illinois, she had even served in his absence as the don. Indeed, the black-clad lady in the pinned hat and flowing skirts who descended through the drizzle toward the banks of the South Canadian on that particular February eve was anything but a lost soul or a dissolute woman bested by fate. No, she was triumphant in that propitious moment, she was criminal royalty—truly an outlaw queen.

But moments are precisely that. And while the first thunderclap that resounded through the river bottoms in the chill and rainy twilight may have been disregarded by those gathered at the Rowes', the second one, delivered just a moment later, would have been harder to ignore. And when her horse, spooked and riderless, came galloping frantically into Younger's Bend, its sidesaddle askew, still wet from swimming the river, even Pearl knew that something had gone terribly wrong. She immediately raced down the path and jumped a ferryboat across the Canadian. Upon landing, she met one of their Choctaw neighbors, a twenty-year-old named Milo Hoyt, who told her he had just seen Belle lying in the road. Pearl jumped up behind him onto his horse and they rode there together.

Darkness had fallen when Pearl found her mother. She was still breathing but wouldn't be for long. Her daughter screamed and crouched beside her, pleading for a response, but she was unconscious—she probably had been since the second blast of lead shot had torn into her face. There was simply no saving her. Two barrels were just too much for even a tough Missouri girl to take.

When death came for Belle Starr at last, when she slipped into the vale and gave up the ghost, it happened in her daughter's arms, and in a place she loved like no other—a daughter whose forgiveness she had desperately sought and a place where she had come alive, that had set her very soul on fire. In that, if nothing else, perhaps the mother and daughter alike would have found some comfort.

One thing Pearl did notice, however, and that she would later recall when asked for her official testimony at the Commissioner's Court in Fort Smith: though unarmed, her mother still had her riding whip clutched fiercely in her hand when she found her, defiant to the very last, ready to give her own killer a little something to remember her by before galloping off into eternity.

Because real outlaws don't go down without a fight.

CHAPTER 9

A Final Mystery to Solve

A NATION SHOULD BE WARY of glorifying its criminals. Of glamorizing its outlaws. Wanton violence and Machiavellian greed are hardly traits to celebrate, regardless of how alluring they can sometimes appear with the cleansing distance of hindsight. Recognizing a country's trailblazers, on the other hand—that *is* a worthy exercise. And in her transcendence of the patriarchal structures of nineteenth-century American life and in her rise to a position of influence and power, at a time when American women were unequivocally denied both, Belle Starr blazed an impressive trail indeed.

Granted, her path-clearing involved considerably more gunpowder and whiskey than that of the suffragettes and activists who would emerge in her wake, but like the disenfranchised urban gangsters who would also follow her lead, she chose the way of the gun because there *was* no other way. On the surface, it's hard not to see the outlaw Belle Starr as a kind of agent of chaos, a queen of all mayhem—a problematic figure who left nothing but broken bodies and broken lives littering her way. Even her own children would suffer from the lifestyle she had subjected them to. In the years after their mother's death, Pearl would find herself impoverished and working as a prostitute at a string of Arkansas brothels, and Eddie would attempt to go straight after a stint in prison, even trying his hand as a lawman, only to get gunned down in a saloon brawl at just twenty-five. Indeed, the life Belle Starr sought—and won—came at an enormous cost, and in the end, she paid the ultimate price.

But what she achieved, as an American, was extraordinary in its own right. No one else, no other train robber or roughrider or gunslinger, could have accomplished what she did at Younger's Bend in such a short span of time, and that's not taking gender into consideration. If the Appalachian writer Thomas Wolfe was correct in his surmise that what all men ultimately crave, and with a mad devil's hunger at that, is "darkness, the wind, and incalculable speed," Belle Starr not only helped herself to a portion that put virtually any man of her era to shame, she cleaned her plate and went back for seconds. She plunged into that mystic darkness— she *reveled* in it—and the truth that she found there must have ignited her soul, with a heat that melted the shadows of her past, if only for an instant. But as is so often the case with those that deal in darkness, in the end, the darkness won. Two quick blasts of a shotgun, and the instant was gone.

The life of Belle Starr ended with that pair of gunshots—on a mud-choked road just a river away from her home in the Cherokee Nation. Her life story, however, would come to a close at her actual burial three days later. After washing her body clean of all blood and anointing it with pine resin and oil of cinnamon, a small party of Cherokee women dressed her in her finest black riding habit, crossed her arms upon her chest, and placed her most treasured revolver—the pearl-handled pistol that had allegedly been given to her by Cole Younger—to be forever clasped in her bruised right hand. Her pine-board coffin was carried by a coterie of Cherokee pallbearers, all heavily armed, to rest beside a hole that had been dug just a few paces away from her cabin at Younger's Bend. There was no funeral ceremony, Christian or Indigenous, to accompany her interment—Belle was never one for such things, always opting instead for the simple, the sincere. However, per tribal custom, all those in attendance dropped a small piece of cornbread into the casket while filing by and paying their last respects. Pearl and Eddie were given a few extra minutes to say goodbye to their mother, and then the lid was nailed shut and the coffin was lowered into the ground. The sound of shovelfuls of gravel and wet clay thudding against hollow pine was the only dirge to be heard. In that moment, silence reigned. The peace and quiet Belle always claimed she had been seeking when she came to Younger's Bend was at last completely hers, after a thunderous life that had yielded her naught but the smallest servings of either.

The wind stirring in the cedars. The clouds hovering over the hilltops. The all-nourishing waters of the South Canadian slipping gently by. The kingdom she had always wanted, that she had spent a lifetime fighting for, now hers until the very end of time.

WHERE THE LIFE ENDS, the legend begins. News of Belle Starr's death began thrumming across the nation's telegraph wires within hours of the shooting. The very same day the Cherokee pallbearers, with pistols and hatchets tucked into their belts, slid her pineboard coffin into the ground, the story broke in the *New York Times* half a continent away, some editor evidently finding the violent murder of a female bandit in Indian Territory just curious enough to be newsworthy. It's not unlikely that a copy of that same February 6 issue was slapped down upon the desk of Richard K. Fox at the *National Police Gazette*, who must have read the short article with wide-eyed wonder. An Irish immigrant from Belfast with a predilection for prizefights, Fox had hardly been outside the Big Apple during his tenure as a journalist in America, barring an 1882 bare-knuckle fight he had helped to promote on the Gulf Coast of Mississippi. He knew nothing of frontier saloons, six-gun shootouts, or the ways of the Cherokee, but he knew a good story when he heard one. He promptly dispatched a writer to Fort Smith and had a book ready for publication just a few months later: *Bella*

Starr, the Bandit Queen or the Female Jesse James. While adhering to the general contours of Belle's life, the account took shocking liberties with the details. Fox didn't care, though, and neither did the general public. The book was a hit. And with a rapidity that would have surely made the farm girl from Jasper County in her chuckle, Belle Starr became a household name, even among Yankees and city folk back east. And while her biography was certainly entertaining in its own right and made for compelling reading at a moment when interest in the nation's fading frontier was at its zenith, Belle Starr's posthumous rise from local pariah to American legend was buoyed most significantly by a mystery—one that remains unsolved to this day.

Who killed her?

It is a question that has been raising rumors and generating conspiracy theories for more than a century. Old neighbors of Belle Starr have spoken up; alleged deathbed confessions have been cited; people claiming to have overheard conversations and in some cases to have been eyewitnesses have given lurid recollections to local reporters. Even the legendary teller of tall tales Frank Eaton, better known as Pistol Pete, claimed to have danced with Belle Starr shortly before her demise and to know the identity of the jealous man who had sworn revenge. Rival ranchers, former lovers, and even her own children have at various times been implicated in her murder. While no one was ever convicted of the crime, and most of these scenarios are *possible*, the wildest theories simply don't pass the smell test—particularly the ones that involve her children.

Belle did indeed have a complicated, at times contentious, relationship with both Pearl and Eddie. But the adoption issue and the rumors of the occasional quirt-whipping aside, there's no evidence to suggest either harbored a grudge fierce enough to ambush their own mother and shoot her point-blank in the face. Some, including S. W. Harman, one of Belle's earliest biographers, have suggested her harsh corporal punishment of Eddie was what had led him to quit Younger's Bend for the Rowe's several weeks prior in a murderous rage. This theory is technically possible, although it's worth considering that by that point, Eddie was nearly eighteen years old—it's hard to imagine Belle was still spanking her full-grown son with a riding whip at that age. If anything, it was probably friction with Jim July, who Eddie did not get along with, that had caused him to leave home. Regardless, there's no clear motive for Eddie's or Pearl's being behind the killing. The fact is, both siblings had solid alibis, and both were distraught by their mother's death. Nobody in the community considered them suspects. Pearl would personally write out a poem to be inscribed on her mother's tombstone, and Eddie would spend hours furiously tracking the boot prints her killer left in the mud in hopes of discovering their identity.

The prime suspect in the murder—and the one who would eventually be arrested for it—was Edgar A. Watson, the disgruntled sharecropper whose lease Belle had revoked. The alleged motive was that Watson feared that Belle Starr, in the wake of their dispute, would reveal to authorities the details of his criminal past and inform them that he was still wanted on charges back in Florida. Gunning her down was thus a means of ensuring her silence. There were many in the community who were aware of the disagreement and believed Watson to be guilty, particularly among Belle's own family. In fact, Jim July, who had rushed back from Fort Smith upon learning of his wife's death, effectively held Watson up at gunpoint at the conclusion of her funeral. And while Jim and Eddie may not have agreed upon much, both were convinced of Watson's guilt to the point that together they frog-marched him straight to Fort Smith, along with a witness to ensure his safety during the journey. Their strong suspicions were enough for the U.S. commissioner on duty, Stephen Wheeler, to put Watson under arrest, with a hearing scheduled before the Commissioner's Court just three weeks later, to establish whether more formal charges were warranted. Jim July, Eddie Reed, Pearl Starr, and a host of others who had been in the vicinity of Younger's Bend at the time of the killing came to Fort Smith to testify, with many of those close to Belle voicing their convictions that Watson was to blame.

There was compelling, albeit circumstantial, evidence. Watson had been seen at the Sunday gathering at the Rowes' and was believed to have left shortly after Belle's arrival. The shooting took place just a short distance from the farm he was renting from Jackson Rowe, practically on the edge of his property. And there were even witnesses who testified that the boot prints they found in the mud—size 7—matched with Watson's size, and led, albeit in a circuitous fashion through some dense woods, back in the general direction of Watson's house. Watson did own a double-barreled shotgun, which in and of itself wasn't damning, as many residents of the area did. One peculiarity, however, was that Belle had been struck in the back with heavier buckshot and in the head with a lighter load of "fine shot"—an unusual ammo combination for an assassin, as fine shot was not usually effective on a human except at very close range. This combination was sometimes used by farmers and hunters, though, to cover variables like distance and size of prey. Charles Starr, one of Tom Starr's sons, gave sworn testimony that he'd examined Watson's shotgun the day after the killing and found it loaded in a similar fashion, although Watson also swore that he'd never fired or reloaded it. But even with speculation about the murder weapon aside, Edgar A. Watson was the only member of the community known to have had an active dispute with Belle Starr at the time. And her threat to reveal his status as a wanted criminal to local law enforcement was, according to the proposed motive, enough to push him over the edge and silence her for good.

There were, however, some obvious flaws with this theory. For one, the motive put forth for the Florida transplant simply didn't make any logical sense. If Watson was concerned about garnering unwanted attention from local authorities, as his accusers claimed, gunning down a well-known resident practically in broad daylight paces from his own house would seem a poor strategy. And Watson didn't attempt to hide or flee during the aftermath. He attended Belle's funeral, alongside his wife, three days after the killing—three full days he easily could have used to put hundreds of rail miles between himself and Indian Territory. By all accounts, Edgar A. Watson was a relatively intelligent, well-spoken, and sensible man. Even if he was wanted back in Florida or did have criminal leanings, nothing about him suggests he was foolhardy or naive enough to think gunning down Belle Starr was a good idea.

If Edgar A. Watson did in fact kill Belle Starr, it seems far more likely that it was a crime of passion concocted in the heat of the moment—not a premeditated act of criminal cunning. Belle was known to have a sharp temper and was not above delivering a fierce tongue-lashing to those who crossed her. It's been well established that she harbored strong opinions about the white sharecroppers who were pouring into the Cherokee and Choctaw nations at that time. Perhaps a more plausible scenario is that Belle, cold and wet and in a foul mood from the road, crossed paths with Watson while attending the gathering at the Rowes'. Subsequently, their old lease dispute was brought up and harsh words were exchanged, with Belle pulling no punches when it came to sharing her opinion that Watson and his kind were nothing but "a low-down class of shoddy whites." This, or a similar such statement, would definitely have qualified as fighting words in the Wild West, at a time when many impoverished, uneducated migrants were arriving on the frontier and extremely sensitive about their origins. In fact, a greater insult to a lower-class Anglo-American from the Deep South, intensely aware of the racial implications of such language, is difficult to imagine. And it's not unthinkable that Watson, a newcomer to the area, would have been unaccustomed to anyone, let alone a *woman*, speaking to him in such a fashion. In this scenario, the enraged and possibly drunk sharecropper storms off, grabs his shotgun from his shack, walks to the road where he knows Belle Starr will be passing shortly, and blows her away. When his blood cools, he realizes the enormity of what he has done, while also realizing that fleeing will only make his guilt that much more obvious. So he stays.

This theory, while perhaps more probable than the "criminal past" motive that's been espoused for nearly a century and a half, also has holes. Most notably: multiple witnesses testified to having heard Edgar A. Watson calling in his hogs just minutes after gunshots were heard, and at least one witness—another local sharecropper named Ansel D. Terry—claimed to have been "sitting on [a] woodpile" within sight of Watson, who had just returned from the corncrib and was "at [the] fence calling his hogs" when the pair of shotgun blasts resounded through the February twilight. This same witness would also attest to having seen Watson's shotgun "on Monday in rack," meaning the morning after the crime, no effort had been taken to hide or destroy what would have been the murder weapon. Regardless of whether such testimonies were reliable or not, they were sufficient to convince U.S. Commissioner James Brizzolara, who presided over the court that day, that further proceedings were unwarranted. Beyond rumors of lease disputes and bad blood, there was simply no hard evidence linking Watson to the crime, and several witnesses whose testimony seemed to preclude it. He ordered the defendant discharged, and Edgar

A. Watson immediately hightailed it out of Indian Territory, well aware that many of those close to Belle still believed him to be her killer, and to stay would have been a death sentence.

Assuming that the witness testimony on behalf of Edgar A. Watson was legitimate and that the decision reached by U.S. Commissioner James Brizzolara to release him was the right one, then the question remains: Who else stood to gain from the death of Belle Starr?

One obvious place to look—and many have—is closer to home. More specifically, Jim July, Belle's own husband. Belle never seemed to have quite the same affection for July as she had for Sam, and there has long been the assumption that their marriage was more or less one of convenience. Belle was able to keep Younger's Bend by incorporating a tribal citizen into her household, and Jim July, fifteen years her junior, was given a comfortable place to live and a lifetime of financial stability in return. And there is a clear motive. On February 25, less than three weeks after her funeral, a formal verbal will was validated, based on sworn statements from multiple witnesses—all of whom testified that Belle Starr had, prior to her death, insisted that "if anything should happen to befall her, or that she should die and leave the improvement on which she was then living not disposed of, the said improvement would be James [July] Starr's." In short, Jim July knew that if Belle Starr was out of the picture, Younger's Bend and the structures built upon it would probably become his—a transfer of title that was even more likely to be upheld by the tribal courts with a will attached. And were he to aid in her departure from said picture, well, he certainly would not be the first person in history plotting the removal of an older, wealthier spouse in the interest of winning a substantial inheritance. Plus, there may have even been a strategic precedent. It's worth noting, there was never a clear explanation as to why Mose Perryman, the Creek relative of July's, had shot

Eddie in the face while he was sleeping. It's perhaps a bit of a leap, but is it possible Jim July was already conspiring to get Eddie out of the way before going after Belle? That putting a hit out on her hotheaded son was the first step in removing a rival claimant to Belle's inheritance—which would have included valuable farm animals, implements, and furniture—as well as a potential avenger?

If this was the case, at least this much can be said: Jim July was almost certainly not the one who pulled the trigger on February 3. Despite long-standing rumors and some testimony to the contrary, his alibi is fairly airtight. An article that appeared in the *Fort Smith Weekly Elevator* stated that Jim July had received a telegram on Monday morning in Fort Smith, informing him that his wife had been killed. According to the dispatch, there was bad blood in Jim July's eye upon reading the news, and forsaking his outstanding larceny charges, he "saddled his horse, provided himself with a quart of whiskey, [and] struck out on a run for home, saying somebody was going to suffer." Logistically speaking, it would have been virtually impossible for July to have doubled back after parting ways with Belle Sunday morning, followed her all the way back to the edge of Younger's Bend, gunned her down in the evening, then galloped back to Fort Smith to be there in the morning to receive the telegram. Not without riding full speed the entire way, in pitch-blackness, and changing horses multiple times, at any rate. A seasoned Comanche warrior with a string of ponies might have been able to pull it off, but Jim July was not that.

This doesn't necessarily mean, however, that July couldn't have been behind the crime. There was even one claim, allegedly put forth by a retired Fort Smith deputy marshal, that July had previously attempted to recruit Milo Hoyt, the Choctaw youth who had first found Belle lying in the mud, to murder her for $200. The account goes even further than that, asserting that Jim July then decided to frame Edgar A. Watson by using his shotgun for the crime. The story may sound fanciful, but perhaps July's immediate certainty of Watson's guilt—not to mention his placing him under citizen's arrest rather than killing him outright—is worthy of a closer, more skeptical look. After all, Sam Starr, Belle's previous husband, had had no compunction about slaughtering a member of tribal law enforcement on sight, simply for wounding him and killing his wife's favorite horse. Jim July's reaction upon encountering the man who he claimed had actually *killed his own wife* was surprisingly mild in comparison—almost suspiciously so, one could argue. Is it possible that July was behind the murder, and that he quickly singled out Watson and turned him over to authorities to hide his own involvement?

It certainly is, although there is a troubling flaw with this theory as well. If Jim July's motive for murdering his wife was to inherit Younger's Bend along with all her possessions, it makes sense that he would have stayed behind following the killing to collect his inheritance. If there is any truth to the theory, then Jim July should have become the lord of the manor, so to speak, immediately following Belle Starr's untimely demise, presiding over all that acreage and spending the profits that the sharecroppers brought in. But far from enjoying the fruits of any calculated inheritance scheme, Jim July Starr appears to have gone totally off the rails in the aftermath of his wife's murder. He skipped out on bond, never to answer to his outstanding larceny charges in Fort Smith, and instead went on a criminal rampage across Indian Territory. He joined a band of desperadoes, proceeded to get in further trouble with the law, and eventually suffered the same fate as virtually all of Belle Starr's lovers, going down in a hail of bullets in the Chickasaw Nation while resisting arrest. He died in a Fort Smith prison hospital on January 26, 1890, just under a year after Belle's own passing, "conscious to the last," according to an obituary that appeared in the *Gainesville Daily Hesperian*, and "without a murmur."

Even if the notion of Jim July acting as a lone agent in Belle Starr's murder seems unlikely, it is worth at least considering the possibility that others from within the Cherokee Nation may have been involved. There had long been whispers, going back to her arrival in Indian Territory and marriage to Sam Starr, that some tribal elders saw her as a grave threat and urged Tom Starr to kill her as a preventive measure—a request that Tom Starr refused to grant at the time, allegedly responding that "he could not harm a woman." Such stories may well be that and nothing more, but there's no doubt that by 1889, Belle had provoked considerable ire from the Cherokee National Council. As a body, they may have accepted the fact that she was not worth the trouble to remove, but it's possible—particularly with the context of the Cherokee civil war in mind—that certain members of the Cherokee government or the Cherokee tribal police had simply had enough and decided to orchestrate an assassination. This brings to mind the paranoid tone of Belle's original prison letter to Pearl, her visceral fear of certain unnamed parties from within Indian Territory discovering her daughter's whereabouts. What if, in hindsight, those fears weren't paranoid at all, but prophetically well founded? If this had been the case, then the decision to take out a white woman on Cherokee land would not have been arrived at lightly; it posed a potentially serious entanglement with the federal government. But perhaps some members of tribal leadership were convinced this was a risk worth taking. Framing Edgar A. Watson—a white resident with a criminal past—for the crime would have mitigated that risk considerably.

As to the somewhat unusual timing of the assassination in this scenario, that has a possible explanation as well. By the year 1889, Belle's criminal activities had been toned down considerably, and any factions of the government or tribal police that wanted her dead could have easily done so prior, when their relationship to her was far more adversarial. And while the answer to that delay could simply be found in the deliberate, "best served cold" flavor of Cherokee revenge—that was, after all, how Tom Starr had slowly taken out virtually all the men who had killed his father—it may also be directly related to Tom Starr himself. According to inmate records from the Southern Illinois Penitentiary where the elder Starr had been serving time on trumped-up whiskey smuggling charges, he had been admitted to the prison on November 27, 1886, and released from its confines on March 27, 1888. And it's hard to imagine that old Tom Starr, grim-faced and coughing while staring out the window of his railroad car, had a great deal of love for Belle Starr upon being set free. His family had been running a successful yet low-key whiskey smuggling and protection racket for years, with the understanding that as long as they kept their activities out of the public eye, authorities would give them a pass. That all had ended when Belle Starr came to town, flashing her plumed hat and silver pistols, daring lawmen to try and arrest her.

All of this was surely weighing heavily upon Tom Starr's mind when he came weak and shivering back to his home in the Cherokee Nation. During the year that followed his return, his health only declined further, no doubt giving way to concerns that his death was not far off. Which would have provided a perfect moment for Belle Starr's tribal enemies to come forward and confront the weakened patriarch of the Starr family about his problematic daughter-in-law. A younger, stronger Tom Starr may have tried to protect her out of some lingering sense of familial loyalty or even personal pride. This Tom Starr, however, weakened from his time in prison and still saddened by the loss of his son, may have finally relented to those forces that had lobbied for her killing since the beginning. Of course, this is all conjecture—there is no substantive evidence that any tribal member had a role in Belle Starr's death. But given her hostile relationship with tribal authorities and the number of uninvited white federal lawmen she had brought into the Cherokee Nation, it's at least worth considering. After being lied to and abused for more than a century by the U.S. government, all the Cherokee wanted was to be left in peace—a goal that Belle Starr's criminal presence in Indian Territory had made increasingly difficult to achieve.

But what if her killing had nothing to do with any immediate or even recent motive at all? Given Belle Starr's long criminal history and the kinds of people she had associated with since girlhood, the possibility that some long-forgotten wrong was never really forgotten at all, does merit consideration. That some malevolent actor, still bearing a grudge born from the past, came back to haunt the outlaw queen at a vulnerable moment. Considering how much of her illicit dealings are still unknown, the possibilities are literally endless, although over the years, a number of revenge theories have been posited, many involving siblings of those whose death Belle was believed somehow responsible for, even if indirectly.

These suspects have included Jim Middleton, the brother of the "drowned" outlaw John Middleton; John West, the brother of the duel-dead Frank West; and even Solomon Reed, the younger brother of Jim Reed, who, according to some crackpot theories, blamed Belle for the tip-off that led to his brother's demise. The problem with all these theories, however, is that there's no solid evidence to even indicate Belle's involvement in the deaths mentioned above, let alone any indication that their siblings—who were all otherwise law-abiding citizens—were silently harboring grudges severe enough to cause them to slaughter Belle Starr after waiting years in the shadows.

There is one revenge scenario, however, that does warrant pondering, if only because there is evidence of a long-standing grudge, and because virtually no other historians or biographers have ever fully explored it as a possibility. And the best place to start is with a question. Looking back over the full criminal career of Belle Starr, *all* the way back to the very beginning, is there any act of banditry she was involved in that resulted in serious harm for another individual, for which retribution was never fully achieved, and for which the aggrieved party would have been in a position, even years later, to extract their revenge? As it turns out, there most definitely is: the infamous Grayson robbery of 1873, one of the first major heists Belle ever participated in, even if her involvement was somewhat peripheral. And the reason practically no historians have probed this area is probably due to a kind of inherent, albeit subconscious cultural bias. It's well-known that Watt Grayson was a citizen of the Muscogee Creek Nation and that Jim Reed and his gang robbed him of a considerable sum of money. But perhaps because of Watt's identity as a Native American, few if any historians have bothered to look into exactly what kind of family the Graysons were.

In many ways, the Graysons were much like the Starrs: a prominent family of mixed Indigenous and European lineages, descended from both tribal elites and white traders. Like the Starrs, the Graysons came west to Indian Territory in anticipation of the Indian Removal Act; they had supported the Confederacy during the Civil War when some factions of their tribe had not, and they had risen to a position of considerable power and influence in the bloody conflict's wake. Besides being a prosperous rancher, former slave owner, and elder statesman of the tribe, Watt also had powerful familial connections of his own. He was the great-uncle of George Washington Grayson, also known as the Yaha Tustunugge, Creek for Wolf Warrior, a sobriquet he had earned while fighting for the Confederates. The two men were close; in fact, it was "Uncle Watt" who had supplied his nephew "Wash" with the initial investment capital for Grayson Brothers Mercantile, the beginning of a business, publishing, and ranching empire that would eventually propel him to the position of tribal chief. During his many years of service as a representative of the Creek Nation, George Washington Grayson would mingle with titans of industry in the gilded parlors of the Willard Hotel, rub shoulders with U.S. presidents as an honored guest at the White House, and help guide his people through the difficult transition into full Oklahoma statehood.

Clearly, Jim Reed and his thugs had not simply mugged some senile old "Indian" with a pot of gold hidden under his cabin, as so many Belle Starr biographies have led readers to believe. They were robbing one of the most respected and influential men in the entire Creek Nation, and in a brutal fashion at that. They strung him up by the neck and tortured him at gunpoint, even threatening to hang his wife next, until he finally divulged the location of his money—at least $32,000, most of it in gold, a considerable sum even by today's standards, but a veritable fortune at the time. And it was not a trespass that Watt Grayson or his kin took lightly. Indeed, they sent a war party after the fleeing outlaws, with the intent to kill, and when they did not achieve their aim, Watt personally put a $2,500 price on their heads and hired a bounty hunter named A. J. King to track them down and recover his money. King was successful in apprehending one of the suspects, but not in retrieving any of the missing gold.

Watt Grayson didn't give up there, however. He hired a lawyer and petitioned the U.S. government for the return of his money, citing an old Act of Congress from June 30, 1834, which stated that the Treasury of the United States was liable for any property stolen "by a white" from "friendly Indians." Of course, this first attempt failed—nobody in a Congress that was openly hostile to Native American land claims was interested in budgeting $32,000 to compensate an aggrieved Creek elder. However, Watt Grayson's legal efforts did compel the testimony of a recent widow who, at that time, still went by Myra Maybelle Reed. The woman who would later be known as Belle Starr made a sworn statement before U.S. Commissioner Benjamin Long on December 16, 1875, in which she explained her own role in the robbery. As previously mentioned, Belle was extremely careful not to implicate herself in the crime; according to her, she was merely an observer. But from her statement, it's clear that she was part of the gang and present following the heist when the money was being counted. And when the hoofbeats of the Creek war party began rumbling through the trees, she joined Jim Reed and his two accomplices as they rode off into the night, their saddlebags jostling with an unthinkable amount of gold. Watt Grayson died in 1878, but his relatives, led by George Washington Grayson, carried on the fight, continuing to lobby both the U.S. Congress and the Committee on Indian Affairs for nearly a decade.

For most of that decade, Belle, the woman who had been part of the outlaw band that had robbed their patriarch and tortured him at gunpoint, was living just a few miles down the road—with the Cherokee, no less, the ancestral enemies of the Creek. Not only that, she had married into the Starr clan, direct descendants of the same bullet-chewing Ghigau Nanye'hi who had defeated the Creek at the Battle of Taliwa in 1755. To know all this and to see her openly flaunt her gangster lifestyle, brandishing her six-shooters and bragging to newspapers about her outlaw friends—it's not hard to see how this might have rubbed certain parties within the Creek Nation sympathetic to the Graysons the wrong way. Of course, there's no way to know for certain. Maybe what had happened on the Watt Grayson ranch back in 1873 was considered water under the bridge, all but forgotten. Maybe they blamed Jim Reed for the crime and had long since forgiven his accomplice wife. Maybe they even appreciated her testimony before U.S. Commissioner Long, feeling it had bolstered their case.

Then again, maybe not. Given the efforts that Creek tribal representatives were still putting into recovering the stolen funds, even a full decade after Watt Grayson's death, neither forgetting nor forgiving seems very likely. Incidentally, the Graysons also had close business ties to the Perryman family, which included Eddie's would-be assassin, Mose Perryman, and they almost certainly knew Jim July as well—he was of both Creek and Cherokee parentage and had spent some of his formative years in the Creek Nation. None of which points to anything concrete in and of itself. But it does raise interesting questions. Admittedly, the Graysons were regarded as a family of statesmen and entrepreneurs—a few minor accusations of embezzlement aside, they were not gangsters like the Starrs, and there's no direct evidence that they or any other citizens of the Creek Nation were involved in Belle Starr's murder. This is sheer speculation, an exercise in searching out potential suspects and possible motives. But if an open-minded investigator were to try to pinpoint individuals from Belle's past who had very good reasons to still wish her harm, the Creek Nation would not necessarily be the worst place to start looking.

There are even stories, going all the way back to the first Richard K. Fox account published just months after her death, of Belle Starr robbing the Creek Nation's treasury alongside John Middleton in the spring of 1885—and potentially even killing him later for the gold. If there was any truth to such stories, even a kernel, it would have provided even further motivation for certain members of Creek tribal leadership to want the black-clad bandit queen of Younger's Bend dead. To that end, they may have already had Jim July and Mose Perryman acting as Creek double agents, with the former ready to lead Belle into a trap on his way to Fort Smith, and the latter, having already tried once to kill her son, waiting patiently behind, ready to pull the trigger a second time. And while few among the Muscogee Creek would have dared to incur the wrath of Tom Starr back when he was in his skull-splitting, barn-burning prime, in his weakened state following his release from prison, perhaps some individuals would have perceived a narrow window of opportunity for their long-awaited revenge. In fact, it appears that this window of opportunity even matches with the recuperation of the stolen funds. In 1888, a decade of Creek lobbying paid off, and a bill was finally approved by the U.S. Congress mentioning the claim and allocating $32,000 to the estate of Watt Grayson. The money was almost certainly received by tribal representatives later that year. If the idea of eliminating Belle Starr had previously been dismissed because of concerns it might interfere with Creek efforts to secure federal compensation, by the beginning of 1889, with the compensation in hand, it no longer would have been an issue. The timing is interesting, at the very least.

On the subject of timing as it pertains to potential tribal motivations, be they Creek, Cherokee, or otherwise, it is worth considering the larger political context. The year Belle Starr was killed, 1889, represented a terrible moment for the governments of Indian Territory, the "Five Civilized Tribes" in particular. The aforementioned Indian Appropriation Act of that same year, signed by President Grover Cleveland on March 2, would kick off the fabled Oklahoma Land Rush, sending thousands of white settlers, known as "sooners" or "boomers,"[1] flooding in to stake claims on what had been considered the "Unassigned Lands" of Indian Territory. This was a first step in imposing private land allotment and dismantling the assorted Indigenous nations of the territory as totally separate, sovereign entities, and the tribal governments knew this—their delegates in Washington, D.C., had been lobbying frantically against the bill for months. George

---

[1] Sooners were settlers who violated the "sooner clause" of the Indian Appropriation Act and occupied land prior to the time proclaimed by the president. Boomers were the land-hungry settlers who waited until the appointed moment to rush to stake their claims.

Washington Grayson himself, who had met back in December with a colony of sooners camped on the Kansas border as part of a secret Creek delegation, had this to say to the "worthless horde" of white invaders: "We are doing all we can to prevent the opening of the country, and you had just as well go home, for we have bought, and can buy, your Congressmen like so many sheep and cattle." He followed that up with a threat to raise an army of five thousand to drive out their kind if they insisted on entering illegally into Indian Territory. Granted, these threats were largely empty—tribal governments knew the repercussions of armed resistance and relied on the federal court system instead to fight the legality of the act, butting heads with powerful railroad lobbies and ranching interests in the process. But given that large-scale organized violence wasn't realistic, is it conceivable that some elements of Creek or even Cherokee tribal government, one month prior to the signing of the Indian Appropriation Act of 1889, saw the elimination of Belle Starr—a local pariah, and in some ways the original Oklahoma boomer—as a stern warning to other white troublemakers looking to enter illegally into Indian Territory? Belle may have been well liked by her Cherokee in-laws and Choctaw neighbors, and she likely had friends among the Creek as well, but to tribal governments and police forces, she had been nothing but a headache for nearly a decade. For community leaders concerned about the future of tribal sovereignty, the combination of a sickly Tom Starr and an impending white land rush could have readily nudged certain opinions toward a lethal verdict: the time had finally come to make an example of Belle Starr. This would certainly help to explain the somewhat curious timing of the murder, if nothing else.

Admittedly, the notion of Belle Starr's killing being a political assassination is not only a novel idea but a bold claim to make, even as a hypothetical. Is there actually any evidence that this could have been the case? Well, *perhaps*. And it comes from a rather unlikely source. In 1954, a letter was donated to the Oklahoma Historical Society, a missive penned by a British-born New York newspaper reporter named Fred McMahon, to his friend back in England, William Prince, on April 14, 1889. What stands out isn't the actual contents of the formal letter, but rather a note that McMahon added in the left-hand margin:

> *Oklahoma is to be opened for settlement next Monday. I was hustling to go down for a N.Y. paper to report but they won't pay enough considering the risk. Belle Starr, a she-tough, is at the head of 150 boomers, making their way over the Indian Territory, and US Troops have gone to fetch them back if they can.*

As to whether or not McMahon was aware that Belle Starr had recently been killed is impossible to say; it's not at all improbable that he had never read the short obituary in the *Times* from that February. But if there's any truth to his claim—that Belle Starr, the local "she-tough," was leading an army of boomers looking to settle on tribal lands—it does present a clear motive for certain tribal authorities, who recognized the existential threat that these settlers presented, to want Belle gone. As to why she would have supported a rabble of land-hungry boomers in the first place, given her general disdain for her own white sharecroppers, there is a simple explanation for that as well: Younger's Bend. It was widely acknowledged, even by men like George Washington Grayson, that the opening of the "Unassigned Lands" to white settlement was the first step in dismantling the tribal system of communal land ownership and replacing it with private allotments—a step that all parties involved knew would lead to sell-offs and a massive influx of white homesteaders, effectively crippling tribal sovereignty. More specifically, it meant the actual enforcement among the

"Five Civilized Tribes" of the dreaded Dawes Act of 1887, something tribal governments had been desperately trying to avoid.

For Belle Starr, on the other hand, private allotment would have meant that Younger's Bend, the piece of land she had fought so hard to stay on, could finally and officially be hers—she could actually own it, rather than simply being granted a temporary license from the Cherokee National Council to live there. If she was a vocal proponent of the Indian Appropriations Act and if she did actually try to lead a colony of boomers into the Unassigned Lands, her desire to gain official title to Younger's Bend was almost certainly the reason. As to whether such actions may have put a target on her back, it is a compelling idea, but barring the discovery of some document far more damning than Fred McMahon's letter, it will probably remain that and nothing more.

THE VARIOUS SCENARIOS DESCRIBED above—some more plausible than others—represent the most likely answers to the question of who killed Belle Starr. If it was a crime devised in the heat of the moment following a bitter altercation, then Edgar A. Watson, the resentful white sharecropper with the double-barreled shotgun is your obvious killer. If it was a cold-blooded act of premeditated murder, committed with the intent of permanently removing Belle from her roost at Younger's Bend, then parties from within the Cherokee Nation are likely to blame—possibly Jim July, although factions of tribal government or law enforcement, acting with at least the tacit consent of Tom Starr, seem more realistic. And if it was an act of pure revenge, extracted on behalf of some victim from Belle's past who sought satisfaction, there are any number of potential candidates, although the Creek Nation seems to be the only place anyone might have still harbored a murder-worthy grudge. And it's not unrealistic, given the collective anxiety that surrounded the impending Indian Appropriation Act of 1889, that the political climate of the time may have factored into that decision. Any of these cases are theoretically possible.

But as long as theories are being posited, and since it's a mystery that still remains unsolved after almost a century and a half of conjecture, perhaps one more theory is in order. It may come off as a bit too elaborate, even a touch too "Hollywood," but then again, what is the life of Belle Starr if not cinematic? Perhaps a little narrative creativity is required.

What if *all* of the above were somehow true? What if Tom Starr, the aging Cherokee crime boss, returned home from prison having already decided that Belle Starr, the young white woman he had taken under his wing and helped to become a bona fide gangster, had finally grown beyond his control and put his family's future in danger? What if Tom, a brilliant yet ruthless strategist who had spent a lifetime outsmarting powerful enemies, decided that rather than rushing into a hastily planned and politically fraught execution, he would take his time and allow his plan to unfold? What if he first arranged a sit-down with the factions in both the Cherokee and Creek nations that had long railed against the presence of Belle Starr in Indian Territory, using the impending Indian Appropriation Act of 1889 to give their meeting a sense of urgency? What if he feigned initial reluctance before finally agreeing to address their concerns, but only in exchange for major concessions—an agreement to leave his family alone from the Cherokee and a promise of advantageous business dealings from the Creek? What if he then decided to recruit a white outlaw for the job to deflect potential blame—something he was known to do—and found the perfect candidate in Edgar A. Watson, a sharecropper with a criminal past who already harbored a grudge against Belle Starr? What if he met with Watson in secret, instructing him to use heavy buckshot for the initial attack, but to deliver the deathblow with less destructive turkey shot, so Pearl and Eddie could at least give their mother an open-casket funeral? What if he promised to supply Watson with an alibi, not to mention an enormous sum of gold, upon his completion of the high-profile hit? And what if he followed up that meeting with a rendezvous that included Jim July, practically his adopted son, and explained to him that he needed to lure Belle partway to Fort Smith, but then have her return to Younger's Bend on her own? What if Tom Starr went on to tell Jim July that as soon as he returned from Fort Smith, he needed to publicly accuse Watson of the murder and turn him over to U.S. marshals? What if, as the finishing touch on his plan, he told his son, Charles Starr, that immediately after the hit took place, he needed to get his hands on Watson's shotgun and reload it with buckshot in one barrel and fine shot in the other, to match Belle Starr's wounds and set Watson up as the unsuspecting fall guy? And what if the entire plan went off without a hitch, perfectly executed every step of the way, except that Ansel D. Terry, that other white sharecropper who had been staying with the Watsons, bore false witness on his friend's behalf at the hearing in Fort Smith, saving him from the gallows and setting him free? And what if Edgar A. Watson, realizing that he'd been outfoxed, that he had been used, and that nobody would ever believe his story, instead packed up his things and ran for his life, never to speak another word of the murder he had been tricked into committing? And what if Tom Starr, never one to talk about his exploits, kept silent on his role in the assassination plot as well, right up until his passing the following year, at the ripe old age of seventy-seven, having outmaneuvered and outfought practically every adversary destiny had ever thrown his way, with the final exception of death itself?

Obviously, the scenario described above does involve some rather numerous and hefty what-ifs. It is purely an exercise in speculation, and a somewhat fanciful one at that, going in direct contravention to Occam's razor, which would posit that the real culprit was nothing more than a volatile sharecropper with a shotgun. But the Tom Starr theory, as rich in conjecture as it may be, does tie up all the loose ends and address all the inconsistencies—something none of the other theories put forth over the years have ever managed to accomplish. It may indeed be a leap, with its uniquely intricate and murderous choreography, but if there is any truth to it, any at all, then the plot to assassinate Belle Starr was nothing short of a criminal masterstroke on the part of a lesser-known and oft-overlooked American outlaw named Thomas "Ta-Ka-Tos" Starr. And it would serve as final proof that in a story filled to the very brim with some of the most dangerous characters and cunning outlaws ever to inhabit the West, it was he, a transplanted Cherokee largely forgotten by history, who reigned supreme as the true gangster, the original "don." Not Jesse James, not Cole Younger, not John Fisher, and not even Belle Starr— although she did come close. Close enough, perhaps, to have even been considered a rival, a sort of frontier Lady Macbeth who angled for the throne and actually achieved it, only to have it pulled out from under her at the last moment.

THE FINAL RIDDLE OF Belle Starr's killer would be a good note to end on, but there is still one mystery left: the smaller, more personal one mentioned at the beginning of this book; the unknown that I had hoped might become slightly less so during the course of my research and writing. Was Belle Starr a relation on my mother's Scots-Irish side, as family lore suggested? And was there a connection to another story, told to my grandmother by her father on his deathbed, that he had "Cherokee blood"?

To be perfectly honest, I approached the possibility of fully answering either question with some apprehension. My cousin Bruce, the one family member who supposedly remembered the specific details of the Belle Starr connection, had passed away several years earlier. And I was well aware of the spurious "Cherokee grandmother" phenomenon so common to families with roots in the frontier. Finding definitive answers felt daunting, to say the least. Even if there was some truth in both stories, without any specific reference points, it was impossible to know where to begin. I wasn't sure if the connection to Belle Starr was linked to the old Cherokee claim or simply the Scots-Irish side of my family in Texas. I wasn't sure if the connection went back to Appalachia or occurred in the period after Westward migration. I wasn't even entirely certain whether it was on my great-grandmother's or my great-grandfather's branch of the family. Needless to say, attempting to locate any point of commonality on sprawling and oftentimes poorly documented family trees was an exasperating task—like trying to locate a needle in a haystack, when I wasn't even sure if the needle existed, what form it might take, or which haystack, if any, it might be in.

However, an initial search on an online genealogical database produced a surprising result: I was related to Belle Starr on both my great-grandmother's *and* my great-grandfather's sides of the family. The former was through a relation to Jim Reed, Belle's first husband, and the latter through Bruce Younger, her second husband. But both of these connections were fairly distant, going back to the British Isles, which perhaps isn't so surprising in the end, given that the Scots-Irish immigrants who settled so much of the American frontier tended to be of a common Northumbrian stock. And I harbored a suspicion that this was probably *not* the connection to Belle Starr that had spurred so much banter at family reunions. So I continued my search, digging through genealogical charts and interviewing family members, making some intriguing discoveries in the process.

My great-grandparents' ancestral farm in Texas is located right on the border of Cherokee County, so named because it was one of the only major Cherokee settlements in the state. The vicious ethnic cleansing campaign of Mirabeau B. Lamar, president of the short-lived Republic of Texas, drove the Cherokee as well as most other Native American groups out of the area in 1839, although a fair number of settlers of mixed Cherokee and white ancestry did stay behind. Could that have been the source of my great-grandfather's claim? I also noticed that one of the families allegedly robbed at gunpoint by Belle Starr during the Farrill episode shared my great-grandfather's surname. Is it possible that the story became garbled over the years and that I was actually related to one of Belle Starr's victims? And lastly, while perusing lineage charts of the Starr family, one name stood out: Griffin. Looney and Felix Griffin, the two outlaws who had ridden with Sam Starr, were related to him through marriage. Griffin was also the maiden name of my great-grandfather's mother, the one who, if there was any truth to the story, was of at least some Cherokee ancestry. Could there be any connection there, perhaps going all the way back to the Appalachian frontier? Or were all these just historical red herrings, small coincidences that held no real relation to an enticing bit of family lore?

These revelations, indefinite as they may have been, piqued my curiosity, and I did consider delving deeper—hiring a professional genealogist, perhaps, or submitting DNA to compare with Belle Starr descendants. It all was tempting. But something held me back.

As Americans, we do need to know our history, if for no other reason than to remember our origins and avoid the same mistakes,

so many of them bloody, that our forebears made. But as human be-
ings, we also need to hold on to our stories—one could even argue
they are the very things that make us human in the first place. And
to be perfectly honest, I felt like this story was one worth keeping
as is, to spur that bit of banter at family reunions and enliven those
bourbons after a Thanksgiving dinner. Always preambled with a
playful "This may or may not be true," and often accompanied by
a mischievous wink, but still, a story that mattered enough to *my*
forebears to be remembered and passed down—a kind of inheritance, if you will, from humble frontier folk who often had little
along the lines of tangible wealth to bequeath. It felt right, in the
end, to let the mystery be.

Relation or not, while conducting research for this book, I did
pay a visit to Belle Starr's grave. It's located on the southern edge
of a sovereign Cherokee Nation that still exists today, having survived both the Dawes Commission and Oklahoma statehood with
its borders more or less intact. Her original cedar log cabin is gone,
has been for years, but her tombstone is still there, perched back
in the woods, overlooking the timeless waters of the South Canadian. A more peaceful final resting place, I remember thinking,
would be hard to find. I didn't bring any flowers—for some reason
it didn't seem fitting—but I did bring along a piece of cornbread,
left over from a lunch at Cracker Barrel no less, to leave beside her
grave. Upon unwrapping my small offering, I stood in the silence of
Younger's Bend and paid my respects to a true American original,
a figure who dared to defy the limitations that her nation imposed
upon her and through sheer force of will bent the very arc of destiny
her way, which may be, ironically enough, the most American thing
of all. And with my hand resting on the weathered white tombstone
of a woman who may or may not have been kin, I read the poem that
Pearl, Belle's daughter, had insisted be engraved upon it:

SHED NOT FOR HER THE BITTER TEAR,
NOR GIVE THE HEART TO VAIN REGRET;
'TIS BUT THE CASKET THAT LIES HERE,
THE GEM THAT FILLED IT SPARKLES YET.

Indeed, in the century and a half since her passing, the dark and dazzling aura that surrounds Belle Starr has lost none of its beguiling gemstone shimmer—perhaps because embedded in every shimmer there is also a reflection. And in Belle's case, what she mirrored of America was stunning in both its complexity and its contradictions. The brilliance, the passion, the violence, the cruelty: facets of a generous yet ruthless woman, the product of a generous yet ruthless land.

ACKNOWLEDGMENTS

Reconstructing a story as elusive as Belle Starr's—actually breathing life back into such an enigmatic and misunderstood character—is a task no writer could possibly hope to accomplish on their own, and this book simply would not exist without the contributions of some exceedingly talented and generous individuals. The project never would have gotten off the ground without the incredible support of my literary agent, Renée Zuckerbrot, and my editorial team, Mauro DiPreta and Andrew Yackira, all of whom saw its potential and stewarded it to completion. And of course, Nick Amphlett—I can't thank you enough for believing in my work, past and present, and for quite literally helping to make my dreams come true over the years, culminating in this book. I also owe a tremendous debt to the Oklahoma Historical Society and the Thomas Gilcrease Institute of American History and Art—Mallory Covington and Jana Gowan, specifically and respectfully—for their invaluable aid in locating archival materials, not to mention some remarkable old photographs. On a related note, I would like to offer a posthumous thank-you to the great Western historian Glenn Shirley as well, for his seminal work in uncovering so many obscure primary sources. Additionally, I'd like to thank the West family, Kurt West in particular, for generously providing such a personal and memorable portrait of the lawman Franklin Pierce West. And lastly, I'd like to extend my gratitude to Paul Stinson, for accompanying me on my research trips, as well as to the residents of Oklahoma and the citizens of the Cherokee, Muscogee, and Choctaw nations, who shared their stories and hospitality along the way and helped to make this such a memorable journey.

SOURCES

Introduction

"A Desperate Woman Killed." *New York Times*, February 6, 1889.

Richard K. Fox. *Bella Starr, the Bandit Queen, or the Female Jesse James*. New York: Richard K. Fox, Publisher, 1889.

"Thrilling Life of a Girl: Belle Starr, Who Shelters Outlaws." *Dallas Morning News*, June 7, 1886.

Burton Rascoe. *Belle Starr: "The Bandit Queen."* New York: Random House, 1941.

Chapter 1

Shane Hegarty. "Scary Tales of New York: Life in the Irish Slums." *The Irish Times*, March 23, 2013.

W. E. Vaughan, ed. *A New History of Ireland, Volume 6: Ireland Under the Union, 1870–1921*. Oxford: Oxford University Press, 1989.

Fred Bateman and Thomas Weiss. *A Deplorable Scarcity: The Failure of Industrialization in the Slave Economy*. Chapel Hill: University of North Carolina Press, 1981.

Alfred H. Conrad and John R. Meyer. *The Economics of Slavery: And Other Studies in Econometric History*. New York: Routledge, 2007.

Charles S. Sydnor. *Slavery in Mississippi*. Columbia: University of South Carolina Press, 2013.

S. C. Gwynne. *Empire of the Summer Moon: Quanah Parker and the Rise and Fall of the Comanches, the Most Powerful Indian Tribe in American History*. New York: Scribner, 2010.

A. L. Kroeber. "Handbook of the Indians of California." *Bureau of American Ethnology Bulletin* 78: 1–995. Washington: Government Printing Office, 1925.

Ralph Strassburger. *Pennsylvania German Pioneers, Vol. I, 1727–1775*. Norristown: Pennsylvania German Society, 1934.

John B. Linn and William H. Egle. *Persons Naturalized in the Province of Pennsylvania 1740–1773*. Reprinted from Pennsylvania Archives, Series 2, vol. II. Baltimore: Genealogical Publishing Company, 1967.

Gary T. Hawbaker and Clyde L. Groff. *A New Index—Lancaster County, Pennsylvania Before the Federal Census, Vol. 3 Index to the 1750 Tax Records*. Hershey: self-published, 1982.

Historic Pennsylvania Church and Town Records. Historical Society of
    Pennsylvania, Philadelphia.

Constance A. Levinson and Louise C. Levinson. *Rockingham
    County, Virginia, Minute Book 1778–1792 (Part II, 1786–1788).*
    Harrisonburg, VA: Greystone Publishers, 1985.

The Hoosier Genealogist, vol. 4, no. 5, 1964, "Abstract of Wills—Book
    A, 1818–1829. Probate court records, 1830–1837. Floyd County,
    Indiana." Indiana State Library, Indianapolis.

Ward L. Schrantz. *Jasper County, Missouri, in the Civil War.* Carthage,
    MO: Carthage Press, 1923.

U.S. Department of Commerce, Bureau of the Census, *Seventh Census
    of the United States, 1850: Population Schedules, Jasper County,
    Missouri.* National Archives microcopy no. 432, roll 402. Oklahoma
    Historical Society, Oklahoma City.

U.S. Department of Commerce, Bureau of the Census, *Eighth Census
    of the United States, 1860: Population Schedules, Jasper County,
    Missouri.* National Archives microcopy no. 653, roll 204. Oklahoma
    Historical Society, Oklahoma City.

"600 Acres of Spring River Bottom Land," *Southwest News,* March 29,
    1861.

"Belle Starr's Mother Dead." *Dallas Daily Times Herald,* January 5, 1894.

Kenneth E. Burchett. *The Battle of Carthage, Missouri: First Trans-
    Mississippi Conflict of the Civil War.* Jefferson, NC: McFarland &
    Company, 2013.

History of Jasper County, Missouri. Des Moines: Mills & Company, 1883.

W. R. Thomason. "An Address on Female Education, Delivered at the
    Close of the Session of the Pulaski Female Academy, June, 1836."
    LC1671.T3. Tennessee State Library and Archives, Nashville.

Chapter 2

"600 Acres of Spring River Bottom Land," *Southwest News,* March 29,
    1861.

U.S. Department of Commerce, Bureau of the Census, *Seventh Census
    of the United States, 1850: Population Schedules, Jasper County,
    Missouri.* National Archives microcopy no. 432, roll 402. Oklahoma
    Historical Society, Oklahoma City.

U.S. Department of Commerce, Bureau of the Census, *Eighth Census
    of the United States, 1860: Population Schedules, Jasper County,*

Missouri. National Archives microcopy no. 653, roll 204. Oklahoma Historical Society, Oklahoma City.

Kenneth E. Burchett. *The Battle of Carthage, Missouri: First Trans-Mississippi Conflict of the Civil War.* Jefferson, NC: McFarland & Company, 2013.

"Noted Woman Dead." *Fort Scott Weekly Monitor*, Thursday, January 11, 1894.

Ward L. Schrantz. *Jasper County, Missouri, in the Civil War.* Carthage, MO: Carthage Press, 1923.

F. A. North. *The History of Jasper County, Missouri.* Des Moines: Mills & Company, 1883.

John McCorkle. *Three Years with Quantrill: A True Story Told by His Scout, John McCorkle*, written by O. S. Barton. Armstrong: Armstrong Herald Print, 1914.

War of the Rebellion: A Compilation of the Official Records of the Union and Confederate Armies. Series I, vol. XIII. Washington: Government Printing Office, 1885.

S. W. Harman. *Hell on the Border: He Hanged Eighty-Eight Men.* Fort Smith, AR: Phoenix Publishing Company, 1898.

Homer Croy. *Cole Younger: Last of the Great Outlaws.* New York: Duell, Sloan, and Pearce, 1956.

"An Old Wartime Story: How Belle Starr Once Attended a Dance—The Killing of Bud Shirley." *Carthage Evening Press*, Thursday, February 5, 1903.

Sixth Plate Ambrotype of John "Bud" Shirley, Missouri Irregular and 8th Missouri Cavalry, CSA, Armed with M1855 Colt Revolving Carbine. Civil War Photographs Box (34–37). Albert and Shirley Small Special Collections Library, University of Virginia, Charlottesville.

Chapter 3

S. C. Gwynne. *Empire of the Summer Moon: Quanah Parker and the Rise and Fall of the Comanches, the Most Powerful Indian Tribe in American History.* New York: Scribner, 2010.

F. A. North. *The History of Jasper County, Missouri.* Des Moines: Mills & Company, 1883.

"Noted Woman Dead." *Fort Scott Weekly Monitor*, Thursday, January 11, 1894.

Burton Rascoe. *Belle Starr: "The Bandit Queen."* New York: Random House, 1941.

Malcolm G. McGregor. *The Biographical Record of Jasper County, Missouri.* Chicago: Lewis Publishing Company, 1901.

William Bulgin, Petition. 31 July 1865, *William G. Bulgin vs. John F. Vestal et al.* Box 47, file 13, Jasper County Records, Missouri.

Cole Younger. *The Story of Cole Younger, by Himself.* Chicago: Henneberry Company, 1903.

James C. Reed to Mira [*sic*] M. Shirley, Marriage Records, vol. 3, p. 49, Collin County Records, Texas.

Dallas Weekly Herald, September 21, 1867.

S. W. Harman. *Hell on the Border: He Hanged Eighty-Eight Men.* Fort Smith, AR: Phoenix Publishing Company, 1898.

Bill O'Neal. *Encyclopedia of Western Gunfighters.* Norman: University of Oklahoma Press, 1979.

"Belle Starr's Mother," an obituary. *Dallas News*, January 7, 1894.

F. M. Shannon, *Fort Smith Weekly Herald*, June 26, 1868.

United States v. John Fisher et al., U.S. District Court, Western District of Arkansas, Fort Smith.

Flossie Doe. "The Story of My Grandmother, Belle Starr." *Dallas Morning News*, April 30, 1933.

Stephen E. Ambrose. *Nothing Like It in the World: The Men Who Built the Transcontinental Railroad, 1863–1869.* New York: Touchstone, 2001.

History of Benton, Washington, Carroll, Madison, Crawford, Franklin, and Sebastian Counties, Arkansas. Chicago: The Goodspeed Publishing Company, 1889.

Charles Dwight Willard. *The Herald's History of Los Angeles City.* Los Angeles: Kingsley-Barnes & Neuner, 1901.

Cole Younger. *The Story of Cole Younger, by Himself.* Chicago: Henneberry Company, 1903.

Dallas Daily Commercial, May 15, 1874.

Chapter 4

"Outrage on the Frontier." *Little Rock Daily Arkansas Gazette*, November 25, 1873.

Letters filed with transcript of *United States v. William D. Wilder*, U.S. District Court, Western District of Arkansas.

Kenneth W. Hobbs Jr. "Jim Reed, South-Western Outlaw and Husband of Belle Starr: A Study of the Watt Grayson and San Antonio Stage Robberies." Master's Thesis, Texas Christian University, Fort Worth, 1975.

Glenn Shirley. *Belle Starr and Her Times*. Norman: University of Oklahoma Press, 1982.

Records of the U.S. House of Representatives, Watt Grayson claim file, Exhibit G and Exhibit H.

"A Highway Robbery in Texas—Passengers of a Stage-Coach Robbed." *The New York Times*, April 9, 1874.

Austin Daily Democratic Statesman, April 9, 1874.

Austin Daily Democratic Statesman, April 22, 1874.

"Tragic Death! The Most Noted of American Robbers! Hands in His Checks!" *Dallas Commercial*, August 10, 1874.

S. W. Harman. *Hell on the Border: He Hanged Eighty-Eight Men*. Fort Smith, AR: Phoenix Publishing Company, 1898.

Denison News, August 10, 1874.

Cole Younger. *The Story of Cole Younger, by Himself*. Chicago: Henneberry Company, 1903.

Fort Smith Weekly Elevator, February 4, 1889.

Kansas County Marriages, 1855–1911, database with images, FamilySearch (https://familysearch.org/ark:/61903/1:1:Q29Q-QK3L: 23 February 2021), Bruce Younger and [*sic*] Maibelle Reed, 15 May 1880; citing Marriage, Labette, Kansas, United States, district clerk, court clerk, county clerk and register offices from various counties; FHL microfilm 1,433,307.

Chapter 5

Lisa L. Moore, Joanna Brooks, and Caroline Wigginton, eds. *Transatlantic Feminisms in the Age of Revolutions*. New York: Oxford University Press, 2012.

Natalie Rishay Inman. *Brothers and Friends: Kinship in Early America*. Athens: University of Georgia Press, 2017.

Emmet Starr. *History of the Cherokee Indians and Their Legends and Folklore*. Oklahoma City: Warden Company, 1921.

James Adair. *The History of the American Indians*. London: Edward and Charles Dilly, 1776.

Jared M. Diamond. *Guns, Germs, and Steel: The Fates of Human Societies*. New York: W. W. Norton, 1997.

John Ehle. *Trail of Tears: The Rise and Fall of the Cherokee Nation*. New York: Anchor Books, 1988.

Carolyn Thomas Foreman. "The Balentines, Father and Son, in the Indian Territory," *Chronicles of Oklahoma*, vol. XXXIV, no. 4 (Winter, 1956–57).

Morris L. Wardell. *A Political History of the Cherokee Nation, 1838–1907*. Norman: University of Oklahoma Press, 1938.

Edward Everett Dale and Gaston Litton. *Cherokee Cavaliers: 40 Years of Cherokee History as Told in the Correspondence of the Ridge-Watie-Boudinot Family*. Norman: University of Oklahoma Press, 1939.

Mary Jane Warde. *When the Wolf Came: The Civil War and the Indian Territory*. Fayetteville: University of Arkansas Press, 2013.

Herman Lehmann. *Nine Years Among the Indians, 1870–1879: The Story of the Captivity and Life of a Texan Among the Indians*. Albuquerque: University of New Mexico Press, 1993.

Jeremiah Curtain. *Seneca Indian Myths, Collected by Jeremiah Curtin*. New York: E. P. Dutton, 1923.

Burton Rascoe. *Belle Starr: "The Bandit Queen."* New York: Random House, 1941.

Thomas Pegg. "Laws Passed by the National Council at Various Periods Commencing at the Council Held in Cowski Prairie in February 1863," 1, frame 101, roll 8, Cherokee National Records, Oklahoma Historical Society, Oklahoma City.

Interview of Morris Sheppard, 1–5, folder 8, box 27, 81.105, Federal Writers Project Ex-Slave Narratives, Oklahoma Historical Society, Oklahoma City.

Chapter 6

Cherokee Volume 1-B, 297, "Marriage Records, Bills of Sale, Court Records, Permits to Non-Citizens," Indian Archives Division. Oklahoma Historical Society, Oklahoma City.

S. W. Harman. *Hell on the Border: He Hanged Eighty-Eight Men*. Fort Smith, AR: Phoenix Publishing Company, 1898.

Ron Lackmann. *Women of the Western Frontier in Fact, Fiction and Film*. Jefferson, NC: McFarland, 1997.

Fort Worth Daily Gazette, vol. 15, no. 25, ed.1, Saturday, November 8, 1890.

Mark Lee Gardner. "The Strange and Mesmerizing Death of the Outlaw Jesse James." *True West Magazine*, January 20, 2023.

"Thrilling Life of a Girl: Belle Starr, Who Shelters Outlaws." *Dallas Morning News*, June 7, 1886.

Fred E. Sutton. "Belle Starr Takes Her Place in History." *Dallas Morning News*, July 28, 1929.

Chapter 7

Mrs. Fannie Blythe Marks to James Carselowery, September 9, 1937. *Indian-Pioneer History*, Foreman Collection, vol. 16, 78–82.

Frederick S. Barde. *St. Louis Republic*, August 20, 1910.

Frederick S. Barde. "The Story of Belle Starr." *Sturm's Oklahoma Magazine*, September 1910.

United States v. Sam and Belle Starr, Case No. 2370, U.S. District Court, Western District of Arkansas, Fort Smith.

Fort Smith New Era, February 22, 1883.

William G. McLoughlin. *After the Trail of Tears: The Cherokees' Struggle for Sovereignty, 1839–1880*. Chapel Hill: University of North Carolina Press, 1993.

S. W. Harman. *Hell on the Border: He Hanged Eighty-Eight Men*. Fort Smith, AR: Phoenix Publishing Company, 1898.

"The Story of Flossie, Belle Starr's Granddaughter." *Dallas Morning News*, May 7, 1933.

Chapter 8

Fort Smith Elevator, May 15, 1885.

Homer Croy. *He Hanged Them High: A True Account of the Life and Deeds of Isaac Parker*. New York: Duell, Sloan and Pearce, 1952.

Fort Smith Elevator, March 12, 1886.

"Thrilling Life of a Girl: Belle Starr, Who Shelters Outlaws." *Dallas Morning News*, June 7, 1886.

United States v. Belle Starr et al., U.S. Commissioner's Court, Western District of Arkansas, Fort Smith.

"Belle Starr's Husband Wounded in a Fight with Indian Police." *Arkansas Gazette*, September 17, 1886.

Ward L. Schrantz. *Carthage News*, January 26, 1953.

Ted Byron Hall. *Oklahoma, Indian Territory*. Fort Worth, TX: American Reference Publishers, 1971.

United States v. Ed Reed, July 21, 1888, U.S. Commissioner's Court, Western District of Arkansas, Fort Smith.

Flossie Doe. "The Story of Flossie, Belle Starr's Granddaughter."
    Dallas Morning News, May 7, 1933.
S. W. Harman. *Hell on the Border: He Hanged Eighty-Eight Men*. Fort
    Smith, AR: Phoenix Publishing Company, 1898.
Vinita Indian Chieftain, October 4, 1888.
Muskogee Indian Journal, July 28, 1887.
Burton Rascoe. *Belle Starr: "The Bandit Queen."* New York: Random
    House, 1941.

Chapter 9

United States v. Edgar A. Watson, February 22–23, 1889, U.S.
    Commissioner's Court, Western District of Arkansas, Fort Smith.
"Verbal Will of Belle Starr." *Cherokee Records*. Vol. II. Indian Archives
    Division, Oklahoma Historical Society, Oklahoma City.
Elmer LeRoy Baker. *Gunman's Territory*. San Antonio, TX: Naylor
    Co., 1969.
J. T. Leonard. *Gainesville Daily Hesperian*, January 29, 1890.
Illinois Department of Corrections and Predecessor Agencies. "Menard
    Correctional Facility. Volume 1." Illinois State Archives: Register of
    Illinois Prison Records (Illinois Digital Archives), n.d., http://www.
    idaillinois.org/digital/collection/p16614coll29/id/11774. 2023-09-11.
Mary Jane Warde. *George Washington Grayson and the Creek Nation,
    1843–1920*. Norman: University of Oklahoma Press, 1999.
Records of the U.S. House of Representatives, Watt Grayson claim file,
    Exhibit G.
The Statutes at Large of the United States, 50th Congress, 1st session,
    vol. XXV.
Grayson to the National Council, October 1881, 30780, microfilm reel
    37, Oklahoma Historical Society, Oklahoma City.
Sumner County (Kansas) Press, December 23, 1880.
Letter 8. Fred McMahon to William Prince—April 14, 1889. Historic
    Oklahoma Collection. Manuscripts: Land Openings. Oklahoma
    Historical Society, Oklahoma City.

INDEX